3 9351 004501146

D0906085

Ezra Stone

Ezra Stone
A Theatrical Biography

by

KENNETH L. STILSON

WITH A FOREWORD BY
HAL KANTER

McFarland & Company, Inc., Publishers
Jefferson, North Carolina, and London

Frontispiece: Ezra Stone as Henry Aldrich in 1939 on radio.

All photographs, except those whose captions state other-
wise, are printed courtesy of Ezra Stone and his family.
The entire Ezra Stone Collection is located in the New
York Public Library for the Performing Arts (Bill Rose
Theatre Collection) at the Lincoln Center.

British Library Cataloguing-in-Publication data are available

Library of Congress Cataloguing-in-Publication Data

Stilson, Kenneth L., 1960–
 Ezra Stone : a theatrical biography / by Kenneth L. Stilson.
  p.   cm.
 Includes bibliographical references and index.
 ISBN 0-7864-0122-2 (lib. bdg. : 50# alk. paper) ∞
 1. Stone, Ezra, 1917– . 2. Actors—United States—Biography.
 I. Title.
 PN2287.S74S75 1995
 792′.028′092—dc20
 [B]   95-17277
                                                              CIP

Manufactured in the United States of America

McFarland & Company, Inc., Publishers
 Box 611, Jefferson, North Carolina 28640

Table of Contents

Foreword

(by Hal Kanter)

When one is invited to write a foreword to any book one should first read the entire manuscript, which I have neglected to do.

But let me assure you that the first 135 pages so intrigued me that I will have devoured the rest of it by the time you nibble on these words.

Why did I not gulp down the book in one sitting? Because I had to stop often to wipe tears from my eyes — tears of shared laughter remembered, tears of sudden sadness recalled — and also — I was reading this in California — to hold on to the furniture as the earth moved.

The movement — ah! — there it goes again! — is what seismologists call aftershocks following more severe earthquakes, such as the 6.8er that had its epicenter in the San Fernando Valley on January 17, 1994. Among the considerable mischief done to our home that morning was the crashing of our large collection of glassware when it leapt from the bar shelves to the floor. Among the drinking vessels that were shattered was a set of Norwegian crystal brandy snifters that we prized not only because they were exquisitely beautiful but also because they had been a gift from a dear and valued friend, Ezra Stone.

Scientists call them aftershocks; how do they know they are not foreshocks for the Really Big One? As the ground continued to rumble, I looked up from reading the typescript of this biography at our nearly empty shelves to the one remaining snifter.

For more than sixty years, Ezra Stone was an undersung hero of the American theater's war against mediocrity. Now his victories can be sung, thanks to Kenneth Stilson, who has provided us with the lyrics in this book. He gave us not only the words but the music as well, for this story bounces along to the fervid tempo of the fertile life Ezra led.

It is my proud boast that Ezra Stone was my frequent collaborator in the vineyards of Twentieth Century Fox and Warner Brothers, where we earned our ulcers stomping the sour grapes of television comedy while still remaining constant friends. Fifty years before we labored together to create laughter, I had become his fan when Ezra proved that a truly talented actor did not have to be a tall, thin leading man to play a short, fat teenager.

But Ezra was more than an actor, much more, as you will read. He is the only person listed in *Who's Who* as an actor, director, writer, producer, teacher and farmer. While I hesitate to vouch for his agrarian expertise, my judgment of Ezra's contributions to the world of theater places him among the most gifted and prolific artists in our generation.

One of the first Broadway shows I ever saw when I moved north from my native south was the comedy *See My Lawyer*. It made an indelible impression on me because I was told at the time that its director, Ezra Stone, was just a kid, even younger than I.

I later learned—to my relief—that Ezra was one year and sixteen days older than I. He was also more gifted, more versatile, more energetic, and vastly more polite. In the company of women Ezra was downright gallant and with children engagingly didactic and amusingly avuncular.

I discovered all that after somebody suggested that Ezra Stone was the ideal man to direct some episodes of my new television series *Julia*, which starred Diahann Carroll and Lloyd Nolan.

When we met for the first time in my offices at Twentieth Century Fox studios, I learned who had suggested Ezra Stone as the ideal man for the job: it had been Ezra himself.

He had seen the pilot that I had written and directed myself, and because its aims and philosophy were consistent with his own he contended that he simply had to work on the show. Ezra confessed that he had fallen in love with my characters and flattered my writing so profusely that I was compelled to make one of my wisest decisions: I engaged him forthwith.

Ezra's theater experience had been primarily with comedy, but in television he was directing everything from two-hour Westerns to thirty-second commercials. Busy as he was during that period, he seemed to see every stage production done in Southern California and as a result encouraged many young actors by bringing them in to read for parts in *Julia* and *The Jimmy Stewart Show*, which he subsequently directed for me at Warner Brothers.

Ezra would wrap an hour-long western, go on to an episode of *Lassie* and without a rest return to our sets, relieved (as he once told me) to get back indoors with honest dialogue and no animals.

I do not know when he found time to do his homework, but Ezra was always prepared. He arrived with copious notes for the actors, suggested cuts for the writers, lists for the prop men and the wardrobe people, diagrams of the sets with shots already blocked out for the camera. The cast, the crew, and the front office adored him because Ezra always knew what he wanted and never wasted their time to get it or his to find it.

As you will find out in reading this biography, my friend was in every sense a civilized gentleman and a scholarly artist, a true patriot, and a liberal, compassionate citizen with wit, grace, loyalty, and justifiable angers.

In the spirited biography of this rolling Stone, you will gather some backstage eye-witness history of our comedy and musical theater, radio, movies, and army life during World War II. All of them would have been different had there never been an Ezra Stone.

Hal Kanter
Encino, California
June 1994

Preface

In fall 1986, while attending Dr. Larry D. Clark's seminar on theater history, a class focused on American theater in the 1940s, I became fascinated with the contributions of entertainers to the morale effort during the Second World War. Although performers played an important role in previous and subsequent military conflicts, I came to believe that the entertainment community was particularly consequential during World War II, as thousands of actors, musicians, dancers, comedians, and other performers provided entertainment and diversion for the young men and women headed to Europe or the South Pacific.

While conducting research for various other projects in this area, I came across several articles about Irving Berlin's hit musical *This Is the Army*. Fortuitously, that spring Ezra Stone, the original stage director of Berlin's musical, and his wife, Sara Seegar, conducted an actor's workshop at the University of Missouri–Columbia. At the time, I knew little about Ezra, but he was exceedingly pleasant and provided keen insight into American theater during the forties.

This meeting piqued my curiosity, and I began rudimentary research on his career. I was amazed to discover that although he had received a wealth of newspaper and magazine press during the late thirties and throughout the forties and although his biographical entries in several *Who's Who* volumes occupied more space than those of most seasoned professionals, nothing substantial had been written about Ezra Stone. In 1944, he and Weldon Melick had published an anecdotal book, *Coming, Major!*, concerning Master Sergeant Stone's life in the army, but it provided little insight into the man and the rest of his vast career.

When I first wrote Ezra a letter asking permission to author his biography for my doctoral dissertation, he promptly returned a note—on the backside of some recycled paper—that read: "Thank you. I'm flattered, but my life is not worthy of a biography . . . ." Fortunately, he changed his mind, and for three years he embraced my dissertation, and for three years after that he helped me take the dissertation out of the biography.

Many people have graciously donated their time and energy to my project. I particularly wish to acknowledge the late Ezra Stone and the late Sara Seegar for their hospitality, time, and candid responses to my questions. Ezra not only spent over eighty hours talking into my tape recorder, but on many occasions he allowed me to rummage through his boxes of old scripts, reviews, letters, newspaper and magazine articles, books, and other memorabilia located in his office and home in Bucks County, Pennsylvania, and in his house in Brooklyn. For more than five years he also spent countless hours serving as my master editor.

Over the years, numerous people graciously took time to answer my letters, return telephone calls, provide needed help and information, give personal interviews, and offer gracious hospitality. I extend my gratitude to Francine Bakewell-Stone, Josef Stone, Jack Kelk, Eddie Bracken, Garson Kanin, Charles Moos, Anthony Scully, Joy Claussen, Mrs. Rudy Vallee, Laurence Bergreen, Harry Harris, Robert Oberreich, the late Mrs. Stanley Broza, Maryann Connelly, John and Larry Gassman, Lori Seward, Gene Leitner, Barclay Goldsmith, Joseph Tomes, Regis and Suzanne Caddic, Ellen Dillon, Miriam L. Golub, and Marilynn Huret. At the University of Missouri–Columbia, my heartfelt gratitude goes to Dr. Weldon B. Durham, James M. Miller, Patrick Atkinson, Dr. Stephen M. Archer, Dr. Carla Waal, Dr. Robert Collins, Dr. Suzanne Dieckman, Clyde Ruffin, Dr. Richard Klepac, and particularly Dr. Larry D. Clark, who took great pains to provide me with constructive criticism in the various stages of this book.

I want to thank Dr. David J. Fowler, research director and acquisitions librarian of the David Library of the American Revolution; Meg McSweeney, assistant to the president of the American Academy of Dramatic Arts; Lynn-Marie Jackson, former head librarian of the American Academy of Dramatic Arts; Sam Brylowski from the Library of Congress Radio Archives; Chuck Schaden of the Museum of Broadcasting and Communication in Chicago; Ron Staley from the University of California–Los Angeles Film, Television, and Radio Archives; Elizabeth W. Adkins, archives manager of Kraft/General Foods; Amy Mihill, director of publicity of the MUNY Theatre in St. Louis, Missouri; Martin Getzler, archives assistant of the Rudy Vallee Collection at the Thousand Oaks Library in Thousand Oaks, California; the staff at the Eunice and James L. West Library at Texas Wesleyan University; the staff at Ellis Library at the University of Missouri–Columbia; Brenda Becker and the Jewish Federation of Fort Worth and Tarrant County; Actors' Equity Association; Dick Moore and Associates; the Archives Department of the Irving Berlin Music Company; and the State Historical Society of Wisconsin, Division of Archives. I also wish to thank Stetson University for a Faculty Development Grant, which funded one of many trips to Pennsylvania and New York.

I want to acknowledge Yael Woll, former vice president of the National Director's Guild, for his valuable comments and recommendations and Judith Royer, C.S.J., of Loyola-Marymount University and Dr. John Rouse of Tulane University for their editorial comments. Thanks to Frank

"Junior" Coghlan, whose autobiography, *They Still Call Me Junior*, was published by McFarland in 1993. A longtime friend of Ezra's, Coghlan graciously spoke with me about my project and steered me toward McFarland. And special thanks goes to Hal Kanter for his time, energy, and gracious words in penning the foreword to this book.

Finally, thanks goes to my family for their ongoing support. And much love goes to my wife, Rhonda Weller-Stilson, who served as my research assistant, travel companion, and sounding board. Without her, this project may never have been completed.

Kenneth L. Stilson
February 1995

Introduction

*He gave me the 8 mm. camera with which he filmed me being born.
He gave me loyalty to friends and thoughtfulness toward strangers.
He gave me a bagel-slicing contraption. He gave me a silver sabbath
cup and saucer. He gave me the tendency to be pudgy and the
tendency to make lists. . . . He gave me my first acting role. He gave
me my first college degree. . . . He gave me a cigar habit, I'm afraid.
From him I got my love of opera and my passion for freedom. He
gave me very late night hours, love of wild mint, sour green apples
and salted nuts. He gave me respect of my elders. He gave me the
discipline of written thank-you's. He gave me my semitic features
and my great-grandfather's mezuzah. He gave me a passion for clip-
boards and spring-binders. He gave me all of my mentors. He gave
me true tolerance, irrespective of creed, color, sex, or credit balance.
. . . He gave me presents wrapped in the very gift paper I had given
him last. He gave me the delicious sense of the surprises that he
would always stage. . . . Clippings significant, clippings ephemeral,
clippings for my interest until they came out of my ears, and cri-
tiques of every show I was ever in. Marsh Wheelings, scrapple, and
horse-radish carried all the way from Bucks County to England. He
gave me the love of Matisse, Pavarotti, Arthur Miller, Noël Coward,
Ezio Pinza, the Philadelphia Eagles, the Brooklyn Bridge, the nightly
news, Harvard yard, Chinese food, and cows coming in from the
pasture to milking. He gave me the thrill of an audience's energy. He
gave me the rigor of doing a job well, and he gave me the respect of
the written word.*

Francine Bakewell-Stone, *Ezra Stone Memorial*

The afternoon of May 28, 1994, was picturesque. Temperatures hovered
in the seventies, while the humidity remained relatively low. Over 350
friends, family, students, and colleagues from the entertainment world
filed into a large tent on the grounds of the David Library of the American
Revolution in Washington Crossing, Pennsylvania, to pay final tribute to
an unassuming man, known by an entire generation of older Americans
as radio's Henry Aldrich. This was the fifth and largest such memorial in

1

slightly more than one month, and Ezra Stone would have denied that his life and career warranted such attention.

Despite more than one thousand credits acting, directing, producing, and writing for stage, screen, television, and radio, Ezra never felt that he had made it. Those who knew him, however, vehemently disagree with his assessment. He had an army of friends who dearly loved him and respected his talents. This became clearly evident as speakers from various walks of life shared stories of "The Little Round Man"—a physical trait caused, as he explained to his granddaughter Jennifer, by swallowing a watermelon seed. Letters from George Abbott, Ronald Reagan, Harold Prince, Garson Kanin, Milton Berle, Ed Herlihy, Hal Holbrook, Hal Kanter, and Jack Kelk served as testimony to his profound effect on his profession.

Following the ceremony, some guests wandered into the Feinstone Conference Center to watch an audiovisual montage of Ezra's life. Others strolled through the Rose Gallery to peruse selected memorabilia on display. Both the David Library and the ground floor of the Feinstone Residence Facility were opened to the public. Visitors slowly passed through his office and gazed at his wealth of mementos: family portraits, photos of him, of his late wife, their two children, four grandchildren, his parents, his grandfather, numerous celebrities, and Americana. Several people commented that they could still smell the smoke from Ezra's sweet pipe tobacco and Marsh Wheeling cigars, the original Pittsburgh stogie. It lingered in the fabric of the room.

This, however, was not the office of a man who had long since retired to rest on the laurels won in his youth. This was the office of a seventy-six-year-old man who had always managed to clock more than a full week's work. Ezra always considered himself "the world's busiest, oldest adolescent." Until his untimely accident on March 3, 1994, he regularly took jaunts to New York and the West Coast for Director's Guild meetings and other business affairs in the entertainment world; however, he spent the majority of his final fifteen years keeping alive his father's dream of America. A picture of George Washington still hangs prominently in the laundry room. "Back in the days of Henry Aldrich," he had reminisced not long ago, "I was considered cute. Now I settle for picturesque."

Ezra had not been a child star like Shirley Temple or Baby LeRoy, but he had barely reached voting age when he became a celebrity. At the height of his career, he was known around Manhattan by such names as "Broadway Dynamo" and "Little Giant." In 1938, when Ezra was only twenty years old, his press agent planted a story that appeared in various syndicated newspapers describing his client's credentials as follows: "Ezra Stone, New York's Busiest Little Man . . . laziest boy in school, he now holds eight important drama jobs at once." When this publicity stunt appeared, Stone not only starred in a Broadway comedy, but also headed the players' cooperative that took over the show, understudied two prominent comedians in a Broadway musical, worked as a casting director and production assistant for the legendary George Abbott, and had become the youngest instructor at the American Academy of Dramatic Arts. At the same time, Ezra was embarking on a radio career that was to make him a major star.

Ezra Stone institutionalized the memorable role of Henry in radio's comedy series *The Aldrich Family*, a program that according to the Hooper Ratings, reached more than thirty million people weekly. Soon after it became a regular weekly series, the sound of Ezra's cracked voice became a rallying cry for listeners. *The Aldrich Family* remained on the air for almost fifteen years, and Ezra, despite a three-year leave of absence during World War II, continued as its cornerstone throughout.

Ezra was not groomed for acting. In fact, his father, a stern man who placed a great deal of pressure on Ezra to earn good grades in school, only unwittingly fostered his son's career. To help correct a slight speech impediment, he arranged for Ezra to take elocution lessons. Inspired by his teacher, the young boy began training and working on the stage. This led to Stan Lee Broza's *Children's Hour* on Philadelphia's WCAU Radio, where Ezra performed such recitations as Poe's "The Raven" or *Spartacus' Address to the Gladiators*. The young boy soon earned the title "Philadelphia's child actor."

Having never achieved the scholarly heights his father expected and having twice attempted to run away, Ezra made an early exit from high school to enter the prestigious American Academy of Dramatic Arts as one of its youngest students. There he came under the tutelage of Charles Jehlinger and Philip Loeb. An enterprising and determined young man, Ezra, after graduating from the Academy, immediately found his way into three successive Broadway flops. Undaunted, he then landed a position as a replacement in George Abbott's production of *Three Men on a Horse*.

Ezra always believed his acting career was a fluke. Consequently, he deduced that in order to stay in the business, he had to learn all phases of theater. Abbott usually looked for talent interested in production, so he hired the eighteen-year-old boy to work in his business office under Garson Kanin and Edith Van Cleve. A production assistant during the day, the tireless young man's career began to soar when he performed small roles evenings and weekends in various Broadway shows. It was during the extended run of *Brother Rat*, the show with which Ezra established himself as a first-rate comic performer, that Abbott discovered Clifford Goldsmith's comedy, *Enter to Learn*. Although Abbott had originally slated Eddie Bracken to play the leading role, a high school kid named Henry Aldrich, it was Ezra who eventually won the job and saw his name in lights when the play, renamed *What a Life*, opened on Broadway.

Soon after *What a Life* began its run in 1938, it caught the attention of Tony Stamford, the producer of *The Rudy Vallee Hour*, who asked Abbott for an excerpt to appear on the radio program. Subsequently, he asked Goldsmith to write two special skits about his characters. The writer undertook the task, and the Aldrich Family came to radio with the original stage cast.

Within two years, *The Aldrich Family* became a solid hit as a half-hour program. Each week, listeners tuned in to hear:

> ANNOUNCER: The Aldrich Family, based on characters originated by Clifford Goldsmith and starring Ezra Stone as Henry with Jackie Kelk as Homer.
>
> MRS. ALDRICH: Hen-ry! Henry Aldrich!
>
> HENRY: Coming Mother!
>
> ANNOUNCER: The Aldrich Family, who live in the comfortable house at 117 Elm Street in Centerville, U.S.A., are friends and neighbors of yours. Sam Aldrich and his wife, Alice, are real parents, and there never was a more typical American boy than their teenage son, Henry. As we join the Aldriches, just see if you don't recognize Henry Aldrich as a boy from your block.

What unfolded then was utter chaos. Goldsmith used the trials of adolescence as a starting point and embellished them with rapid-fire complications. The forerunner of most subsequent situation comedies on radio and, later, television, *The Aldrich Family*, according to John Dunning in his book, *Tune in Yesterday*, revolved around situations involving "the generation gap, teenage love, or that vital something that gets lost (such as Henry's pants) and must somehow be retrieved." Henry's escapades kept him and his best friend, Homer Brown, in perpetual hot water. He was always in trouble, as he could make a crisis out of the simple act of going to the store. If an episode began with Henry and Homer going for a swim on an early spring day, it only followed that a pleasant afternoon would turn into a midwinter blizzard stranding the boys on an island and culminating in a massive search for them by all of Centerville's able-bodied men.

Naturally, working for Abbott combined with his success as Henry created many new opportunities for Ezra. Not long after *What a Life* closed, Ezra undoubtedly became Broadway's youngest director, as Abbott entrusted him to stage Richard Maibaum and Harry Clork's *See My Lawyer*, starring Milton Berle and Gary Merrill. This marked the first time Abbott allowed someone other than himself to direct one of his productions; moreover, the youthful Ezra had never directed a full-length play before— anywhere. Nonetheless, the play met with modest success, and Ezra began a new phase in his long career.

In Broadway circles, some people referred to Ezra as lucky, but it was his determination that made things happen. At an age when most young men were just getting out of college and wondering blankly about their future, Ezra Stone became a figure of importance in the entertainment world.

As a production assistant and casting director for George Abbott, Ezra worked on such productions as *Three Men on a Horse, Boy Meets Girl, Room Service, Brother Rat, Pal Joey, Best Foot Forward, The Boys from Syracuse*, and *What a Life*. As a stage director on Broadway and in various regional theaters, Ezra boasted more than twenty-five major productions, including *Me and Molly, January Thaw, Reunion in New York, Your Loving Son, To Tell You the Truth, At War with the Army, Wake Up Darling*, and *Curtains Up!*, and worked alongside such stars as Philip Loeb, Gertrude Berg, Tony Randall, Gary Merrill, Sam Jaffe, Walter Matthau, Gene Sacks, Jack Klugman, Sara Seegar, Steve Allen, Ezio Pinza, Vilma Kurer, Ty Perry, Jack Cassidy, Bea Arthur, Ethel Barrymore-Colt, Paul Lynde, and Bill Macy. During World War II, Master Sergeant Ezra Stone assembled, staged, and appeared in the all-soldier smash musical production of Irving Berlin's *This Is the Army*, starring Irving Berlin and some three hundred entertainers.

Beginning in the 1950s, television proved a magic medium for Ezra, who directed hundreds of popular programs — among them *I Married Joan, The John Forsythe Show, Bachelor Father, The Munsters, Laredo, Petticoat Junction, Lost in Space, Julia, The Flying Nun, Love American Style, Lassie, Karen, Tammy, Bob Hope's Chrysler Hour, Coranado 9, Affairs of Anatol, Angel, The Debbie Reynolds Show*, "Please Don't Eat the Daisies," and *My Living Doll*—working with Jimmy Stewart, Bob Hope, Fred Allen, Ezio Pinza, Danny Thomas, Groucho Marx, Bob Cummings, Sally Field, Sandy Duncan, Phyllis Diller, Martha Raye, Ed Wynn, John Forsythe, Fred Gwynne, Yvonne de Carlo, Herb Shriner, Debbie Reynolds, and Hollywood's number one canine, Lassie. For the American National Theatre and Academy he created, produced, and directed the memorable Golden Wedding Anniversary Tribute to the Lunts.

He no doubt carried the shadow of Henry Aldrich with him throughout his life, but the role was only a part of his vast theatrical career. To cover Ezra Stone's career in its entirety would fill several volumes; therefore, this biography focuses on the pinnacle of Ezra's career, the years between 1936 and 1953, a busy time that reflected both the venerated traditions and the short-lived novelties of the theater and radio of the period. While this book pays particular attention to the role for which Stone is best remembered, his career prior and subsequent to that event place it in its proper perspective. His career spanned several important decades when the American cultural landscape, broadly defined, changed almost daily. Like many of his eminent contemporaries, Ezra successfully made the transition from stage to radio and later to television, which makes him a quintessential figure of this era. His career, which, as he modestly noted, was marked by more perspiration than inspiration, tells the story of the vital, thriving American theater of the recent past.

1. The Child Actor

Beautiful verse, strains of music, a cathedral window, a sunset over the harbor is apt to bring tears of joy. Try a walk with a friend some snowy Sunday morning in the canyons of lower Manhattan.
Sol Feinstone, *Fellow Passengers*

Solomon loved America; he had loved the new country even before he arrived. "In the old country, Lida, most of us were poor. Life was hard, but no one seemed to mind, because there was hope," he later wrote in *Fellow Passengers*, a book dedicated to his grandchildren and to all grandchildren. "Everyone hoped for something; everyone, young and old, dreamed about something better." Solomon dreamed of America, big ships, the Statue of Liberty, the Brooklyn Bridge, and live Indians.

In 1888, in Lida, a small town that was originally Lithuanian and later became part of Poland, Solomon Bialogrodski was born the son of Josef the Scribe, a profession to which he was initially apprenticed. Solomon's mother was a poor, suffering, sweet woman of Polish descent. She was daughter, wife, sister, and mother (Solomon's older brother) of scribes of the Torah, the first five books of the Old Testament. Lacking a formal education, young Solomon read widely in his father's religious and secular books; he also worked for a time in a large bookstore in the capital city of Vilna. These early intellectual influences and an inquisitive mind instilled in the young man a life-long dedication to learning and questioning. Once he even made the mistake of asking his father, "Who made God?" As a response he received a hard slap on each cheek: "Such questions should never be asked."

Solomon's mother, a kind woman who was loved by her neighbors and who never complained, worshipped her husband. She bore him ten children—five of them died at early ages—and died in her middle thirties. When his father remarried an unloving and often brutal woman, Solomon ran away to Vilna and threatened to kill his stepmother if she did not stop mistreating his older sister and the younger children. After working for a time at Funk's bookstore in that "godless city" (according to Solomon's father) and after an extended visit to his mother's family in Poland, Solomon, then fourteen, received from his brother and sister who had preceded

7

him to America by six months, a ticket for passage from Antwerp to New York harbor. "Both were in New York working in sweatshops," wrote Feinstone. "They bought the ticket for forty dollars, to be paid off in two dollar installments each weekly payday."

Departing by a subterranean route, as most Russian emigrants did, Solomon paid thirty-five rubles to agents, who illegally took his group across the border and transported the emigrants to the port of embarkation. The group traveled by night to escape border patrols, slept by day in "safe" barns and root cellars, and eventually reached the Dutch port city of Rotterdam. Traveling steerage class on a transatlantic ship, Solomon arrived in New York harbor and Ellis Island with one Indian-head penny, which had rolled over to him on the steerage deck when someone on the first-class deck had thrown down a handful of coins and watched the immigrants scramble for them; this he took as an omen for his future in his new country. It was at this time that Solomon, at the suggestion of an uncle, adopted a semianglicized version of his mother's maiden name, Feinstein, and thus Solomon Bialogrodski became Solomon Feinstone.

Feinstone first found work in a sweatshop in New York's garment district, and he eventually earned enough money to attend evening classes at Delahanty School for Immigrants, where most students wished to become policemen, firemen, or postal workers. There, besides learning his new language, Feinstone got a crash course of sorts in the history of New York City. He obtained enough credits to earn his diploma in just over three months. Like many others of his generation motivated by the conservation movement, Feinstone attended several lectures in Cooper Union, where he was inspired by such speakers as Gifford Pinchot and especially Teddy Roosevelt; therefore, in 1911 he decided to study forestry at the University of Missouri–Columbia.

He always remembered his time in Missouri, especially his college forestry summer camp in the Ozarks, as one of the happiest periods of his life. Nevertheless, he moved back to the east coast after his freshman year and entered the New York State College of Forestry at Syracuse University where he became honor man of the school's first graduating class. Here he got his first taste of anti–Semitic discrimination. The school administration designated the second highest ranking student, Joe Sweeney, as "honor man" and placed his name on the marble plaque in the forestry college's foyer. It took over half a century and several hundred thousand dollars to have this planned "error" corrected. In 1916 Feinstone received a master's degree in chemistry from the same school. While enrolled at Syracuse, he married Rose Meadow and eventually sired two children—Ezra and Miriam.

For three years after his graduation, Feinstone worked as a chemist at the Philadelphia Navy Yard. In 1920 he became a partner in a Phila-

delphia construction company. Not content with his success in this oc-
cupation, Feinstone entered the University of Pennsylvania's graduate
school in 1925 to better understand the principles of democratic socialism
he had espoused for years. Subsequently he returned to the business world
as a real estate investor in the Philadelphia area, where he attained the
financial success that allowed him to pursue his intellectual interests.

That was the world into which Ezra Chaim Feinstone was born on
December 2, 1917. No one in the immediate family had theatrical aspira-
tions, but the Feinstones enjoyed the arts, especially the performing arts.
Feinstone and his wife subscribed regularly to the Metropolitan Opera,
which every so often presented children's programs, such as a one-act version of *Hansel and Gretel.* These children's shows were typically performed
as matinees at the Academy of Music in Philadelphia, and it was there that
Ezra received his earliest exposure to live theater.

As time passed, the Feinstones further exposed their children to legitimate theater. At age six, Ezra saw Max Reinhardt's spectacular production
of Vollmoeller's *The Miracle,* starring Gifford Pinchot's daughter, Rosa-
mond. As he had done with New York's Century Theatre, Norman Bel
Geddes transformed Philadelphia's Metropolitan Opera House into a simulated cathedral; the spectacle simply overwhelmed the boy—and apparently everyone else who witnessed the production.

Saturday was a shopping day for Rose Feinstone, Ezra, and his sister,
Miriam, a time to buy shoes and clothing at various Philadelphia children's
stores and larger department stores. On those Saturdays they would invariably congregate with other ladies at the famous Golden Eagle in the
main court of John Wanamaker's department store and enjoy a seventy-five
cent Chinese lunch along with a fourteen-piece jazz dance band. Ezra
amused himself with watching the ladies dance with one another. After
shopping and lunch, they often attended the B. F. Keith Vaudeville matinee on Chestnut Street. Performances by Sir Harry Lauder and Belle
Baker stood out in the young boy's mind; however, no memory was more
special than the afternoon when he witnessed a matinee show of Harry
Houdini at the Chestnut Street Opera House.

During the course of the two-hour magic show, Houdini, of course,
asked for volunteers from the audience. Young Ezra wasted no time jump-
ing on the stage, presumably to inspect the locks that entrapped the magician. Assistants had manacled Houdini at the wrists and ankles before
dropping a spot line from the grid. They hooked him by the feet at the end
of the line and lifted him high above the stage floor. After rolling a vertical
glass tank filled with water beneath him, they lowered him into the chamber. Assistants unhooked the line and attached an ornate lid with clasps on
all sides. A curtain fell before the tank, and music played as one assistant
kept time and another stood ready with a fire axe to smash the glass tank

Ezra Chaim Feinstone, age 3, 1921.

if necessary. The mesmerized audience had previously been informed that if Houdini failed to emerge within six minutes, he would drown. Just before time expired, of course, an assistant ripped open the curtain to reveal the dripping wet magician with his hands free from the manacles. Witnessing the entire trick from a chair on stage, Ezra undoubtedly thought he played a significant role in this powerful theatrical event.

Friday nights the Feinstones opened their home to their numerous friends and family acquaintances who came by for hot tea and hotter discussions about scientific, historical, and political subjects. Visiting engineers from foreign countries, doctors, bankers, educators, union leaders, and journalists fascinated the young boy with their varied personalities and wonderful stories. Among these visitors was Maurice Sloan, a colorful and splendid actor who had been forced to give up a promising career on the New York stage because of ill health.

Sloan, an expert cigarmaker by trade, had a tremendous theatrical instinct and love for the stage. As was the custom in the cigarmaking trade, one member would be chosen on a rotating basis to read aloud from literature, poetry, drama, novels, or the daily news. Many times Sloan was selected as the reader of choice. With his colleagues helping him during their meal and rest breaks, he made up his work quota.

Feinstone had lent the failed actor money and then became fearful that Sloan would attempt to pay it back, which was not Feinstone's way of doing business. To minimize the embarrassment, he suggested the actor repay the loan by giving Ezra elocution lessons. The boy had developed a slight lisp and needed improved posture and proper breathing technique.

Sloan agreed, and he and Ezra spent numerous hours several times a week in the dark front parlor of a rented older home in the Strawberry Mansion area of Philadelphia. Sloan instructed the boy in the same voice, diction, and breathing exercises that he had learned while attending the prestigious American Academy of Dramatic Arts in New York. During these elocution lessons, Sloan also taught Ezra the so-called "old war-horse recitations." The boy learned to declaim "The Raven," *Spartacus' Address to the Gladiators*, "The Seven Ages of Man," and "Oh! that this too too solid flesh would melt." When not performing for his teacher, Ezra spent a great deal of time watching the elder actor perform; thus, Ezra became the audience Sloan no longer had as a professional actor.

The child became so engrossed by the beauty of the language, the actor's magnificent use of his voice, and the atmosphere of the dimly lit surroundings in this front parlor that he resolved to become an actor. When Ezra found he could get people to applaud his performances and to laugh at things that were intended to be humorous, he was hooked for life. On many an evening his parents and their guests had to suspend their conversation to witness a sleepy-eyed performer in droopy pajamas attempt Shakespearean resonance and feign complete understanding of one of Hamlet's soliloquies or Poe's "The Raven." He later explained his early fascination with performing:

> I guess what I liked most was doing something by myself. Not team sports, not working on the class work that other students were doing. . . . It made me feel rather special to have this activity that no one else in the school at that time had. So I became a known individual recognized for that skill. And then the general applause and the audience concentrating and

Pupil and first dramatic teacher, Ezra Chaim Feinstone and Maurice Sloan, 33rd Street and Columbia, Philadelphia, Penn., circa 1925 or 1926.

applauding. And my father loved to have me recite, that was the phrase used at the time. You would learn these recitation pieces and you reeled them off. . . . And then going to worker's guild meetings or organizations that my father would belong to. I'd be so-called booked on the program and I remember standing on tables of restaurants and reciting.

Unaware of his talent to teach, Sloan had not considered this profession as a career. Encouraged by the elder Feinstone, he then took on other students and eventually supplemented his income with a small paying job as theater director at the Philadelphia branch of the Young Men and Women's Hebrew Association. After a year of study, Sloan cast his star pupil as the impish youngster in the organization's production of Franz Molnar's one-act play, *Phosphorous and Suppressed Desires*. For this role, Ezra received his first favorable notice in his hometown press. Sloan went on to become a successful and inspiring teacher, counting playwrights Clifford Odets and Joseph Kramn among his many students with careers in the theater.

Ezra's association with Sloan took him directly into early radio, a medium that provided teachers like Sloan with a place to parade their students. At that time commercial radio was virtually unknown, and few listeners tuned in; therefore, sponsored programs were infrequent. For talent, stations such as WPEN Radio in Philadelphia used almost any available performers. Dance instructors rolled out the tap mat and had their kids tap into a foot mike. Singing and elocution instructors displayed their students in front of the old carbon microphones. Needless to say, Ezra first found his way into radio by performing his "well-worn" recitations.

Ezra continued his association with Sloan until the fall of 1927 when his parents sent him to a progressive boarding school in Pawling, New York. Manumit School was part of a new educational movement that was free and experimental, "bound by no worn-out traditions, limited by no fixed procedures, not preparation for life, but life itself," according to a brochure distributed by the school. In the twenties, this was an extremely avant-garde teaching concept, heavily influenced by the progressive thinkers of the day.

During the boy's short tenure at the school, the instructors encouraged his sixth-grade class to write a play; thus, *The King of Cobble Hill* was created, whose title referred to a wooded hill located on the 177-acre eighteenth-century farm that housed the various classrooms, dormitories, administrative offices, and a gymnasium. Having chosen Ezra as the king of Cobble Hill, his classmates created for him a beard constructed of moss attached to gauze with ear pieces to hold it in place. The faculty considered the play uncommonly well written and performed, and to prove how creative their pupils were, they scheduled the show to tour two locations. First, the students played in a nearby outdoor theater at a girl's school in Poughkeepsie. Then the faculty loaded the young thespians into an old bus and transported them to the Ethical Culture School in Manhattan for one performance. Ten-year-old Ezra had broken into New York City as a leading actor.

Ezra's stay at Manumit was brief, for during a school holiday his father questioned the boy as to what he had learned. He could not remember anything from his classes but he explained in detail how the students had built a manure pit, converted an ice house into a dormitory, and dammed a stream to provide a swimming pool. Nellie Seeds, the wife of Scott Nearing, a leading socialist and famous progressive educator of the day, had put Ezra in charge of making the marker stakes for the school's vegetable garden. Ezra also supervised making hand-cranked ice cream, which turned a healthy profit during parents' day festivities. The industrious young boy even found a way to earn money by selling a pocket adding machine to classmates and later to the president of the First National Bank of Pawling. Feinstone, convinced that practical knowledge was not what his son needed, sought a school with a more rigid curriculum.

Ezra Feinstone (bottom right), age 12, eighth grade, Oak Lane Country Day School, 1930.

The Feinstones withdrew their son from Manumit School and enrolled him in another progressive boarding school, Oak Lane Country Day School in Philadelphia, where the boy remained from seventh grade through high school. Oak Lane had a fine reputation and an excellent faculty; it focused on purposeful activities to stimulate original thinking. The instructors thought of themselves as "creative educators." The small school enrolled children primarily of upper-middle class and, in some cases, wealthy parents. Many of the families had been friends since the Philadelphia suburbs developed at the turn of the century. The Feinstones were by no means part of this clique, and until Ezra became an upperclassman, he was not socially included in the "crowd." The teenage boy was always short and far from a serious student or a proficient athlete, all of which made him even more self-conscious than the typical teenager.

Upon his arrival at Oak Lane, the scions of Philadelphia's better families properly snubbed him. This, however, simply sharpened his naturally acute wits, and he took to business in revenge. For example, he opened a yo-yo repair service, at which any of the little snobs could get their ten-cent yo-yos repaired for the small sum of twenty-five cents. "The thing was almost pure profit," he later told Kyle Crichton of *Collier's Magazine*. "I got the repair parts by unravelling the string from the girls' hockey sticks."

During his second year at Oak Lane, Ezra found his way into a key role in Charles Wharton Stork's prize-winning three-act play, *The Flower Seller*, presented by the Arts Alliance at the oldest and best city community theater, Plays and Players, which still operates today on DeLancy Street in Philadelphia. This was an old organization consisting primarily of professional and society people who raised funds to sponsor the arts. To enhance the play's chances of success, the organization imported New York director Charles Allais. Through Owen Roberts, the family's lawyer who later became a U.S. Supreme Court Justice, Feinstone received word that the organization needed a boy to portray Nicolo, Poldini's son.

By that time, young Ezra had gained something of a reputation as Philadelphia's child dramatic actor, and they offered him the role. Although the script and production received rather cool reviews, Arthur Tubbs, the *Philadelphia Evening Bulletin's* leading theater critic, cited the child actor as the shining star of this allegorical play.

> It is in a prologue and three acts and runs the entire theatrical gamut from humor to pathos. The humor is principally supplied by a youngster who unquestionably deserves as much praise as any member of the troupe. He is Ezra Feinstone, cast as the little waif of a cruel and scheming father in the lower reaches of Greenwich Village. The youngster is a gamin, a product of the gutters, and young Feinstone plays the part admirably. His youthful indifference, his boyish devotion even to his father in his cruelest moments, the ability with which he is swayed by suave words, every action of the youngster is plain street boy.

Following this critical bouquet, Ezra became more highly visible to the local art patrons, especially J. Howard Reber, a leading attorney. One night just prior to a Theatre Guild performance at the Garrick Theatre in Philadelphia, Reber arranged for the boy to meet Theresa Helburn, the codirector of the Guild, where he was touted as an up-and-coming young actor. As a result, whenever a child was needed for a Philadelphia engagement of a national touring show, Ezra's name appeared among the top prospects. The important result of this introduction was not that he landed several bit parts but that he made connections there that later allowed him to join the National Junior Theatre.

When Ezra became associated with the three-year-old National Junior Theatre in 1931, it had already gained critical approval from both adults and youth in Washington, D.C., and Philadelphia. The company had been founded and directed by Glenna Smith Tinnin and Katherine S. Brown. Both ladies had begun their careers in Chicago but did not work together until after the First World War when they founded and operated Cleveland's Chronicle House Theatre for two seasons. Next they managed and became travel agents for E. H. Sothern's national Shakespearean lecture tour. The ladies claimed that Sothern gave them the idea to originate a junior theater, because it had long grieved the renowned Shakespearean actor that children had little opportunity for theatrical exposure. The two ladies decided this woeful lack had to be filled immediately.

The National Junior Theatre, whose avowed purpose was to present good adult plays for the benefit of youthful audiences, performed on Saturday mornings and in some cases on Saturday and Sunday afternoons. They began their operation in Washington, D.C., but soon branched out to other east coast cities such as Philadelphia, Richmond, Boston, Brooklyn, and finally Manhattan. The company traveled by bus to most cities, leaving Friday afternoon and setting up and rehearsing that evening. Generally, the cast performed around ten o'clock in the morning at theaters where no other productions were currently scheduled. The company operated with only rudimentary equipment, and its simple settings mostly stood on a bare stage before black legs or a colored cyclorama. After a performance, the company immediately returned to base, an inn in the beautiful small town of Haddonfield, New Jersey. The younger actors returned home in time for Monday classes, so for young professionals, like Ezra, acting remained a weekend operation.

Ezra's first assignment with the Junior Theatre was in James M. Barrie's *Quality Street* as one of the small boys in the dancing class. When the production opened at Philadelphia's historic Walnut Street Theatre, the two ladies assigned an experienced actor to dress with each of the children and show them the ropes, to shepherd them. It was here that Ezra met a life-long friend, John Shellie, who first introduced the boy to the art of makeup, later one of Ezra's many passions. Other supporting roles followed, but the boy remained the company's "second" child actor, as the leading roles went to another young boy, Preston Dawson, Jr.

The Feinstones found it difficult to reconcile Preston's continual good fortune in landing leading roles, such as Tom in *Tom Sawyer* and Jim

Hawkins in *Treasure Island*, with his lack of exceptional talent. Feinstone deduced that the roles came in return for some sort of subsidy or grant from Preston's parents. Therefore, when Tinnin and Brown announced that three plays were scheduled to play in repertory at the Alvin Theatre, a large Broadway musical house on 52nd Street now known as the Neil Simon Theatre, Feinstone negotiated a deal. In exchange for a five-hundred dollar contribution young Ezra would make his Broadway debut alternating with Preston as the lead in Robert Louis Stevenson's *Treasure Island*. The ladies, always in need of financial assistance, agreed.

As usual, Brown functioned as director of *Treasure Island*, but the cast also supplied a great deal of the staging. In rehearsal, the company's leading character man, Robert deLany, choreographed a chase sequence with Ezra and Preston. The scene took place on deck and moved to a rope ladder with the rigging coming down from the upper grid. During the chase, deLany's pirate character pursued the boy with a knife, while Ezra (or Preston) carried a horse pistol. DeLany suggested that the scene end with the boy climbing the rigging followed closely by the elder character. The small, wiry deLany carefully checked how much weight the safety lines could support, and the boys were told exactly on which rung they were to stop. Sight lines were also considered. Once in position, the boy would fire the gun and deLany would fall backward, hanging by his knees on the rope ladder.

During his first performance, Ezra got carried away and let the elder character get too close. Perhaps he got nervous, or maybe he intuitively sensed that the closer the villain got, the greater the tension. When deLany came up the ladder, he grunted through his teeth, "Fire! Fire!" Finally, young Ezra fired the shot and the man fell backward. After the scene, deLany grabbed the boy and screamed that he could have lost an eye being so close to that blank-loaded gun. Ezra was not yet the most disciplined actor.

Soon after departing from the National Junior Theatre, Ezra discovered another weekend performance outlet through the *Children's Hour* on WCAU Radio in Philadelphia, a variety program that showcased the talents of local children. Even though producers normally did not pay for talent, local teachers brought in a steady stream of pupils for auditions. Such programs were typically hosted by an adult or team of adults, and in this case that duty fell to Stanley Broza, whose wife, Esther, served as producer, writer, and director. Shortly after the program began airing, its sponsorship fell into the hands of Horn and Hardart, a Philadelphia and New York chain of restaurants made famous by a patented device called the Automat. Unlike other haphazard children's variety programs of the time, the Horn and Hardart's *Children's Hour* became a scripted theme show.

The interesting thing about this show for Ezra, however, was the couple in charge of production. As a relative of William Paley, founder of the Columbia Broadcast System, Broza became program manager of the CBS-owned and operated WCAU radio station and assigned himself to host the *Children's Hour* as a source of additional income. Stanley Broza used a stage name that broke his first name into two words—Stan Lee—and he suggested to Ezra that Feinstone was not a theatrically appropriate name. He recommended the young actor abbreviate it to Stone, saying "It's shorter and people will remember it better. And as time comes, maybe you'll be in the theater, and it's easier to get on a marquee." Broza was right, and as time passed Ezra Stone saw the wisdom in his advice.

The Brozas' most significant contribution to Ezra's career came when Mrs. Broza, realizing the young man's organizational skills and keen interest in the production phase of radio, made Ezra her production assistant. While the other children headed across the street to Horn and Hardart's for a "free" lunch—in lieu of pay—after a Sunday morning program, the Brozas invited Ezra to their home in Marion on Philadelphia's Main Line. After a hefty beef roast midday meal, he worked for hours with Mrs. Broza in her room sorting through music and discussing themes for the next week's show. During these times together, Mrs. Broza grew extremely fond of Ezra. "Ezra Stone is one of my favorite people of all times," she wrote in a letter just before her death in 1990. "I have two sons whom I adore, and next to them comes Ezra. I always felt as close to him, as if he were my third son. And throughout the life of the *Children's Hour*, whenever we needed Ezra, he was there ready to serve." And as he did with the National Junior Theatre, Ezra left the Broza's house and returned home by Sunday evening to do homework for Monday's classes.

Ezra performed many different sketches and recitations for the weekly radio program, and one of his big dramatic numbers became a showstopper. Reciting from Geoffrey O'Hara's *Guns*, Ezra portrayed a shell-shocked World War I veteran who tried to exorcise the sounds of war from his mind. Mrs. Broza thought musical accompaniment would give the recitation dramatic effect, and so Billy James, WCAU's musical director, played the piano as background to the boy's monologue. Ezra also performed lighter and more comic selections set to music. Occasionally, he worked with a young lady who would sing, recite poetry, or dramatize such romantic scene extracts as Cyrano's "What is a kiss?" speech while Ezra recited literature. Although Ezra had little musical ability, Mrs. Broza continuously found ways to enhance his performances with music.

The Horn and Hardart's *Children's Hour* became so popular that various groups, such as the Reading Carnival and the Dupont Estate, Longwood Gardens, booked them for special engagements. As an executive at WCAU, Broza sometimes had other responsibilities and could not attend. On those occasions, Mrs. Broza pushed Ezra to play the child host. The

Dupont Estate was modeled after the Palace in Versailles, and the *Children's Hour* performed on its outdoor stage along with the Monte Carlo Corps de Ballet and the United States Marine Corps Band; a spectacular fountain display followed the live entertainment.

On one particular evening, the gathering lasted until early morning. The young performers and the WCAU band then piled into buses and headed for home. Trying to impress Jeannie Watson, a young lady in the cast, Ezra said, "Let's not ride in the bus with the kids. Let's ride with the band." Ezra had hosted this particular show and was also testing his new stature within the company. On the road, however, the bus collided with a car that had run a stop sign. When the vehicle came to rest against the sidewalk, the bus driver yelled back for assistance. The musicians remained motionless; some checked their instruments, which were apparently more important to them than the people in the smaller and more vulnerable automobile. Ezra, a coward at the sight of blood, decided the best thing he could do to help in this crisis was to find a telephone. He ran to the nearest lit porch and telephoned the police and an ambulance. Shaking uncontrollably, he returned to the bus and his girlfriend. All six occupants in the car had been killed, including a two-year-old child.

The *Children's Hour* also exposed Ezra to vaudeville. For one week during the summers of 1932 and 1933, the children performed five to six shows a day at Atlantic City's Steel Pier. Broza again had commitments at the radio station, so Ezra filled in as host. By the second summer, the boy had been with the program longer than most and had gained a reputation as the younger performers' surrogate big brother. This was reflected in the following *Children's Hour* vaudeville script.

BOTH:	Ladies and gentlemen!
BOBBY:	We are not the midgets!
JUNIOR:	In fact we think we are very grown up.
BOBBY:	Yes, two big fellows, starring in a sure fire revue.
JUNIOR:	You said it Bobby. You said it.
BOBBY:	And now let me introduce to you the Daddy of the WCAU *Children's Hour*, Stan Lee Broza!
EZRA:	Just a minute, Junior and Bobby, just a minute. After all those rehearsals it's about time you knew that Mr. Broza is unable to be here for the matinee shows. Now start over and introduce me, not Mr. Broza.
BOBBY:	Ladies and
JUNIOR:	Gentlemen.
BOBBY:	Let me introduce for the first time.
JUNIOR:	And we hope the last.
BOBBY:	The big brother of the WCAU kiddies hour,
BOTH:	EZRA STONE.
	(*Applause maybe*)
EZRA:	Now I want to tell you something that hasn't been rehearsed.

> Being one of the kids myself, I know that we are all tickled pink to be back on the pier this year. We only hope you're as glad to have us as we are to be here. Yes sir you've heard them on the air every Sunday morning. Now meet them in person.
> (*Song*)
>
> EZRA: Say, Ellen, please don't kid me about getting old, you little rascal. After all big brother Ezra is only a few years older than you. Why I'm full of pep, vim, and vigor and there isn't a thing you kiddies can do that I can't.

And, of course, the children then proceeded to roller-skate, dance, and sing — all things Ezra could not do with any proficiency.

Although he was there for only a short time, Ezra learned a great deal from his vaudeville experience, including the difference between amateurism and professionalism. The headliner that second summer was the great star of silent and talking film, Edmund Lowe. He performed a specially written dramatic sketch in which he played a gentleman cat burglar. Although the audience perceived him as a smooth performer, backstage he was a lush. When not performing himself, Ezra often observed the other performers from the wings; more than once he witnessed Lowe's road manager propping up the star as he peered through the split in the traveler curtain and introduced his act.

Louise Groody, the original "Tea for Two" girl, on the other hand, was to Ezra the model of professionalism. She performed a song and dance with two men. In the middle of one particular week, she developed a blister on the sole of her foot. Between sections of her act, she had time to take short breaks. Ezra noticed during one performance that she almost fainted. She collapsed; her knees went out from under her in the wings as she made her big exit, but the audience applauded and the orchestra continued to play. Her maid held smelling salts under her nose and removed the shoe, revealing the enormous blister, which had burst. Nevertheless, the maid pulled her together again, and Louise danced out to do the tap dance reprise on her raw wound.

After gaining a considerable reputation as a child actor, Ezra felt different but not special at Oak Lane Country Day School. "I knew that I had a different image in school with my schoolmates, because of what I was doing as a performer," he later said. "I think they were a little more forgiving of my lack of scholarship as a student. That, I rather enjoyed. Then again, there were classmates who had outstanding talent in other areas, and they stood out in their respective areas." Ezra was unaware of having a following, but as a performer he was so obviously in a class by himself that the other students reportedly stood in awe of his talent. Ezra, however, had no pretensions with regard to his talent, and there was neither competitiveness nor jealousy of his achievements on the part of fellow students.

In fact, by the end of his senior year Ezra had also become popular, having been elected president of the dramatic club and selected as an actor for several school plays.

Although his classmates admired his experience, however, a couple of the teachers who directed the productions became a little tense when the precocious young man occasionally questioned their stage technique. Nevertheless, Ezra continued to land leading roles in an extremely wide variety of plays. He played Simon the cobbler in Leo Tolstoy's *What Men Live By*, Driscoll in Eugene O'Neill's *Bound East for Cardiff*, a blackfaced Dreamy in O'Neill's *The Dreamy Kid*, and the lead in Kenneth Webb's farce comedy *One of the Family*.

Ezra was so conspicuously affable that in short order he became popular with most of the faculty as well as the students. He became a mascot of sorts. During high school, he also wrote a gossip column for the school paper, managed the varsity athletic teams, let the air out of faculty tires, and fell in love with every girl he met. In fact, he did everything but study, except when his father would force him to do so after revealing report cards or ominous notes from the headmaster and various teachers.

Ezra had the impossible dream of attending the famous Yale Baker School of Drama, but he had several scholastic deficiencies, particularly in the area of chemistry. Considering that his father held a degree in that subject, had worked as a chemist in the Philadelphia Navy Yard during the First World War, and had taught chemistry at Syracuse University, the potential consequences of his failure seemed unbearable. Feinstone had always taught the virtues of a sound education. He believed all children should possess a curious intellect and be eager to learn. With this in mind, Ezra lacked the nerve to bring home his final handwritten evaluations from his teachers, and instead he made plans to run away from home. He set out for New York, determined to change his name, get radio work, and pay his way through the actor's training program at the American Academy of Dramatic Arts, a school, he was told, that required neither Latin nor chemistry. For these reasons, the academy seemed much more suitable than Yale. Besides, Ezra remembered that his former elocution teacher had graduated from there.

Ezra began hitchhiking from Philadelphia and made it to Trenton before getting hungry. In typical juvenile fashion, he realized how convenient it was to have his Aunt Ida living in the vicinity. The moment he arrived at her door, however, she spotted trouble. She telephoned the Feinstones and instructed her daughter, Estelle, to escort the young vagabond to a Philadelphia bound train. Ezra's father met him at the station and properly chastised him.

Ezra stayed home for a while, but the pressure put on him by his father soon caused him to take another stab at running away. This time he was

on Roosevelt Boulevard, U.S. Highway One, north of Philadelphia, trying
to hitchhike his way to New York when he accidentally thumbed the wrong
car. Thinking it to be his lift, Ezra approached the automobile only to spot
his father, who had been notified by Oak Lane, and was in hot pursuit with
a business colleague at the wheel. Upon seeing his mistake, Ezra turned
and ran toward safety into the huge Sears-Roebuck store. His father, who
had hopped out of the car to chase him, enlisted the help of a park guard.
Not knowing what kind of criminal he was pursuing, the guard drew his
gun and joined the chase. When Ezra turned back to measure his advantage, he saw the gun. "He was going to shoot over my head, I guess. I hope,"
Ezra later said. Many things entered his mind, but when the guard accidentally dropped the weapon, Ezra, out of a strange sense of good sportsman-
ship, stood waiting for the guard to pick it up, then he continued his sprint.
Other people coming out of the store realized the men were chasing this
juvenile, so they surrounded and seized him. The guard grabbed the boy
and pulled him down the steps to his father. Along the way, Ezra stopped
to pick up a shiny brass object; it was the guard's uniform button, which
he carried on a chain in his stage makeup case throughout his life. Of these
episodes, Ezra recently wrote,

> It would take a shrink a couple of years of therapy and thousands of dollars
> to dig for the real reason for my running away. I guess I realized I would
> never be a scholar and that I would never possess an exceptional brain
> like my father. In fact, this has been my fate through the years. My wife,
> my two kids, my four grandchildren all have better brain power than I
> have. That's why I have to work longer, harder than my many more tal-
> ented colleagues to produce a usable product.

Following these escapades, Ezra and his parents sat down for a serious
discussion about the boy's future. His father, conceding that his son had
no scholarly ambitions, made a deal with him. "If you want to be an actor,
if you want to be anything, you've got to learn to do it right. And the only
place to learn is at an accredited school." Feinstone agreed to let his son
take a one-year sabbatical before entering college in order to attend the
American Academy of Dramatic Arts. Needless to say, the young man immediately sent for a catalogue, which he read thoroughly several times.
The program was, of course, exactly what he wanted.

The American Academy of Dramatic Arts, originally entitled the
Lyceum Theatre School of Acting, had opened in 1884 when Franklin
Haven Sargent, a Harvard graduate, quit the faculty of that university after
his suggestion to set up a drama department had been ignored. His new
school, which opened in New York, became the first training school for
actors in the English-speaking world. In the beginning, the academy based
its training on the theories and techniques of François Delsarte, an external

approach centered around stylized control of gesture and attitude—actually acting by numbers. Sargent, however, soon perceived the need for more naturalistic acting to fit the work of the new dramatists such as Ibsen, Strindberg, and Maeterlinck. By 1891 "Life Study" and "Improvisation" became part of the academy's curriculum. Charles Jehlinger, an early graduate and academy teacher, carried Sargent's concepts forward when he became director of instruction in 1900. He became one of America's first master acting instructors, pressing his students beyond the conventional histrionics of the time to genuine emotional involvement, truthful behavior, and simple, honest communication.

Ezra arranged an audition with the prestigious academy on December 1, 1933. When the long anticipated weekend arrived, Ezra and five companions of various ages from Oak Lane loaded their automobile and headed for a lively time in the big city. Ezra's primary mission, of course, was to audition, but the remainder of time was free to "raise hell." On the highway, a billboard advertising what was then the newly built Hotel Edison at the reasonable price of two dollars per night attracted their attention. The hotel limited the number of occupants per room, but the six young men convinced themselves that no one would be the wiser if they all stayed together. Ezra registered the room under his name and the boys went upstairs to unpack.

Mr. Flood, the hotel detective, who no doubt had grown accustomed to youthful groups overcrowding rooms, saw the boys enter and grew suspicious. After an exciting night that included seeing Charles Laughton's *Henry VIII* and a titillating venture into one of the Times Square taxi dance halls, the boys retired to their room at the Edison. Around three o'clock in the morning, Flood, a middle-aged James Cagney–type, entered the room and accused the boys of being illegally registered. He commanded every boy to sign the ledger, which he conveniently carried with him. In terror, they did as instructed, paid the additional money, and the Edison had a bonanza of three times the normal bounty for that room.

The following day, Ezra went for his audition at Carnegie Hall, the academy's home at that time. He entered the elevator with a small yet distinguished gentleman, shorter than himself. The budding actor did not recognize the man and simply assumed that he worked as a businessman in the building. Upon arriving at the fourteenth floor, Ezra started to exit the elevator when the man placed his hand before the lad. The well-dressed stranger then preceded him out into the hall. Ezra realized he had just been chastised for his lack of courtesy to an older person. The man disappeared down the hall as Ezra entered the school's front office.

There the receptionist met him and introduced young Ezra to Emil Diestel, a tall, slim man with buck teeth, who together with Jehlinger owned and operated the academy. He was not an actor but loved to act, and he typically showed each applicant how to audition. Diestel expressed concern about Ezra's age—it was the day before his sixteenth birthday—and the school had a policy against accepting high school students because the owners believed taking them on did not work socially. There had been one prior exception to this rule, however, when Rudolph Schildkraut came to the academy and obtained special permission for his son, Joseph, to enter at the age of fifteen. Ezra became the second exception when Diestel allowed him to audition.

Ezra performed a recitation from Marc Connelly's *The Green Pastures*, a selection he had previously used on the *Children's Hour*. Diestel was obviously impressed with Ezra's talent. On his audition form the teacher commented that the boy had "unusual reading ability" and was "exceptionally intelligent for his age." He also noted that Ezra's spontaneity, versatility, characterization, and pantomime skills were exceptional. Diestel saw him as "a boy of unmatched ability and instinct with fine equipment" whose biggest handicap was his height.

In the 1930s, an AADA student had to complete two terms, the first referred to as the junior and the second as the senior year. Training could either begin in April and end the following May, or the courses could be spread over two regular academic years beginning in October and finishing the following year in May. After his audition and interview, Ezra handed Diestel his father's check for five-hundred dollars, which covered the tuition for his first year. Upon signing the necessary paperwork and registration forms, Diestel sent for Jehlinger to meet the new student. A short time later, the small man who had silently reprimanded Ezra in the elevator entered the room; it was Jehlinger. Jehlinger, although shorter than the five-foot-three-inch Ezra, looked at the boy and then turned to Diestel and said, "He's quite short to be an actor." He then turned on his heels and walked out. Diestel reassuringly said, "Since he didn't say no, that means you're in."

Diestel informed Ezra that entering the academy as an April junior was best, but this was contingent upon whether Oak Lane would grant him an early release. High school graduation was not until June, and Ezra wanted out in April. This seemed an impossible request from this less-than-perfect student. However, Headmaster Arthur M. Seabold, a rather large, utilitarian educator from the Midwest, seemed more than happy to rid the school of a boy he considered a troublemaker. Upon his recommendation, the Oak Lane instructors exempted Ezra from finals and graced him with passing grades. They even allowed him to return and graduate with the class, by which time Ezra had become, at least in his own eyes, an important man who had entered an independent training program. It was with some sense of arrogance that he walked down the aisle with what he perceived to be less experienced "kids."

Charles Jehlinger. Photo: Courtesy of the American Academy of Dramatic Arts.

Ezra began his study at the American Academy of Dramatic Arts in spring of 1934. He and the other April juniors had the special advantage of working with Jehlinger, sometimes referred to as Jehli, for four hours per week for six weeks in the summer in scene study class. The October juniors, on the other hand, only worked with the master teacher only as seniors during their final examination play. Jehli, to use Kirk Douglas' description in his autobiography, *Ragman's Son*, was known as the great director, the great teacher of acting who had taught Spencer Tracy and Rosalind Russell and Sam Levene, and who would later teach Jason Robards and Jennifer Jones and Anne Bancroft and Grace Kelly and so many others. He was almost eighty years old, slightly deaf, a little gray-haired man about five feet two with black eyebrows and piercing eyes that looked out at you from behind thick glasses.

Although many of his students feared and even hated Jehlinger at times, most of them later became his disciples. Nevertheless, many stories circulated about Jehlinger's harshness and cruelty in rehearsal, and Ezra's experiences with him were no different from those of the hundreds of students who had passed through the doors before him.

Ezra first suffered a tongue-lashing from Jehlinger early in the summer while working on a scene from Elmer Rice's *Counsellor-at-Law*. Ezra had been cast as a communist supporter opposite his classmate Daniel Marcus, who later changed his name to Marc Daniels and pioneered the three-camera technique on the television comedy series, *I Love Lucy*. During the scene from Rice's play, the tension of an argument was to build until Ezra picked up a chair and threw it at his classmate. Apparently the pair of student actors got a bit carried away, for Jehlinger stopped the display and proceeded to criticize the falseness and pretentiousness. He said, "Mr. Stone is thinking more of Mr. Stone than he is of the character he is supposed to be portraying. You're acting like a high school idiot." He continued the verbal assault for several minutes until Ezra became so angry he almost threw the chair at his instructor. Jehlinger instructed both actors to immediately perform the scene again. The second time it became a simple, straightforward, emotional scene without the added dramatics. This was of course not to be the only tutorial attack suffered by the first-year student.

Years later, during a social weekend with Jehli at the Santa Barbara Hotel, Sara Seegar, Ezra's wife, asked him why he ranted and raved at his students and insulted them by calling them idiots and idiotic amateurs thus reducing them to tears. The older man replied, "Tears are the release of tension. Young people learning to act are very tense, but remember this, I never called anyone an idiotic amateur," he said. "You're forgetting the most important little word. What I have always said is 'You *act* like an idiotic amateur.'"

As juniors, the students had to participate in a fixed number of examination plays, and the faculty then tallied up points to determine whether or not a student was to be invited back for the senior class. Tension ran high, because a great number of students did not make the transition from the junior to the senior year. During a dress rehearsal of one of these productions, Ezra experienced what was perhaps one of his worst attacks from Jehlinger.

The student actor had been cast as the cockney window washer in John Galsworthy's *Windows*. One of Ezra's other instructors had recently given a lecture on the importance of the actor's research, a lesson that struck a chord in Ezra, and he went to the New York Public Library where he discovered period pictures of British workmen. Ezra also studied dialect books to help create an authentic accent. "Now I'm going to show Jehli just what I can do," he thought. After waiting anxiously in the wings, Ezra made his entrance. He had not walked more than a few feet onto the set when from the back of the house the little old man roared, "Stop!" "Go back!" He mocked and jeered for what seemed an eternity. The actors then started over and again gave Ezra his cue. He walked on the stage only to hear the same remarks. He did not understand this and whirled around and said, "Mr. Jehlinger, I'm sorry. I'm ready to go back, but I don't know what you want me to do." "Well, I want you to take off that absurd mustache," Jehlinger replied. Ezra had proudly pasted on a Herbert Mundin–type of mustache that completely obscured the lower third of his face, and he proceeded to tell the old man that he had gone to the 42nd Street Library to research his makeup, which had convinced him that this style of facial hair was typical for the period. A long, frightening silence followed, and then Ezra heard the familiar sound of his teacher mounting the shaky ramp temporarily joining the auditorium and the stage during rehearsals. The master teacher walked to the boy's side and said in a cooing tone, "Mr. Stone, that's the youth of it. The stage magnifies. When you put on all that hair on your cherubic face, you look ridiculous. You don't look like a British workman in his middle age. Wear a smaller moustache for the performance."

Nevertheless, Diestel and Jehlinger saw promise in Ezra, and the young actor made the cut for the senior year. In fact, in his senior year the Feinstones arranged for Ezra to become a scholarship student. Since the academy always had a surplus of women and a shortage of men, Ezra did not see this as a huge compliment to his talents. At any rate, he figured he was receiving his professional training for only five hundred dollars.

During his junior year, Ezra lived on three and a half dollars a week in an apartment on 14th Street owned by friends of relatives. Everyday Ezra had to walk up to 57th Street and 7th Avenue to school. When it rained, he rode the subway for a nickel. He had breakfast in the apartment, followed by a simple lunch at Nedick's orange drink stand located near the academy. For ten cents he could purchase a watered-down orange drink, a cup of coffee, and a hot dog. On the way home, he usually passed Hanson's Bakery, where for a penny he picked up a large loaf of day-old bread. He then improvised the remainder of his dinner.

Ezra toyed with the idea of augmenting his income, so he took a job as a dishwasher in a cafeteria one block away from school. Such a job was not for him, however, and he lasted barely a week. His parents sent him an allowance, which he usually squandered on books or girls, and this forced him to again improvise with his finances until the next week. Although money was not plentiful, Ezra was never deprived of anything. Unlike some of his classmates, he did not have to struggle or work extra hours at outside jobs in order to survive.

By his senior year Ezra had made many new friends and had picked a roommate, a Hoosier from Indianapolis named Robert Oberreich and affectionately known as Obie. Moving to the Village just off Sheridan Square, the two young men envisioned themselves as Bohemians. They lived in a one-bedroom, studio apartment with an extra bed in the living room. Soon after they had moved into their pad, Feinstone came from Philadelphia to visit. Naturally, he had several concerns. Himself an immigrant kid from New York, he knew the neighborhoods, knew the tone of the town. He thought all Greenwich Village people, all artists, were phonies. On the night he stayed with Ezra and Obie, a group of singers formed a chorus just outside their window singing Christmas carols — although it was only early fall. Feinstone assumed they had escaped from an insane asylum.

A set of low French windows in the front of the apartment looked out onto the street; this, too, concerned Feinstone, who wanted bars placed in front of them for safety. The boys, however, were simply renting the place for ten dollars per week and could not alter the apartment. Obie was an ingenious, artistic young lad, and he satisfied the old man's concerns by affixing to the window a cobweb of sorts with lashline and eyescrews to detract intruders.

Obie was also an eccentric young man who, much like Ezra, had been interested in theater since his childhood. He and Ezra both also expressed a love of the sea and ships. They therefore decided to walk around the island of Manhattan in easy stages to explore the waterfront. The first night, the two adventurers got as far as Battery Park from the Village. In order to get a few hours sleep, they boarded a subway for the trip home. The next night, they rode back to Battery Park and started up the East River. They continued this ritual for several nights until one evening Obie got angry at his roommate for something unusually petty and disappeared. Ezra was terrified because every few blocks along the river sat empty warehouses filled with homeless men. He did not know whether Obie had fallen prey to these vagabonds or had slipped through the planks into the river. He searched for a while then decided it was best to return home.

When he reached the top of the stairs leading to the apartment, he found a locked door. He tried his key; the lock had been packed. Ezra banged on the door, but his pleading fell on deaf ears. After sleeping that night on a park bench just beneath his own window, Ezra confronted Obie when he made his departure for school the next morning. Backing him against the wall, Ezra said, "What the hell do you think you're doing?" "Just wanted to see how flexible you were," Obie replied, and off to school he went.

At the academy, Ezra sailed along rather smoothly for several months. He was assigned to numerous noteworthy roles, one production per month to be exact. In October, he portrayed Peter Cope in Philip Barry's *Paris Bound*; he followed this in November as Oliver O'Shaughnessy in Lennox Robinson's *The Far-Off Hills*. However, during his December assignment as Bobby in A. A. Milne's *The Romantic Age*, Ezra had his next major confrontation with Jehlinger. While rehearsing this romantic comedy, the old man challenged the honesty of his love for Dorothy Sparks, a young woman in the cast. He claimed in no uncertain terms that Ezra was a phony, a liar, and a cheat. He suggested the young actor had not even read the script and should go back to high school. If not for the period coming to an end, the boy felt the tongue-lashing would have continued well into the night. Jehlinger had really hurt him this time, for Ezra had deep feelings for Dorothy. The insensitive instructor had attacked not only his artistic ability but his feelings for Dorothy. He had shamed Ezra in front of the class. Later in life, Ezra reflected that perhaps Jehli was trying to steer him and the young actress clear of what he knew would be a dangerous course for them to pursue. The old man knew only too well that many drama school romances had tragic endings.

At the time, however, Ezra felt that Jehlinger was the devil himself. That night he went back to his room and resolved to give up the whole business. He pored over the school catalogue, which a year before had seemed to him so glamorous. In it he found a statement saying that a student who was undesirable could be asked to resign his seat in the academy. He decided to beat them to the punch.

That night, he sent a telegram to Diestel explaining his position and intentions, and the next day he stayed home from classes. Just after ten in the morning, he received a telephone call from Marie Meyer, the beloved secretary and school sweetheart. Diestel wanted to speak with him. After a little coaxing, Ezra withdrew his resignation. He now believed the school's instructors had had a change of heart and wanted him. Since he was a scholarship student, money had no bearing on their position. He thought that perhaps he did have something to offer the theater, so he returned to classes with his confidence restored. Jehli never said a word about the incident, and from that day on he seemed to go out of his way to talk to Ezra and help him. Because Ezra did not own a suit, Jehli sometimes even lent the young actor his personal wardrobe to wear on stage. Several years later, after Ezra had become a teacher at the academy himself, Jehli even invited him to lunch in the Oak Room of the Plaza, where he lived, to counsel him.

Philip Loeb. Photo: Courtesy of the American Academy of Dramatic Arts.

Ezra met many people and made a lot of contacts during his two terms at the academy, but none were more special than his relationship with Philip Loeb. Loeb was an outstanding teacher, and although he was stern, unrelenting, and demanding, the majority of students adored him. In a letter written a few years after his graduation from the academy, Ezra described Loeb as "a fine actor, understanding teacher, inspiring director, and the swellest guy on Broadway." Their first association was as teacher and student, but Ezra and Loeb quickly developed a deeper relationship. He became Ezra's cherished friend, his New York surrogate father, and his connection to the professional theater world.

Ezra's most vivid, early memory of Loeb grew out of a lesson that changed the young actor's entire career. A senior's greatest concern lay not in the classroom but rather in what role he or she would land as a "lead" in the downtown production at the grand old Empire Theatre where agents, casting directors, and producers might see their work. When Ezra learned he was to play Maxie, the older, wisecracking, Tin Pan Alley piano player in Ring Lardner's and George S. Kaufman's comedy hit *June Moon*, he exploded with anger. Since his days as Philadelphia's child dramatic actor, he had pictured himself as a great tragedian. Comedy was beneath him. He did not want to destroy his dramatic talent by begging for laughs.

Again Ezra sent a short, snappy letter to Diestel resigning his seat in the academy. And again Diestel summoned the lad to his office. This time his cajoling could not break Ezra's stubbornness, until he revealed that Loeb, the director of *June Moon*, had requested Ezra for the role. Reluctantly, Ezra rescinded his second resignation.

That night Ezra received a telephone call from Loeb. "Who the hell do you think you are?" his teacher screamed. "I asked them to cast you in that part! You're not a kid actor from Philadelphia anymore! Why did you come to the academy in the first place?" Ezra was reminded of Jehlinger's verbal attacks. "Do you think you know more than people who have been training professional actors for half a century and doing a damn good job of it?" his teacher continued. "Maybe you should go back to Philadelphia. Maybe it would be the best thing for you, for the theater and for your father. Save him all the dough it's costing him. You're a loser! Give up!" By this time Ezra had broken into tears. He pleaded, "I'm not a funny guy! I can't tell jokes like Maxie!" "Who asked you?" Loeb countered. "Kaufman and Lardner are pretty funny guys. They don't need you." He explained to his pupil that his job as an actor was to find and project Maxie's mental attitude. "Let the playwrights supply the jokes! Now just get your ass down to the first rehearsal tomorrow and tear up that stupid letter of resignation." Loeb hung up and left Ezra sobbing.

Four weeks later on February 21, 1935, a Thursday afternoon, the select cast of academy seniors presented *June Moon* on Broadway at the Empire Theatre. Another group of seniors presented the first act of W. Somerset Maugham's *The Sacred Flame* as a curtain-raiser. Typically, the school presented its matinee series on Fridays, but this eighth matinee production of the season was moved up one day because of Washington's birthday. The students' hard work paid off, and the show had no obvious weak spots. The comic bits and timing, although not up to professional standards, were surprisingly good for a student group. On the whole, this production turned out to be the best of the academy season.

Despite Ezra's original misgivings about his character, his performance stole the show. In addition to the agents and producers sometimes attending these matinee performances, a writer from *The Billboard* reviewed the young thespians. Aside from the appearance of his name in the cast list of the National Junior Theatre productions of *Treasure Island* and *Tom Sawyer*, this was Ezra's first legitimate New York appraisal. Eugene Burr, the reviewer, singled him out as the most exciting performer with the most promise in the cast.

> Perhaps outstanding (tho there were plenty that deserved that description) was the performance of Ezra Stone, as Maxie. Stone, according to reports, is just about leaving his middle teens, but if he keeps on the way

he's been going, he'll be a finished and professional character man before he graduates. He has an imposing gallery of stage portraits already, and all of them excellent.

Loeb was correct, and Ezra's career took a propitious turn. He would no longer play the dramatic roles of his youth.

2. The Young Professional

Years after Ezra Stone had established himself on Broadway and radio, reporters often asked him to describe the one chance occurrence to which he attributed his success. Ezra usually turned to the story of the American Academy of Dramatic Arts' production of *June Moon*. With this show, Ezra had proved to himself that he could perform comedy, but, more importantly, it was during its matinee performance that Broadway producer Harry Moses happened to walk through the theater and witnessed the young actor's work.

At the time of *June Moon* a hit show was running in the Empire Theatre — Zoe Akins and Edith Wharton's *The Old Maid*, starring Helen Menken and Alice Brady. On this particular Thursday afternoon in the middle of the students' production, Moses descended from his office to retrieve something from the backstage area. His normal route was to exit through the front door onto Broadway at 40th Street, walk around the corner and back to the stage door. But it was cold and raining, so he altered his course through the lobby and pass door to get backstage. As he walked behind the orchestra, he heard the audience laughing uproariously. The timing could not have been better, for it was Ezra's juiciest moment. Hearing the laughter, Moses stopped to listen to the entire scene, after which he went about his business.

The next morning the producer called the academy and asked for the name of the student who had played the Harry Rosenthal part in *June Moon* — Rosenthal having originated the role of Maxie. Miss Meyer, the secretary, quickly identified young Stone, whereupon the producer summoned the actor to his office. Ezra still had several months to go before graduation, and he knew that Moses did not have a show in the works; nevertheless, he immediately answered the producer's call.

After a secretary in Moses' front office announced him, Ezra was permitted to enter the inner sanctum and meet the kindly, white-haired gentleman. As Ezra stood in silence facing the first real Broadway producer he had ever seen, Moses burst out with, "I'm sorry to tell you this, but there must be some mistake. The school sent the wrong student. The actor I saw was much older." "No, Mr. Moses; that was me in makeup," Ezra explained. They carried on the discussion, but Moses continued to fret that he had somehow been misled about Ezra's age. He conceded, finally, that Ezra had considerable talent and questioned him about his future goals.

"I want to be a working actor when I graduate," Ezra responded. "My father wants me to go to college. I'm really only supposed to get a year off to go to the academy, and then I'm supposed to go to Yale if they'll take me. But, if I can get work, I know he isn't going to make me register." This reply impressed the producer, but he lectured Ezra on his decision to forego an education, momentarily convincing the lad to register for the fall term at Yale and join the professional theater after college.

Before they parted, however, Moses told Ezra of his plans to produce a show in the fall, provided he could put all the production elements together. He said, "If you're not in college and you read that I'm ready to go into production, contact the office and I'll see what I can do." Ezra, of course, needed no more incentive than that.

Ezra returned to his apartment to plan his attack on the uncertain future. Because his parents continued to press him to enter college, he had to quickly find work as an actor. Fortunately, not long after this episode, Philip Loeb began to find employment for some of his students. From the senior class, he selected Ann Landers, Lois Leng, and Ezra, who were all short in stature, to make their professional debut as kids in the Theatre Guild's production of *Parade*, an avant-garde musical revue starring Jimmy Savo and Eve Arden. The guild had hired Loeb to direct this show, which would be its final production of the 1934–35 season.

The Theatre Guild had been established in 1919, and by the 1930s it was considered by many American and European critics without question the foremost American theater organization. Although the 1934–35 season had two relatively successful shows—Maxwell Anderson's *Valley Forge* and S. N. Behrman's *Rain from Heaven*—it was clearly the most lackluster season in the guild's seventeen years. Finally, *Parade*, originally written by Paul Peters and George Sklar for the Theatre Union on 14th Street, ended this mediocre season in atypical fashion.

"At the close of the season it is customary for the Theatre Guild to lift her skirts cautiously and to skip a little; that frivolous gesture is not always becoming to so staid a body," said Brooks Atkinson in a *New York Times'* review. In other words, the guild's typical practice of ending the season with a fairly conservative production was shattered when they opted to produce the left-wing play *Parade*. The guild described *Parade* as "1935 set to music." The production's playbill explained

> We are living in unusual times. We are inclined to take some of the foibles of the day too seriously. Others we pass by too lightly. *Parade* is designed to give you a perspective. It is bright, witty and nimble, yet it has a sting. It is, in fact, a revue with a definite idea and not just a potpourri of songs and sketches about sex and love and the moon up above.

From 1921 to 1927, Loeb had worked with the guild as general stage manager. During this period, he had played an instrumental role in organizing young performers, known as Guild Juniors, who later went on to coordinate a highly successful production of the revue *The Garrick Gaieties.* Directing a second edition of *The Garrick Gaieties* thrust Loeb to the top of the line among revue sketch directors on Broadway. It was thus only natural that the Theatre Guild now entrusted him with the direction of the revolutionary revue *Parade.*

Parade represented Ezra's first association with a full union production. Actors' Equity Association, which had been established in May 1913, had two membership classifications: seniors who had been in the union longer than two years, and juniors. Nonunion actors could not appear in equity productions; therefore, before Ezra could accept his role in *Parade,* he had to join the union as a junior member.

Ezra immediately telephoned his father, who also acted as his advisor on legal and business matters, and explained his obligation to join the union. Dues were eighteen dollars per year. Although equity had no initiation fee, new members were forced to pay the first year's dues in advance before they could receive their member identification cards. Since Ezra's weekly allowance amounted to only twenty-five dollars and went toward living expenses, he could not afford union dues until he received his first paycheck. He therefore had the ominous chore of requesting a loan from his father.

Unexpectedly, this proposition pleased Feinstone, which in turn led Ezra to suggest a bigger proposal. He told his father, "By paying ten years' dues, one-hundred-eighty dollars, I can become a life member, which I know is a lot of money." His father pondered the situation for a moment and said, "Well, do you figure that you're going to be an actor for the rest of your life?" Ezra, of course, answered affirmatively. "Then it's a good investment," Feinstone concluded.

According to equity rules, a musical could rehearse five weeks before opening; nonmusicals were given only four weeks. There was no rehearsal pay, and the producer had to open a show after this time and begin paying his cast performance salaries. Incidentally, Philip Loeb later headed a group of left-wing equity rebels who fought for and achieved rehearsal pay for all union members. But in 1935, if management fired an actor in a musical within the first seven days, he or she received no salary. If released after the seventh day, however, the producer had to pay two weeks of contracted performance salary.

Needless to say, on midafternoon of the seventh day of *Parade* rehearsals, the Theatre Guild fired Landers, Leng, and Stone. The producers reasoned that the show would go through many changes; sketches and numbers would be taken out and replaced with new ones. To save money

Ezra receiving lifetime membership into Actors' Equity Association from James O'Neill, 1935.

they intended to hire young actors, rehearse them for a short period, and fire them on the seventh day. They could then replace them with new young people and use them for a week without pay. If *Parade* showed promise during the last week of rehearsal, the guild could always hire three new kids for the permanent company.

Loeb, however, not realizing the guild's plans to use and then release his students, challenged the guild "powers that be" and demanded the young actors remain in the cast. He also told the three academy graduates to attend the eighth day of rehearsals, but when they arrived, the stage manager would not allow them onto the stage. The three found themselves sitting in the house waiting for their teacher-director to rescue them. Fortunately, Loeb carried sufficient clout in the organization, and the matter was quickly resolved in the young actors' favor. Ezra Stone had been initiated into the professional ranks.

Parade opened in New Haven, Connecticut, as was customary for musicals in the 1930s. Following a split week there, the show moved to Boston's Colonial Theatre, where the audience was clearly divided into two camps. The *New York Times* reported, "The difference in opinion was amusingly apparent at the first performance in the Colonial Monday evening, when the galleries and standees were enthusiastic in approval of the satirical sketches, and the lower part of the house took it gamely but quietly." The revue sparked lively debate in Boston. One side held that the guild had misled its subscribers. They thought *Parade* was dull entertainment filled with a lot of propaganda and that its performance would drastically hinder chances for a successful guild subscription drive in Boston the following season. The other side argued that the show marked a new development in the field of revue, that it reflected a radical yet significant theatrical trend, and that the guild was fulfilling its proper function by producing it.

Since Ezra was one of Loeb's favorite students, the director assigned him to many numbers as a nonspeaking, nonsinging character. For example, in the opening number, "The Police Station," the five-foot-three-inch actor, complete with his Herbert Mundin mustache, played a Keystone Cop amidst a chorus of other cops, all of whom stood over six feet tall. To prepare for this particular number, Ezra went into the chorus girls' dressing room thirty minutes before each performance. Following a few moments of sight-seeing, Ezra approached each girl, especially Stella Clausen, about whom he was "gaga" and Billy Rose's sister, Polly; each would kiss a different part of his face with their lips painted with reflective red lipstick. As a result, this short Keystone Cop made his opening appearance with lip marks spread over his entire face.

During one of the early performances of *Parade*, Ezra learned a difficult lesson in professionalism. The sketch, "The Dead Cow," which featured Charles D. Brown and Eve Arden, examined the plight of a hungry Southern farm family in the middle of a drought. They could not afford paint or wallpaper, so old newspapers decorated their walls. The blackout of this sketch occurred when the character Johnny, played by Leon Janney, followed by a newspaper photographer and reporter, dragged a full-sized, papier-mâché cow onstage. The impoverished farmer then raised his gun to shoot the intruders. Ezra, who imagined himself the busiest actor in the show, played the reporter in this scene.

On one particular evening, Ezra was gossiping with the stagehands instead of listening for his cue. Meanwhile, the fake cow had been set up just offstage, and the photographer and Johnny stood in position. The cue came and Ezra, of course, was nowhere to be found. The two young men attempted to move the cow onto the stage without him, but the clumsy property caught in the doorway. The blackout joke was lost, and the sketch ended with a great hush.

The stage manager, Dennis Murray, had no choice but to signal an early blackout for "The Dead Cow." Ezra, who had a quick change from that sketch into his next big part, dashed upstairs to his dressing room. He had just stripped off his clothing revealing his Indian body paint when the second assistant stage manager issued a summons that the stage manager wanted to see him immediately. Ezra explained that he had no time before his next entrance, but the assistant declared that Murray had banned him from the stage for the remainder of the performance. This shocked the young actor. He did not understand how the show could continue without him. Little did Ezra realize that this silver-haired, square-jawed man with steel blue eyes—a veteran of the Ziegfeld Follies—was the most feared stage manager in the Broadway musical world.

Ezra arrived at Murray's desk to find him preoccupied with throwing cues. After completing his work, he turned to Ezra and instructed the lad to follow him for the remainder of the show. Before his eyes, Ezra saw every one of his roles instantly replaced or edited out completely. Every once in a while, as Murray went about his business, he turned back to Ezra and said, "Smart-aleck, huh? You think you're going to be an actor? What in the hell did they teach you at the Academy? I think you need to go back and spend four more years there!" The lecture continued until the final curtain fell. Ironically, several years later, Murray enrolled his son, Don, in the academy when Ezra was one of its instructors. Years later, Ezra helped Don's career by hiring him to play the juvenile in the prologue of *June Moon*, which was presented on television on NBC's *Fred Allen Show*, a show Ezra produced and directed.

Parade opened in New York at the guild's 52nd Street Theatre on May 23, 1935, to cool reviews. Most critics could not understand why the Theatre Guild took over the production when the smaller Theatre Union had refused it, and most agreed that the show was more appropriate for a smaller house outside the Broadway district. As the guild operated on a subscription basis with seven weeks representing a minimum guaranteed run, the production closed after seven weeks. Nevertheless, it drew a fair attendance, had lots of energy, and featured an excellent director, scenic designer, cast, and crew. Ezra learned much from both the successes and failures of this show, and it exposed him to the world of Broadway musicals.

Several weeks before the cast and crew of *Parade* received their final notice, Ezra and most of the others suspected the show's ultimate demise. The enterprising young man immediately made alternate plans. With Sol Hoff, an elder AADA classmate who was a bandleader and singer turned actor, Ezra concocted a plan to put together a social staff for the Hotel Hoffman on the Borscht Circuit in the Catskill Mountains in upstate New York. The company was to consist of ten academy-trained actors, all with musical as well as other performing talents. They would perform sketches, musical numbers, and one-act plays. Hoff, whose stage name was David Ainsely, decided that whether *Parade* remained open or not, he would take the group to work in the hotel. If *Parade* closed, Ezra would join them; if it continued to run, he would of course remain with the Broadway company.

When *Parade* folded, the guild dismantled the set and hauled the pieces that could not be recycled to Secaucus, New Jersey, for eventual incineration. As was typical of Broadway shows in the thirties, the reusable elements were carted to Cain's Warehouse, a sort of scenic cemetery for closed shows. Local colleges or stock companies could sometimes obtain these items for the price of transportation. Ezra recognized a potential use for some of *Parade*'s smaller, collapsible scenic units and arranged to pick up those pieces small enough for use in a social hall. For an outlay of eight dollars, Ezra and a load of beautiful Broadway scenery designed by Lee Simonson headed for a hotel in Nappanock, New York.

The Stone and Hoff Stock Company operated for ten weeks during the summer of 1935, billing itself as "the most versatile and energetic company seen in the vicinity for many a year." The producers' objective was to present quality performances, stirring and true-to-life dramas mixed with comedies and musical revues. Audiences apparently enjoyed the young thespians' work, but in a letter the following year Ezra admitted their lack of experience with which they had embarked on this venture. Less than ideal performances and living conditions affected the enterprise. "I'm not exaggerating when I tell you that I never knew where I'd sleep one night to the next," Ezra wrote. "I slept on a cold leather divan in the musty lobby, a two-legged cot in the basement, a mattress in the attic and one nite on a dew-soaked hammock on the lawn. I lived out of a trunk for 10 weeks. I know my work suffered. But it taught Sol and me a lesson."

The season ended in the mountain resort just after Labor Day, and Ezra immediately returned to New York and began searching for employment. He walked from one producer's or agent's office to another, read theater notes columns, checked on films, attended large "cattle-call" auditions— anything to find work before his parents began applying additional pressure to get him to enroll in Yale. One afternoon as Ezra walked the theater district, he by chance ran into Philip Loeb, who grabbed Ezra, saying, "You gotta come with me right away, right across the street here to the Music Box Theatre. I'm gonna get them to hire you for a show I just signed for."

As luck would have it, the producer of *Room Service*, a comedy by John Murray and Allen Boretz, was looking for three actors to play New York public school students who appear at the end of second act in search of their teacher. In pursuit of one of those roles, Loeb marched the young professional directly into the office of one of Broadway's most important men, Sam Harris. Harris' line of successes had temporarily secured his reign as Broadway's top comedy producer. Once inside his Music Box office, Loeb shoved his former student toward Harris and said, "Here's your Abie Applebaum; don't look any further." Ezra stood agog as Harris offered him the small role on sight. Once again, he had avoided the clutches of Yale.

Ezra was still a junior equity member, and Harris signed him at the minimum pay of twenty-five dollars per week. The company rehearsed in the Music Box Theatre before starting out-of-town tryouts at the McCarter Theatre in Princeton, New Jersey. Starring John Litel, Paul McGrath, Hardie Albright, and Dorothy Vernon, with Loeb in support, *Room Service* opened to a responsive house filled to capacity. The optimistic production staff and cast moved on to Philadelphia, and Harris scheduled their Broadway debut for the first of December.

Once they arrived in Philadelphia, Ezra convinced Loeb, who had yet to meet the young man's family, to eat dinner with them and stay the night. The Feinstones lived in Oak Lane at the north end of the city in a large older home that had been subdivided into apartments—Feinstone being practical about things like that. Rose Feinstone assigned her son and Loeb to the annexed downstairs bedrooms, which were not as well insulated as the rest of the stone house. Following the Feinstone household custom, they sipped tea before retiring for the evening, and Rose offered sandwiches to the two young men. Ezra, not wishing to impose, declined for both; however, the always hungry Loeb retorted, "Why are you speaking for me? I'll tell her if I'm hungry or not!"

After the late-night snack, everybody retired. But just as Ezra had donned his pajamas, he heard a shriek from Loeb, who was in what used to be Ezra's sister's room. "It's cold in here! What are you trying to do to me? How will I ever be able to perform!" Typically, Loeb was feigning wild extremes for humor, but on Ezra's conservative parents he made a deep and lasting impression.

Room Service did not do well at Philadelphia's Broad Street Theatre; in fact, most critics agreed the show should close immediately. Unfortunately, the advance publicity had not adequately promoted the production. Furthermore, *Room Service* was a fast-paced farce requiring responsive audiences, and the show opened in Philadelphia with a Wednesday matinee. Ezra, hearing nothing but silence during the first act, peered through the curtain and counted only six people in attendance, half the size of the cast. Moreover, he knew most of those people probably had complimentary tickets. Needless to say, the Harris production of *Room Service* never made it to Broadway, closing out of town after two weeks.

In the 1930s many so-called shoestring companies operated on the outskirts of Broadway; one of these was managed by Oscar Wee and Jules J. Leventhal, a pair who persisted in regarding drama not as an art but as a business. "So 'phooey,' please on the player's inner radiance, the playwright's astonishing dramaturgy, the director's sublime interpretation and the producer's masterly supervision," wrote Jack Gould of the *New York Times*. "J. J.'s stethoscope is trained on the theater's heart, which is the box office; his aim is not to bring the theater to the masses but the masses to the theater." This production team belonged to the carrion crows of Broadway, swooping down on dying shows and negotiating contracts with the original producer and cast. To the business of reviving dead shows they brought assembly-line techniques, more often than not forsaking all artistic values.

Wee and Leventhal became known as the Goldwyns of the suburbs, the sahibs of the so-called subway circuit. In other words, to get to a Wee and Leventhal show, one had to take the subway. In the middle thirties, they developed a rotary stock circuit with theaters in Boston, Springfield, Massachusetts; Providence; Hartford; New Haven; Newark; Jackson Heights; Brooklyn; Atlantic City; Trenton; Philadelphia; Baltimore; Washington, D.C.; and Chicago. They also owned a warehouse full of scenery, costumes, and properties in Fort Lee, New Jersey, having bought most of it just before it was to be incinerated. Both men reported annual incomes in the seven digits. The more artistic producers disapproved of their methods, but Wee and Leventhal boasted a much better credit rating. Since they targeted the original cast, they found rehearsals unnecessary. In fact, they did not rehearse at all unless they had a change in a major role. If the smaller roles needed to be recast, they ignored the original director and hired the stage manager, who knew the blocking and served as an adequate surrogate director.

Wee and Leventhal negotiated the rights and purchased the costumes, set, and properties for *Ah, Wilderness!* from the Theatre Guild, which produced most of Eugene O'Neill's plays during the Depression. Of course, George M. Cohan, the leading player in the Broadway production, did not consent to continue his performance, but they obtained his understudy, Seth Arnold, a person known to be something of a lush but a good character actor. Arnold's wife, also an understudy, agreed to portray the female lead opposite her husband.

Ezra auditioned and received the role of Tommy, a chubby, sunburnt boy of eleven with dark eyes, blond hair wetted and plastered down in a part, and a shiny, good-natured face. Although Ezra's hair was much darker, his cherubic look allowed him to play young boys. He also understudied the juvenile leading role, Richard, the seventeen-year-old son. Ruth Gillette, an AADA actress who had appeared with Ezra in the Sam Harris production of *Room Service*, signed on as Muriel McComber, a fifteen-year-old girl and Richard's first love, and Betty Field, another academy actress who later appeared with Ezra in *What a Life* and radio's *The Aldrich Family*, was hired to play Belle, the pretty peroxide blond who taunts Richard for not sleeping with her after he has given her five dollars. To receive a contract from Wee and Leventhal, Ezra also had to agree to assist the stage manager, Irving Stiefel, who played as the bartender in one scene.

At the time, Ezra believed *Ah, Wilderness!* represented an extremely important step in his career. He had made two previous Broadway appearances, but this show was an established hit. Since this was his third such show in less than one year away from the academy, Ezra thought he was well on his way toward making a name for himself on Broadway.

Leventhal was a stubborn man with little respect for directors, designers, and playwrights. *Ah, Wilderness!* was scheduled to open and play for one week at the State Theatre in Trenton. The beach scene between Richard and Muriel represented a key moment in the play. Lee Simonson's set for this scene required the use of the entire cyclorama and mounds of sand that broke into sections. Most of the remainder of the play occurred in the sitting room of the Miller home, designed as a rather shallow room and readily mobile. Since the single beach sequence occupied the entire stage, it was clear that the shift was potentially clumsy.

To prepare the State Theatre for the performance, stage hands worked long and hard. At that time, union laws regulated that members working past 11:30 P.M. receive double their regular pay scale. That magic hour was fast approaching as the stage crew struggled with the mounds of sand and a cyclorama hung by an outmoded hemp line system. Leventhal, watch in hand, paced before the footlights. "Set me up the bitch scene," he demanded in his thick accent. "If you ain't got this bitch scene set up before midnight, I'm cuttin' the whole ting." O'Neill had refused to let the Theatre Guild, or anyone else, cut a syllable from any of his plays, but Leventhal was casually threatening an entire scene.

After a week in Trenton, the company moved to the Erlanger Theatre in Philadelphia. One of Ezra's duties as assistant stage manager was to inform the actors how much time remained before curtain. Ezra, at this point in his life, did not manage his own time well, which made him a poor candidate for this position. He frequently got sidetracked in conversation, then ran down the hallway yelling "half-hour!" . . . five minutes late. By his own admission, he practically never announced an accurate call. Nevertheless, the elder cast members liked Ezra and forgave his tardiness. In fact, his mismanagement of time became a running joke with the company.

During this period Ezra enjoyed playing poker, and the stage hands frequently had a game in progress on the scene dock on stage left. One night as they played a dealer's choice, high-low hand, Ezra and a stage hand held unusually good cards. A lot of money, in their terms, began to accumulate in the pot. The tension mounted as the two continued to raise each other. Suddenly, Ezra heard the cue for the curtain to fall on the bar scene, and he had given neither the warning nor the cue. Irving Stiefel, the stage manager turned bartender in this scene, again gave the cue line. By now Ezra had arrived at the stage manager's control panel on the stage left prompt side. Ezra detected the anger in Stiefel's voice as he threw his onstage cue one final time. The assistant stage manager punched the warning light on and off. Nothing happened immediately, but soon Ezra heard footsteps running up the iron stairs leading to the fly gallery. He then realized that his poker opponent was the flyman responsible for dropping the curtain. Meanwhile, Stiefel ad-libbed to the others on stage that he was closing the bar early. He kicked them out, swiped the bar with his towel and walked off stage where he grabbed Ezra by the lapel and shook him until he had vented his anger. Ezra's career as an assistant stage manager ended when *Ah, Wilderness!* closed a week later.

Following the failure of *Ah, Wilderness!*, Ezra again returned to New York in search of employment. Almost before he got settled, he read audition notices for a new play by Zoe Akins to be produced by Harry Moses. "Harry Moses!" thought the young actor. He saw the opportunity and prepared to take action. The play was *O Evening Star!*, a story derived from the Marie Dressler legend, which chronicles her rise, fall, and difficult return as the Queen of Hollywood.

Jobyna Howland, one of the original Gibson Girls and a former top model for John Howard Christie, was scheduled to play the lead. To direct the production, Moses imported an extremely sought after female director from Germany, Leontine Sagan, who had recently directed a highly successful silent film entitled, *Das Mädchen in Uniform*, which concerned lesbian activity in a German school and predated Lillian Hellman's *The Children's Hour*.

Ezra went to the Empire Theatre and waited his turn to visit with Moses and remind him of the offer he had made the previous spring. To his surprise, Moses recognized him and offered him the role of the auctioneer's assistant in the prologue. The play began with the auctioning of Amy Bellaire's (Marie Dressler's) estate and then flashed back to her former glory. Moses said, "They're casting now. I'll take you to meet Miss Sagan and her codirector, Frank Conroy."

Moses graciously introduced Ezra to the director, but she looked at the short actor and shook her head as if to say no. Sagan couldn't speak English but her interpreter informed Moses that visually Ezra did not fit the role of the auctioneer's assistant. Moses turned to the translator and said, "Tell Miss Sagan that she'll just have to get used to that, because this young man is going to be hired for the production." Although Ezra did not even read for the role, he soon found himself in rehearsal.

As the fifth day of *O Evening Star!* rehearsals approached, the young equity actors grew increasingly nervous. Unlike musicals, producers of straight dramas could fire an actor without pay only within the first five days. If an actor returned for the sixth day, it meant a guaranteed two-week's salary. Ezra anxiously anticipated this moment, for his experience with *Parade* was still fresh in his memory. To his dismay, the stage manager, Lionel Bevens, called him over at the end of the fifth day. Ezra fully expected to receive his walking papers. But instead of firing the young man, Bevens invited him to stay late and assist with readings for another role for which an actor had received notice, thus leaving a vacancy that had to be filled immediately.

Moses' casting office arranged for several actors to come to the theater to audition, and Bevens assigned Ezra the task of throwing cues in the selected scene. After several conservative and rather artificial actors dressed in typical three-piece suits with ties, a casually dressed young man with a large, sunny smile and closely cropped blond hair walked onto the set. The character to be recast was based on Jack Oakie, a famous screen comic and a lovable drunk. The scene, set outside the famous Paramount Studio gates with their corkscrew columns, required the Oakie character to stumble and fall into the gutter. The well-dressed actors reading for the role skipped the business of hitting the deck; one merely pointed to the ground cloth and rotated his hand, indicating that his character was rolling in the gutter. The more casual young actor, however, chose not to feign the action but staggered and collapsed on the stage floor and crawled around holding the playscript in his hands. The onlookers immediately recognized his talent and his winning personality. Thus Ezra had his first encounter with Eddie Albert. After the audition, Moses promoted Ezra to the role of Ed, the mailroom kid from the studio, and hired Albert to play the small role of Ben Martin.

O Evening Star! opened at the Empire Theatre on January 8, 1936, to grudgingly bad reviews. Although some critics said the play had moments of emotional triumph, most of them agreed that it wallowed in sentiment. Grenville Vernon captured the general reaction when he wrote, "*O Evening Star!* is filled with theatricality and unrestrained emotion. It is Zoe Akins at her worst." After only four performances, management distributed closing notices to the cast and crew. Once again, Ezra found himself unemployed.

Prior to graduating from the academy, Ezra had become acquainted with two of the school's recent alumni, Martin Gable and Garson (Gar) Kanin, both of whom frequented the school's greenroom between auditions and interviews. Kanin had also taught a scene study class and had directed several student productions. In a recent letter, Kanin remembered his first impressions of Ezra's work as a student.

> I had seen Ezra and thought very highly of him and his work, and had him in several plays. . . . It was clear from the first time I saw him in a scene in class at the AADA that Ezra was a remarkably talented, imaginative, daring young actor. He went on to prove the veracity of my first impression. He played a variety of parts at the AADA, as indeed did all the students. The difference was that most of the students had certain parts they were good in while they failed in others, but to Ezra it was all one great lark and he enjoyed each and every part he created.

Soon after Gable and Kanin had graduated, they struck a deal with WMCA Radio, an independent New York station, to broadcast thirty-minute biblical stories on Saturday mornings. During many performances, both actors played more than one role; at times they even enacted two or three characters in a scene by themselves. But if the script required more than six or seven characters, they offered academy actors work. Ezra had become part of this pool of extras when he was still a student, and, more important, he had befriended Gar Kanin.

At the time of *O Evening Star!*, Kanin was playing a small part in *Three Men on a Horse*, a farce comedy by John Cecil Holm and George Abbott and the hottest legitimate play on Broadway at the time. During a Saturday morning biblical performance, Kanin informed Ezra that Mr. Abbott, the director, intended to remove him from *Three Men on a Horse* so he could take on a larger role in Bella and Samuel Spewack's *Boy Meets Girl*, a new comedy also to be produced and directed by Abbott.

In *Three Men on a Horse*, Kanin played the small role of Al, a wisecracking photographer from the *Newark Gazette*, who entered in the last act with Gloria, a reporter from the same paper. The entire role consisted of snapping a few pictures and referring to his cohort as "Toots," but Kanin also understudied all the larger male roles. His departure left an opening for Ezra; however, Mr. Abbott was vacationing in Miami and therefore was not available to audition new cast members. This situation left Edie Van Cleve, the head of the Abbott casting department, with the authority to make the decision.

Van Cleve, another academy graduate, played the role of Gloria in *Three Men on a Horse*, understudied the female leads, and directed all three road companies. If she liked Ezra's audition, he was assured employment.

Before Ezra arrived to visit with Van Cleve, Gar Kanin telephoned her in his behalf. Surprisingly, Harry Moses also found time to speak with her about Ezra. Van Cleve scheduled the appointment with the young actor just thirty minutes before a Sunday matinee performance of *Three Men on a Horse*, an arrangement Ezra was informed of by Kanin. When he arrived at the Playhouse Theatre, an extremely punctilious doorman informed him that Miss Van Cleve did not expect him and that she never spoke to anyone prior to a performance. Deciding he had received misinformation, Ezra wandered up and down 47nd Street, rationalizing the situation and marking it off as a lost cause. But as he walked home, he suddenly changed his mind. Concluding that he had no other prospects, he had nothing to lose. By the time Ezra arrived back at the Playhouse, the matinee had begun, which forced him to wait alongside the unpleasant doorman.

After a while, as Ezra stood outside the theater waiting to see Edie Van Cleve, the audience began to file out. About the same time, two men slammed open the stage door. Both were yelling, and the smaller one screamed, "Shut up and don't you talk to me that way! And don't you hit me!" Ezra recognized Teddy Hart, who played Frankie in *Three Men*, running from Sam Levene, who could be extremely emotional and volatile and was now throwing a barrage of foul language at the petite man for something that had occurred during the performance. Ezra began to have serious doubts about whether he should get involved with this group of characters, but he stayed and eventually received permission to enter backstage.

As Ezra climbed up to Van Cleve's second floor dressing room, he noticed a sign reading "Ye Olde Dressing Room for Edith Van Cleve, Betty Field, and Garson Kanin." He stepped into this communal area where Van Cleve, a curt and businesslike woman, waited. She said, "They tell me you're an up-and-coming comedian, Mr. Stone." They exchanged pleasantries and began reading the script aloud. Displeased by his audition, he later wrote, "I never realized how lucky I was that Mr. Abbott was in Miami and was unable to hear what appeared to me to be a horrible reading." To his surprise, she offered him the job but warned him that if Abbott did not agree with her decision, Ezra would be given his notice and receive two weeks' salary, which had now climbed above junior equity minimum to thirty-five dollars per week.

Since 1932 Abbott had produced nearly every show he directed, but *Three Men on a Horse* was produced by a Broadway gambler-type press agent named Alex Yokel. After discovering a script entitled *Hobby Horse* by John Cecil Holm, Yokel had gone to Warner Brothers for financial support, which they promised only if Yokel could find someone to doctor the script and direct the production. Yokel approached Abbott, who immediately recognized the play's potential, rewrote it, split the author's royalties, and retitled it *Three Men on a Horse*. The play opened to fine notices, but no one, including Abbott, realized just how big it was to become. At the height of its popularity, the show boasted a Broadway company, three road companies, and a London production. Many critics described it as the biggest nonmusical hit of the 1930s.

Abbott and Yokel worked well together for the first couple of years. Just prior to Ezra's arrival, however, the director and producer had ended their friendly relationship. Abbott explained the details in his autobiography, *Mister Abbott*.

> People react to success in various ways. . . . He [Yokel] started out as a meek little man eager to do anything he could to help; now all of a sudden he began to feel important, imperious, to give violent orders. My contract specifically stated that he was to have no authority whatever behind the curtain, but as soon as I was out of town, he would be backstage giving notes to the actors. . . . When I got to Boston to see the company playing there, I was shocked to discover a red light on the bar in the second scene

which flashed on and off advertising a roadhouse nearby. Not only did the blinking light have a rather distracting effect on the audience, but the roadhouse which it advertised was in Boston, whereas the action of the play was in New York. I quashed this and left my stage manager in charge of the various productions and went to Florida. The next thing I knew a friend sent me a program from the London production which stated that Alex Yokel had directed the play. That was the end of our relationship.

Ezra, however, was not aware of this feud. In fact, he became one of the few of Abbott's actors who actually liked Alex Yokel. This relationship would later pay off for Ezra.

Although Ezra played only a small role, he believed his involvement with *Three Men* taught him more about the technique of playing comedy than any prior experience. The academy had provided proficient training in script and character analysis and basic stage technique. Now by sitting in the house at many performances and watching the scenes preceding his entrance, he learned the meaning of comedy—what gets a laugh and what doesn't. He was discovering how important timing was and how to build a scene so as to prompt laughter.

Ezra's observations also taught him the negative effects of a two-year Broadway run. At that time, he believed the show had already become somewhat flat, lacking the indescribable spark that had originally brought *Three Men on a Horse* to prominence. Ezra's observations of the cast appeared in a paper written for his Monday night English composition class at the City College of New York.

> . . . it must be pointed out, that the company, with the exception of Shirley Booth, who plays the ex–Follies girl and James Lane, the bartender, has become quite stale. . . . Sam Levene, whose characterization of Patsy, a gambler, the most dynamic of the "Three Men" was studied and detailed the first few months of the run and now has become unbearably wooden. . . . Shirley Booth, however, outshines all her colleagues. She is ever fresh, ever funny, and never for a moment fails to give the illusion of the first performance.

In a 1936 *New York Times'* article, Abbott mirrored Ezra's assertion in more articulate language. Concerning the two-year run of *Three Men*, he wrote:

> My claim is that any group of actors who have played the same performance 200 times or more is on the way to becoming very mechanical, . . . Every actor knows what horrible things a long run can do to the performance. Unconsciously the actor, bored with saying the same old inflections night after night, changes his readings. If it is a sad play, he becomes more sad (what a time we had in *Coquette* to keep it from being a funeral). If it is a funny play, he becomes more funny, and then you have nothing . . . Few of them do it on purpose. It is the inevitable consequence of monotony.

But as Ezra grew older, his attitude toward the company's overall performance softened; presumably Abbott's perspective did not change with the years. When Abbott returned from Miami, he attended one of Ezra's understudy rehearsals. Although he always remained a gentleman, he could appear foreboding because of his straightforward manner. "Mr. Abbott didn't demand respect; it was automatically there," said Eddie Bracken, a later Abbott actor. "His presence demanded respect. Abbott was a father figure, a big brother figure, a friend figure. You couldn't get away with murder with Abbott because just one line would put you right down to the ground. You knew that the boss was speaking and you paid attention." So the master director witnessed Ezra's work and spoke to the new member of his company in his typical fashion, with precision, clarity, and economy. And in his own way, he was complimentary of Ezra's work. The young professional remained in the cast and thus became a member of the "Abbott company," an informal distinction resulting from Abbott's allegiance to a core group of favored actors he used in various productions.

In the 1930s and beyond, George Abbott established himself as one of Broadway's top producers, directors, and writers. He achieved a reputation for "pulling rabbits out of shabby theatrical hats and turning them into ermine." Prior to *Three Men on a Horse*, his extensive list of Broadway successes included *Broadway* (1926), *Coquette* (1927), *Twentieth Century* (1932), *The Drums Begin* (1933), and *John Brown* (1934). Abbott had once dreamed of directing significant pieces of literature, of becoming a directorial Shakespeare of sorts, but with *Three Men on a Horse*, he established himself as Broadway's preeminent director of farces and musical comedies. In 1936, George Jean Nathan of the *Theatre Arts Monthly* wrote, "His is the theatre of snappy curtain lines, wisecracking dialogue, mention of favorite brands of champagne, periodic, humorous excursions to the lavatory, sentimental relief in the shape of tender lovers, and various analogous condiments, all staged as if the author had used a pepper shaker in lieu of an inkwell." By the time Ezra joined Abbott's company, he had few rivals in the field of popular entertainment.

Ezra remained as Gar Kanin's replacement as the photographer in *Three Men* at the Playhouse Theatre. Kanin, in the meantime, moved with Betty Field across the street to the Cort Theatre to play in *Boy Meets Girl*. Since Ezra's role was relatively small, he had a lot of time before making his entrance. Kanin took advantage of this situation and hired Ezra as his valet for five dollars per week. Ezra picked up Kanin's laundry, laid out his makeup, handled his mail, and did whatever else needed attending to. Once he had checked in with the Playhouse stage manager half an hour before curtain, Ezra crossed the street and helped his new unofficial employer. He then returned in time to make his appearance in the third act.

Sometime during the late summer of 1936, Kanin suggested to Abbott that Ezra might work well in the business office; the valet *cum* actor had always maintained a sincere interest in the production and directorial phase of show business. Abbott asked the young actor to talk about his ambitions. "I'd like to write and someday like to direct," Ezra answered. Abbott invited him to come to his office, located at 220 West 42nd Street on the twentieth floor next to the New Amsterdam Theatre. He left Ezra with the notion that his people would find a place for him somewhere. Abbott often employed young performers he felt possessed drive and talent. He did not pay everyone in his office, but each received something much greater, the privilege of observing and learning from Broadway's master producer and director.

When Ezra arrived for his first day of work, Abbott introduced him to his press agent, Charles Washburn. Although extremely bright, Washburn, a former newspaper man, was an acerbic, growling Irishman. After Abbott assigned Ezra to assist him, Washburn took one look at the young man and said if that was what the boss wanted, he would oblige. Abbott went to his office leaving Ezra to the mercy of this curmudgeon. Washburn began by informing young Stone that he had no use for him; nevertheless, he allowed his new assistant to sit in an old chair, which he usually kept piled high with magazines, and observe.

Ezra sat in that chair the entire day. He had no desk, no typewriter, no errands, no assignments; his job was to watch and listen. When he arrived the second day, Washburn again ordered him to get back into the chair and watch. Finally, the older man asked if Ezra could write. The helper said he believed he could. Washburn then said, "Write me a story for the *Journal American*." "On what?" Ezra asked. His new mentor said his job was to figure that out.

Following that night's performance, Ezra went home and wrote a publicity story, a short feature piece on the life of an understudy in *Three Men on a Horse*. The next day, he presented it to Washburn, who immediately began editing it as he read. Apparently the older man liked it, because he handed it to his secretary and told her to type it up as a press release and send it to the newspaper. When the *Journal American* used the entire article, Ezra thought he had found his second calling; if he did not make it as an actor, he would become a press agent. But his success didn't alter Washburn's view of him, and their working association lasted only a couple of weeks.

One afternoon, Kanin asked Ezra to step into the restroom for a chat. Standing at the urinal, Kanin informed his friend that Samuel Goldwyn had offered him a chance to break into the film industry as a director. Believing his future was in Hollywood and having discussed the matter at length with Abbott, Kanin was preparing to accept the proposition. He realized Ezra's displeasure in working with Washburn, and he suggested that the younger associate ask to be moved to the casting department, working under himself and Van Cleve. Wasting no time, Ezra cleared the move with Abbott and became the low man in that division.

Kanin did not have to leave for Hollywood until fall of 1936, so Ezra learned his new role from both his elder associates. He worked diligently as a general go-fer, scheduling casting sessions, readings, and interviews. After making the initial arrangements, he coordinated the backstage operation. When it came time for Abbott or the playwright to hear a reading, Ezra worked with the stage manager, distributing scene excerpts, pairing actors, and even reading with unmatched performers.

After Kanin's departure, Ezra moved up one rung. The casting department now consisted primarily of Van Cleve and Stone, whose responsibilities increased. While Van Cleve was working on a show during its production phase, Ezra would be assigned to the next script. He also began to familiarize himself with the theater market by attending non–Broadway shows, and catching out-of-town tryouts. His purpose in all this effort was to find undiscovered talent. When Abbott announced auditions for a new play, Ezra would handle the flood of telephone and mail inquiries. He then set up interviews and readings with performers who looked good on paper, especially if he had seen them in outside shows. He typically held initial screenings in the Abbott office. Once his boss gave final approval to the script and set rehearsal dates, they would have two to three weeks to cast the production. Ezra (or Edie) would then set up readings in the chosen theater and manage the performances and conferences that followed the formal auditions. At this point, Abbott would make his final casting decisions, which would be given to Carl Fisher, Abbott's nephew and his general business manager, who in turn would notify the actor or his agent and set about to negotiate a contract. Since Ezra took no part in the business end, at this point his work was completed unless the producer and actor could not come to terms. Then Ezra supplied information concerning the next actor in line.

Ezra's position with Abbott continuously grew and its boundaries lost definition. He had always had a sincere desire to become a director, and after a while Abbott entrusted him with the supervision of understudy rehearsals and asked him to suggest replacements for both Broadway and road company casts. Ezra also began to read and screen plays. When manuscripts came into the office, he perused them and wrote down his opinion of their quality. This spared his boss the impossible task of sifting through piles of scripts.

Sometime during this process, Ezra discovered a play entitled *Three Steps Down*, by Baruch Lumet, which he hoped to cultivate and perhaps to help direct. Abbott ultimately rejected the script, but he gave his youthful employee some advice. "You know Ezra, I decided not to do *Three Steps Down*," he said. "The people aren't very interesting or likable. Plays I do, I want to have people who are either attractive or interesting." This discouraged Ezra for a while, but Abbott realized the young man's desire to direct and later rewarded him for his hard work.

3. Maturity

Prior to his association with George Abbott, Ezra's attitude toward theater had seemed unbridled, immature, and misdirected. He undoubtedly had a sincere desire to make a career in the business, judging by his relentless efforts to gain employment. He did not believe that he was merely a boy seeking to defy his father's wish that he enter college and train for a stable profession. Nevertheless, even he had to admit that early on he lacked the mental discipline found in most working performers.

Something inside him changed, however, when he joined the Abbott company. Perhaps his evermounting responsibilities turned him about, or possibly his new maturity resulted from his close working relationship with such dedicated professionals as Garson Kanin, Edith Van Cleve, and Abbott himself. Regardless of the reasons, Ezra matured as a person and as a theater artist. No longer a follower, he became a responsible leader who skillfully managed his time as actor, production assistant, assistant casting director, producer of the Stone and Hoff Stock Company, and, later, youngest instructor at the American Academy of Dramatic Arts.

In the summer of 1936 the Stone and Hoff Stock Company entered its second season. That summer they performed at Echo Lake Tavern in Warrensburg, New York. Members of the company, again all graduates of the academy, included Sol Hoff, Rita Kerwin, Ethel Korosy, Charles Thomas, Fred Sherwood, John Most, Norma Lehn, Glenn Sherman, and Deborah Dryman, most of whom had appeared in Broadway productions during the 1935–36 season. Since Ezra had commitments to Abbott and *Three Men on a Horse*, he stayed in New York and communicated with the company by telephone and mail.

The troupe diligently rehearsed during the month of June, and Hoff showed his pride in their progress by describing them as true professionals with whom he worked "easily and naturally." They opened on Friday, July 3, with a one-act farce playing to a large and enthusiastic crowd. "The Friday and Sat. shows were smashing hits," Hoff wrote in a letter to Ezra. "Some of the remarks about *Thank You Doctor*: 'Like a B'way show.' 'Best show we've seen here and we've been coming here for years.' 'Better than professional.' 'We've never seen such a smoothly acted performance in any camp or hotel.'" Hoff later wrote, "I'm so confident of this group it's not even funny. They're a perfect bunch of troopers. I tell them what to do and it's done five times as well."

The company sailed smoothly along, presenting a variety of musical revues and relatively unknown one-act plays to an apparently spirited audience. Not all the shows, however, played equally well. For example, Hoff described *Wrong Number*, a one-act play presented late in the summer, as a poorly written script. "It was well done, but God and the Group Theatre couldn't make a good play out of it," he wrote. Such problems were rare, and Hoff's correspondence with his partner, who worked on press releases, letters, and financial matters from New York, remained extremely optimistic throughout most of the summer season.

In the middle of August, however, a severe problem arose between the Echo Lake management and the acting company. The hotel administration began to censor scripts, delay salary payments, edit news releases, and behave audaciously toward company members. The troupe retaliated in an equally unprofessional manner; they refused to perform. Upon hearing the news, Ezra discussed the matter with his Abbott associates and with Philip Loeb, all of whom advised austere consequences for the unruly actors. Ezra then swiftly responded with a telegram threatening their careers, but he soon realized he had reacted as irrationally as his company. "My telegram I repeat was written in anger and disgust, and I retract the last statement I made," he wrote. "It would be foolish and unfair for me to attempt to harm your respective careers. You are too good actors to curb. You shall learn I hope." Ezra had absorbed difficult lessons about producing, and he invited the actors to discuss the matter further upon their return to Manhattan.

In the year and a half after graduating from the AADA, Ezra's talents had developed considerably, and during the fall of 1936 his development intensified when his alma mater invited him to return as the school's youngest instructor and director. At that time the academy offered classes such as voice, speech, movement, fencing, dancing, theater history, theory, and scene study; in other words, it anticipated contemporary conservatory programs. Ezra earned just over two dollars per hour supervising scene study classes. The students chose partners and selected scenes prior to his arrival. They then presented their work to Ezra, who in turn offered criticism and suggestions. He eventually directed a few examination and senior plays. He enjoyed his work and devoted as much time to the school as his busy schedule allowed.

Ezra later maintained that he learned more from Jehlinger and the academy as an instructor than he had as a student due to working in close proximity with all the other teachers. Time permitting, he attended others' rehearsals and classes to observe their work. But true to form, just as Ezra began to feel comfortable with his fledgling career, Jehli took him aside and attacked his lifestyle, his habits, his thoughts. Ezra had made a conscious decision to make acting and directing his career, but he had accomplished this feat without experiencing life outside the theater. In an unpublished article written in 1952, "A Man of Iron Named Jehli," Ezra explained Jehlinger's lecture.

> "Theatre," Jehlinger reminded me, "is the mirror held up to nature, and to be forever standing in front of the mirror and gazing narcissus-like into it would be an artist's downfall." My position should be behind or alongside that mirror to be able to freely observe and understand that which was before it so that when called on to reproduce any part of the image of life it might be an accurate reflection rather than one blurred and obscured by my own unimportant presence in the frame.

Seeing his son's advancing career in theater and realizing that Ezra's rather limited education—especially in math—would be detrimental to the business side of his career, Sol Feinstone continued to handle all of his son's contracts and business affairs. Ezra lived on a nominal allowance, while his father invested the remainder of Ezra's earnings. The Feinstones also realized that their son was fast approaching a marriageable age, and they wanted to assert their influence over his choice of a future wife; therefore, the family made plans to provide a stable home environment in New York City. Throughout Ezra's childhood and early professional career, his family had essentially been based in Philadelphia. Feinstone, however, concluded that moving to New York would not affect his own business affairs as his activities were equally divided between both cities.

Despite his rather shrewd business dealings, Feinstone never had an office, never had a secretary. His transactions, in a sense, were always out of his hat. Upon purchasing property, investing in construction projects, or going into partnerships with small development companies in which he held an interest but wished to remain anonymous, Feinstone would many times go to Metropolitan Life in New York to borrow money. He spent the majority of his time, however, hitting the auction galleries and libraries and following his other intellectual interests in both cities. "Business was never a major part of what I remember as my father's activities," Ezra explained. "Occasionally he would take me to see a property that he had just bought, or I'd meet him in Philly for lunch and to meet some of his cronies."

When it came time to relocate the family to New York, Ezra and his father looked at several places. The prospective house had to have a nice view, as this constituted one of Feinstone's major requirements. The two had looked at several houses on Riverside Drive when the fiancé of Ezra's maternal aunt suggested they look in the Columbia Heights area of Brooklyn Heights. Upon investigation, Feinstone discovered a brownstone for sale that had been built around 1865 by the Squibb brothers and had later been willed to Fordham University. The first Squibb pharmaceutical factory had once sat on the bank of the East River directly below the house. From the living room Feinstone could in one panoramic view look up Wall Street, take in the Brooklyn Bridge, the Statue of Liberty, Ellis Island, and Governor's Island. It was perfectly situated to suit his taste. Ezra immediately fell in love with the house and claimed the top floor as his.

When Feinstone asked his wife to inspect the house, she asked a girlfriend to drive her there from Philadelphia. When they pulled up in front of 148 Columbia Heights, Rose Feinstone looked out of the car window at the building and declared that she would never live there. She did not even get out of the car. Nevertheless, the family eventually bought the house and lived there.

A couple of years later, the twin brownstone at 152 Columbia Heights became available, and Feinstone purchased it for investment reasons. Like previous homes, both buildings went through several of Feinstone's mutations — some of which were logical and good and some simply butchered the two beautiful old homes. This was merely his system of splitting larger buildings into separate dwellings on each floor. And so this house served as the Feinstone's primary residence for the next decade. It was extremely handy for Ezra to take the subway from Clark Street into Manhattan, and his sister, Miriam, enrolled in Packer Prep School in Brooklyn. Rose Feinstone never complained, and Feinstone simply went about business as usual.

In the meantime, Ezra continued with his small part in *Three Men on a Horse*, but he spent an increasing amount of time working with Gar Kanin across the street at the Cort Theatre. Sometime in early fall of 1936, a new comedy by John Monks, Jr., and Fred F. Finklehoffe concerning the lives of cadets in the Virginia Military Institute came to Kanin's attention. Although the script had been rejected by thirty-two producers, Kanin saw its potential. He did not believe, however, that it was strong enough to submit to Abbott. Therefore, he arranged to meet with the authors to work on revisions before approaching his boss.

Kanin's dressing room served as a frequent office for the three men to work on the play, and Ezra, of course, was present during many of these sessions. The script contained a character that fit Ezra's body type — a hazed freshman cadet named Mistol Bottome — and as they worked on this character's scenes, Ezra graciously volunteered to read them aloud for the three men. "We would bat the thing around for hours and hours," Kanin wrote in a recent letter. "Finally, it was submitted to Abbott. The three of us waited in a hotel room somewhere and we finally got a call from Mr. Abbott who uttered three historic words: 'Gar, it's wonderful!' So we nearly passed out, of course."

Monks and Finklehoffe had written the original version of their script,

The Feinstones at home at 148 Columbia Heights — Ezra, Miriam, Rose, and Sol.

When the Roll Is Called, while they attended the Virginia Military Institute at Lexington, Virginia, in 1932. During their senior year, the two cadets had suddenly found themselves confined to barracks for a breach of discipline. With nothing else to occupy their time, they decided to write a play, using the misadventure that had caused their confinement as a basis for the plot. It turned out so successfully that they used it for their thesis in their senior English class.

After graduating, the boys went their separate ways, Monks turning to radio and Finklehoffe giving his full attention to Yale University and to law. Three years later, during the summer of 1935, the two young men got together for a session of reminiscing. When the topic of their schoolboy drama came up for discussion, they decided to revamp the script. They changed the title to *Stand at Ease*, made a few changes in the first of three acts, and again relegated the script to the bureau drawer for six months. In early November, after introducing the script to Kanin and following Abbott's suggestions, the final version retitled *Brother Rat*, emerged. Abbott optioned the play and planned to begin rehearsals in the Biltmore Theatre on November 16.

Brother Rat centers around the mishaps and love affairs of three cadets.

Most of the boys' troubles are routine: securing dates for school functions; betting on school baseball games; raising money to place bets; the constant fear of commanding officers. But one cadet, Bing Edwards, the fabulous pitcher, has more serious troubles. He is secretly married to a young girl who is expecting a baby. As one would expect for the 1930s, this peccadillo is grounds for his dismissal. In the end, the boys win the game and the girls and even graduate, escaping a series of frenzied mishaps unscathed.

By the time Abbott held auditions for *Brother Rat*, Ezra had become intimately acquainted with the character of Mistol Bottome. Although he auditioned well, Kanin informed him that Abbott had narrowed his decision to him and Frankie Thomas, Jr., the hottest juvenile on Broadway at the time. Ezra presented reasonable competition for the role, so when word arrived that Thomas had signed a contract to perform the lead in another show, Abbott offered Ezra the job.

Ezra excitedly approached Edie Van Cleve to see what he could do to make himself look more all–American. He thought perhaps if he lightened his hair or changed the color completely, he would appear more appropriate for the type. Ezra then talked to Kanin, who had bleached and dyed his hair for previous roles. Kanin agreed that a change in color would improve the younger actor's appearance. Edie then escorted Ezra to her beauty parlor on 42nd Street. He entered with dark brown hair and emerged as a bright redhead.

Casting *Brother Rat* posed a problem for Abbott. Since he did not believe that famous names were necessary for success, he did not worry about securing a star. Nevertheless, he had to find capable actors and actresses who could believably pass for eighteen-year-old cadets and boarding school girls. He signed Frank Albertson for the lead on the basis of his screen performance in *Fury*. Others in the cast included the then not-so-famous José Ferrer, Eddie Albert, Robert Griffith, and Mary Mason.

After accepting his role in *Brother Rat*, Ezra had the difficult task of giving notice to Alex Yokel, who accused Abbott of stealing his top actors from *Three Men on a Horse*. Customarily, an actor leaving a show would give written notice to the company's stage manager, who then would notify the producer. Ezra decided to forgo custom and speak directly to Yokel. He made an appointment with his producer, whose office was in the Fulton Theatre, to discuss his new opportunity. For some reason, instead of merely informing Yokel of his decision, Ezra asked for the elder man's advice. This display of courtesy impressed Yokel, and although he remained at odds with Abbott, he agreed that Ezra should seize the opportunity. He wished his former employee good luck and even offered to hire him back into *Three Men on a Horse* if *Brother Rat* quickly folded.

Abbott was known to view each show he produced strictly as a business proposition. His actors and employees marveled at the ice water he seemed to have in his veins. On the day after the opening of a play, Abbott usually called his production staff into his office. After having studied the reviews, he would without showing any emotion announce the show's fate. Despite the critics' stranglehold on his business, he seemed to have no sense of discouragement, dismay, or animosity regarding them. He had the ability to walk away from one show and begin with a fresh attitude on the next production. Similarly, he found it useful to sit in the audience during a play's tryouts and use the information conveyed by the audience for revisions. At each performance he became part of the assembly and reacted to what he saw and heard as if he did not know the outcome. He relied heavily on audience reaction and displayed cold logic concerning a show's effectiveness.

When *Brother Rat* opened at the Maryland Theatre in Baltimore on December 8, 1936, the audience responded with such fervor that Abbott followed up with only minor changes in the staging and script. He experimented each night of the tryout period with different curtain or blackout lines including: "A drug store on every corner and you have to ring up a baby." or "Put a flag over her face and love her for old glory!" — spicy stuff for 1936. Boston being the most prudish of the tryout towns, censors made certain such vulgarities would not be heard upon their stages. Nonetheless, Abbott appeared confident that the show was ready to open in New York as rehearsed.

On December 16, 1936, *Brother Rat* opened at the Biltmore Theatre to a capacity crowd, and it received sterling reviews from all the major magazines and New York newspapers. In fact, the notices proved so favorable that Abbott uncharacteristically placed an advertisement in all the major newspapers around New York thanking the critics. He wrote, "We like the critics so much we've decided to make them "Brother Rats." In his review in the *New York Times*, for example, Brooks Atkinson wrote, "*Brother Rat* is only a school play with the usual crises to joggle the funny bone, but it is written and acted with an exuberance that is contagious. . . . This is practically revolution." A reviewer for *Newsweek* reported, "The comedy is gay, and Abbott has directed it with his usual deftness. . . . *Brother Rat* should run until Commencement."

But as much as the critics enjoyed Monks and Finklehoffe's script and Abbott's direction, they also gave much praise to the cast of relatively unknown players. Albert's slow-witted but genuine baseball pitcher, Ferrer's weary voice of experience, Mrs. Curtis Burnley Railing's sapient matron, Anna Franklin's portrayal of the clowning maid, and the capriciousness of Kathleen Fitz, Wyn Cahoon, and Mason delighted the audience. But in the midst of this talented group, Atkinson wrote that "something especially appreciative should be said for . . . Ezra Stone's terrified freshman." Grenville Vernon of *The Commonweal* threw a larger bouquet in Ezra's direction

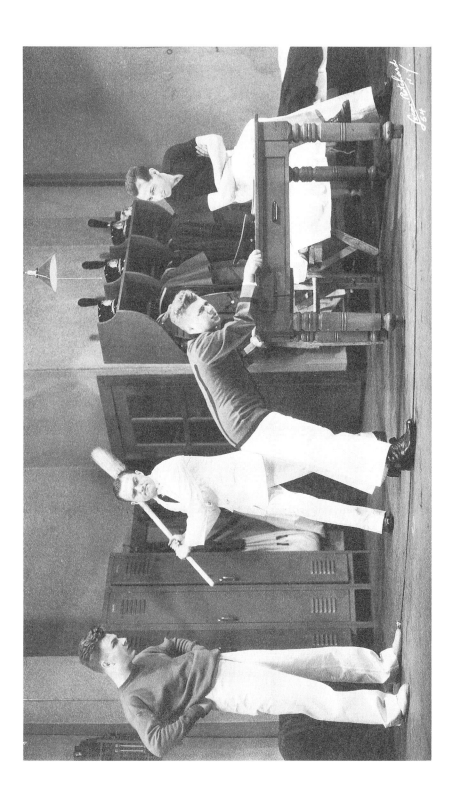

when he wrote, "It is . . . well acted, with special words of praise for Eddie Albert, Frank Albertson, José Ferrer and Mary Mason, and a double special word for Ezra Stone's delightful humorous portrayal of the earnest and courageous plebe."

Ezra, who in his younger days had never revealed a lack of confidence on stage, sensed his success even before the newspapers hit the stands the following morning. The audience chuckled throughout his performance as the older cadets abused the "dumbest brother rat" in the school. He immediately established his rapport with the audience during his first entrance in the second act when Billy (Albertson) forced him to look into a mirror and give himself "pluperfect hell." Bottome (Stone) then proceeded to say,

> Mistol Bottome, what in hell's a matter with you . . . Mistol? . . . You're gross. You're gross as hell. You know it . . . You . . . haven't got enough brains to pour rain out of a boot. . . .

By the time the older cadets enacted Bottome's rights-of-passage ceremony in the third act, the young performer had completely won the spectators' hearts. As he made his final exit, they gave him an appreciative ovation — a response repeated by audiences at many subsequent performances.

When the curtain fell on opening night, Robert Griffith, the assistant stage manager, immediately came to Ezra's dressing room to inform the young actor that Mr. Abbott wished to see him. Ezra went down the stairs past the star's dressing room, a room he would later occupy. By the theater's call-board at the bottom of the steps stood Abbott, dressed in a white dinner jacket; next to him was Douglas Fairbanks, Ezra's idol at the time, and his wife, Lady Ashley. Fairbanks was so tan his face looked to Ezra like leather. This deep color naturally contrasted with the actor's white teeth and bright eyes, causing the young man to stare in amazement. Here stood the most gorgeous couple he had ever seen.

Abbott broke the silence with "Thanks for coming Ezra. I thought you might like to meet Mr. Fairbanks and Lady Ashley, and I wanted them to see your makeup." In addition to bleaching his hair red, Ezra had painted freckles across the top of his cheeks and his nose with brown eyebrow pencil. The cast had poked fun at this during the tryouts, but Ezra had simply ignored their ridicule. But now his boss and his idol stared at his dots. They chuckled for a brief moment while the young actor turned red with embarrassment. And then Abbott said, "Of course you know that from about the first three rows it looks like freckles done with brown pencil. Probably for two rows in back of that they look like freckles. For the rest of the house,

Opposite: Eddie Albert, Frank Albertson, Ezra Stone (as Mistol Bottome) and José Ferrer in the George Abbott production of *Brother Rat* (1936).

they don't even know there's anything there." Abbott was teasing Ezra but at the same time flattering him by introducing him to his honored guests; however, Ezra never painted the freckles on his face again.

The cast of *Brother Rat* worked well together and became friends both on stage and off. Albertson, Ferrer, and Albert were slightly older, but the majority of the cast was approximately the same age as Ezra. In the meantime the show settled in for a long Broadway run, providing these young performers with the inevitable problem of the monotony of enacting the same role night after night. As Abbott had so often preached, their work could easily become stale, so they began to play games with each other on stage to keep spontaneity alive. Beginning in early rehearsals, the three young leading men eagerly anticipated Bottome's rights-of-passage scene.

DAN:	What do you want, Mistol?
BOTTOME:	Mr. Randolph told me to come down here tonight, sir.
BILLY:	Oh, yeah. Anyone taken you in yet, Mistol? (*Crosses to radiator and takes broom.*)
BOTTOME:	(*Painfully.*) Oh, yes, sir.
BILLY:	(*Stern.*) Well, assume the angle, Mistol. (*Bottome bends over table, grasping ends with both hands. Billy takes broom from corner, swings broom menacingly through air, and strikes Bottome on his buttocks with flat of broom. He then extends his hands to Bottome.*) Call me Billy.

The other two characters then followed this same ritual. But the older actors, who had fun with this scene, did not hold back the force of their swing. Ezra foresaw problems with this initiation scene and asked Abbott what he could do to prevent future bruises on his backside. They decided to request the costume shop foreman to insert a pad in the seat of his pants. It took a couple of weeks, but Ezra was finally issued a pad that both absorbed the shock and blended into his physique.

Another game the young actors played occurred during a night scene when the boys sneaked the commander's daughter into the barracks so she could tutor Bing (Albert) enough to pass his examination the next morning. If he did not receive a passing mark, he would supposedly not be allowed to pitch in the upcoming ball game. The cadets also possessed illegal food in the barracks—cream-cheese-and-jelly sandwiches—one of Eddie Albert's favorite snacks. The upperclassmen called Bottome to stand watch. After a short time, Bottome whispered, "Chicky-chicky" indicating the officer on duty had been sighted. He turned off the lights, and the group hid in and under the cots pretending to sleep. The actors, however, also took this opportunity to eat a sandwich during the commanding officer's inspection. On several occasions, Ezra spiked Albert's sandwich with alum, and after the older actor puckered through a mouthful, he would usually retaliate by striking Ezra a little harder during the initiation scene.

Among Abbott's directorial trademarks were his timing and rhythm. During one performance of *Brother Rat*, Robert Faulk and Albertson came running into the barracks closely followed by Ezra. It was a rhythmic entrance timed to the swing of a door. But during one performance, the second man through tripped and disrupted the swing. When Ezra entered, he placed the palm of his hand through a pane of glass in the door, and a long sliver punctured a small artery. In his rush, he did not realize the severity of his wound until the audience stopped laughing. When the other actors began to stare at his blood-soaked sleeve, Ezra silently panicked. He knew he had to compose himself for his rather long monologue in which he had to bawl himself out before the mirror. He thought, "What a silly thing to do, stand here while my life's blood is pouring out," but he simply could not figure out how to get offstage without a cue. In a daze, he walked over to the mirror and began his customary speech. After the first line, Albertson cut in, "All right, that's enough of that. Now get the hell out of here." The cowardly, bleeding actor needed no further encouragement.

The stage manager, who had taken in the situation from the wings, sent someone across the street to retrieve the house doctor from the Edison Hotel. Ezra's arm was so swollen, the doctor had to cut open the sleeve. Then he proceeded to withdraw a six-inch sliver of glass before applying a cold compress. To guard against blood poisoning the doctor insisted on a tetanus injection. After several attempts, the needle finally landed in the proper place— completing the process just prior to Ezra's next entrance. "The moral was morale," Ezra stated in his book, *Coming, Major!*. "An actor, or anyone else who's morale is good, can take a beating when he has to. I took mine in the third act that night on my tetanus injection, with a broom."

Later in the run of *Brother Rat*, Abbott moved his production to the Fulton Theatre, which shared the stage door alley with the Gaiety Burlesque House. At that time Ezra became an aficionado of the bump-and-grind strippers and raunchy clowns. Throughout the summer months of 1937, during intermissions both casts frequently opened their stage doors to ventilate the backstage area. Both the Brother Rats and the show girls would sometimes take this opportunity to wander onto the other group's sets.

One evening when an old friend visited backstage, Ezra took the occasion to flaunt his newfound privilege. Taking his friend on a sight-seeing tour, they entered the inner sanctum of the Gaiety just as the ladies were preparing for their bare-breasted statuette posed picture sequence. Eyes wide, Ezra spotted a familiar showgirl, who stood with both hands covering her bosom. Following an introduction, Ezra's friend extended his hand. To their dismay, she slid her left hand and forearm over to cover the view and shook with her free hand.

About this time, Ezra befriended Joey Faye, one of the headlining comics of burlesque, and eventually got him hired as an actor in one of Abbott's road companies. One evening Faye announced, "I got a date for you, Ezra. She's a new girl in town; she's Carrie Fennell's niece." Well, anyone who knew anything of burlesque knew of Carrie Fennell, and Ezra was no exception. A big, beefy woman, Fennell's gimmick was that she could make each breast pop out of her blouse independently, a stunt she performed with ease during the finale of her act. As it turned out, Ezra escorted her niece, Jean Modé, a small-town girl from Ohio, on a couple of dates.

Billy Friedberg, a cousin of Teddy and Larry Hart and a friend of Ezra's, worked as a leg man for Walter Winchell, a journalist from the *New York Daily Mirror*, who also wrote the number one gossip column in the city. Between Ezra and Jean Modé there existed no real romance, but to tease the young actor, Friedberg and Winchell planted a story with the headline: "Newsome Twosome . . . Ezra Stone and Jean Modé from the Apollo's Strip Pit Choir." Unfortunately for Ezra, his father's sister was then living in Brooklyn and read the tabloids. "She couldn't wait to call my mother and tell her that I was in Winchell's column and read her the item over the phone," Ezra later recalled.

The Feinstones usually retired early, while Ezra routinely wandered home around one or two o'clock in the morning. They understood that their son as a working actor did not maintain a normal schedule. After performing, Ezra had to unwind, so there was never any hassle about his late-night arrivals. On this evening, however, as Ezra unlocked the door, there stood his mother with a long, petulant look on her face. "She just kept shaking her head and saying, 'Ezra, a strip pit choir!'—like this was going to be her daughter-in-law," he said. Mild as it was, that was the only reprimand he received from his mother.

During that same summer Ezra gained a brief reputation as the Broadway actor playing simultaneously in two shows. He had always been a hustler, and the theater community at that time was really quite small. In the backstage area of the Biltmore Theatre, *Brother Rat* actors and stagehands and other area theater folk maintained a running poker game. It sometimes began in the afternoon and lasted until early in the morning, and it resulted in a clique of younger actors becoming poker friends.

At one of these card games, Ezra learned that one of the men playing a small walk-on part in *Behind Red Lights*, a mediocre show in the waning part of its Broadway run, had landed a larger role with a summer stock company and intended to leave the organization. Ezra said, "Hell, I bet I could fit it into my schedule and play the role."

To see if the character's entrance corresponded with his scenes in *Brother Rat*, he got permission from the stage manager to leave the Biltmore Theatre during a performance, walk up 47th Street at a fast clip, through the Edison Hotel to the stage door of the 46th Street Theatre. Calculating his time, he deduced that he could perform both roles. Abbott did not mind. In fact, he thought it might make for a good story, so Ezra approached the producer of *Behind Red Lights*, who recognized him from his notices in *Brother Rat*. The young shark then proceeded to sell him on the idea of hiring him as his friend's replacement.

Behind Red Lights, regarded as the first glorification of a madam on the American stage, starred Dorothy Hall, a featured actress of the day. The second act curtain was a sight laugh with the madam showing two college kids, presumably freshmen in raccoon coats and beanies, into the parlor. The madam stood behind the boys as they chose from a lineup of prostitutes. Disregarding the younger girls, they turned to the madam and said, "You'll do."

Although the simultaneous acting stunt gained Ezra some local notoriety, it induced him to resort to rather devious behavior. His wardrobe in *Brother Rat* consisted of a V. M. I. cadet uniform. He kept the fur coat and beanie from the other show in his dressing room at the Biltmore. After his second act scene in the Abbott production, he quickly put on the fur coat and ran up the street, a curious sight considering the time of year. He cut through the Edison Hotel, where each night he greeted his old friend, Mr. Flood the house detective, and entered the 46th Street Theatre. He usually had a few minutes to spare before walking onto stage with Hall to inspect the girls and throw the curtain line cue.

Although Ezra spoke the last line of the act, the director clearly intended the focus to fall upon the star. It was her scene and her moment. When Ezra said the line, however, he did a double take toward Hall, keeping the focus on himself. This trick upset the actress, and she vowed to confront him after each night's performance. As soon as the curtain fell, however, Ezra avoided Hall's wrath by running back to the Biltmore to make his third act entrance in *Brother Rat*. Fortunately for Hall, this stunt lasted only a short while, for *Behind Red Lights* closed soon after Ezra had taken over the role.

Not long after *Brother Rat* had opened in late fall of 1936, Gar Kanin convinced Abbott to mount a production of Allen Boretz and John Murray's *Room Service*, which Sam Harris had abandoned in Philadelphia. Kanin insisted the play had potential and if Abbott could correct the shortfalls in the script, it would be a hit. Abbott met with the authors and began work on the play.

In the revision of *Room Service*, Abbott, Boretz, and Murray combined the hysteria of Broadway hotel management with the bedlam of a shoestring theater production company, a story loosely based on actual experiences of the original authors. The initial Harris production had succumbed to a disastrous third act, but Abbott helped the authors tighten and blend the story to perfect proportions. Abbott did not alter the play's basic story line of a producer conning a hotel staff into housing and feeding his company while he was trying to find financial backing for his play. He did, however, make many specific changes, such as changing the playwright's hometown from the Bronx to Oswego, a smaller town in upstate New York. This emphasized the contrast between the young man and the shyster Broadway people.

Another reason why Abbott's production of *Room Service* found greater success than its predecessor was the cast. He used only one member from the Harris production, Philip Loeb, a master of timing with a rigid deadpan. He then added actors from what he referred to in his autobiography, *Mister Abbott*, as his "group of old reliables." The show became a huge success, giving the producer and director his third hit running simultaneously on Broadway; the other two were *Boy Meets Girl* and *Brother Rat*.

Throughout this period, Abbott enjoyed hosting postshow parties at New York's Coffee House Club. For entertainment, he often invited the casts of his current shows along with other favorites. Although not treated as servants, the actors nevertheless functioned as minstrels for such New York socialites as the Whitneys, Schwabs, Swopes, and Vanderbilts. Abbott also enjoyed performing at these affairs himself. At one Coffee House Club party, Donald McBride portrayed Sam Harris, Loeb, an incredible mime, played Abbott, and Ezra played a bus boy in a scene they called "An Utterly Impossible Conversation" set in the Times Square Automat after the second New York performance of *Room Service*.

BUS BOY: (*To Harris*) No smoking please.
ABBOTT: I told you cigars are no good for you, Sam. Look at me, never smoke and never drink anything but raw milk. I leave the vices for my authors to indulge in.
HARRIS: Yeh, I saw two slow balls carrying Finklehoffe out of the Picadilly Bar this morning.
ABBOTT: I guess he was waiting up for the *Room Service* notices.
HARRIS: Does he wait up for notices every nite?
ABBOTT: (*At a loss for an answer*) Gee this is good milk. (*Finishes milk*)
HARRIS: What makes you think people will really come to see *Room Service*?
ABBOTT: Charlie Washburn told me. He said if I run ads, *not* presented by Sam Harris and *not* directed by Melville Burke, it would cinch it for three years.
HARRIS: Well, of course, George that would be neither ethical or gentlemanly.
BUS BOY: (*To Harris*) Excuse me can you read that sign? (*Points to sign saying "Gentlemen Will Kindly Remove Hats"*)
ABBOTT: (*Trying to read sign without glasses*) He's not smoking. (*Bus Boy takes Harris' hat off, puts it on table. Picks up Abbott's empty glass and napkin.*)

HARRIS: (*As Loeb*) Hey! Don't take the napkin. He's got business with it later on.
BUS BOY: (*As Stone*) Oh I forgot.
HARRIS: (*As Loeb*) Such insincerity! You'll never be an actor, son. A pupil of mine. Jehlinger would throw a fit. Now go back to where you pick up the glass. Go ahead.
BUS BOY: (*As Stone*) O.K. Pop.
HARRIS: (*As Loeb*) Don't call me Pop, you little Bastard. (*Bus Boy puts glass down. Picks it up again. Bumps Abbott in head with tray as he exits.*)
ABBOTT: God damn it!

"God damn it!" was Donald McBride's running gag line in *Room Service*. Ezra described another routine as the world's shortest blackout sketch, which teased Abbott about keeping *Brother Rat* running by moving it from the Biltmore to the Hudson, to the National, and finally to the Ambassador. As the scene began, Abbott sat behind a desk on stage; Walter Wagner, then the stage manager of *Brother Rat*, knocked on an offstage door.

ABBOTT: Come in.
WAGNER: Mister Abbott, I'm the new stage manager of *Brother Rat*.
ABBOTT: Yes?
WAGNER: Where is it? (*Blackout*)

While *Room Service* scored a hit at the box office and settled in for a long run, Ezra continued as Mistol Bottome in *Brother Rat* and worked in the Abbott office. By fall of 1937, Edie Van Cleve, like Gar Kanin, had left the production team in search of new opportunities. This unofficially made Ezra the top man in the casting office. Abbott, who at the time busied himself with another project, then entrusted Ezra with holding the preliminary casting for the London company of *Room Service*. Abbott, of course, had final say on Ezra's selections, but this represented an important step up for Ezra within the organization.

By this time Ezra had found a girlfriend, Helen Gillette, whom he had recommended as the ingenue in the London cast of *Room Service*. Infatuated with the young lady, he even had intentions of marriage. He scheduled a leave of absence from *Brother Rat* and planned to take a freighter to Ireland and bicycle to England. Marrying his girlfriend in London or Paris seemed romantic to the young actor.

For the hotel manager in the London company, Ezra suggested and Abbott approved William Mendrek, who at the time was playing the bank messenger in the Broadway production of the same show. Ezra himself then replaced Mendrek in the New York play. The relatively small role allowed Ezra to continue his role in *Brother Rat*, so he again became the Broadway actor performing simultaneously in two shows. Before he made

Ezra Stone and George Abbott, 1939.

the scheduled trip to London to marry his beloved, however, Ezra received word that Gillette and Mendrek had begun dating. They eventually married. To add insult to injury, Abbott later cast Mendrek as the assistant principal in his production of *What a Life*, a character who slapped Ezra's character's face in every performance.

Many new scripts passed through the Abbott office, most of which fell by the wayside. But when a play attracted Abbott's interest sufficiently for him to consider an option for production, he devised a system of having that play read to him by a full cast of actors. As the top man in the casting department, one of Ezra's many office duties included the arrangement of these original script readings, known as worklight readings. Beginning with cast lists from current Abbott productions, Ezra assigned appropriate actors to roles. If he could not secure someone from a present show, he turned to previous Abbott companies for names. Abbott sometimes handed him a play with specific instructions as to who should play a particular role. But in the end, Ezra proposed a cast list, and Abbott either approved it or suggested changes. The casting director then contacted actors concerning their interest and availability. If they accepted the assignment, he sent them a copy of the script. Next, he secured an Abbott theater and made arrangements with the house and stage crews to open the doors and set up the proper number of chairs needed for the reading.

During a worklight reading, Ezra's chore was to read the scene description and any actions indicated in the script. Abbott sat in the auditorium with the playwright. Since Abbott directed and produced mostly comedies, farces, and musicals, he felt he needed audience response even at this early stage. Therefore, he instructed Ezra to post invitations on various call-boards of Abbott productions. Without fail, a great number of actors and theater people attended.

Although the arrangement and execution of these readings greatly interested Ezra, he enjoyed and learned the most from the meeting with the playwright and agent that was held in Abbott's office immediately afterward. Here Ezra had the benefit of hearing his mentor's reactions to the script and the reading. Abbott, an expert play doctor, usually pinpointed problems and made suggestions for the revision. Abbott also negotiated with the author and agent varied types of coauthorship credits, and percentages of the playwright's royalties. On some productions, Abbott had income as producer, director, and credited or uncredited playwright.

While *Brother Rat* and *Room Service* continued on Broadway and the road, Abbott discovered a play entitled *Enter to Learn* by a then unknown playwright, Clifford Goldsmith. Like *Brother Rat*, it had been rejected by numerous producers before Abbott declared interest in hearing it read. He warned Ezra not to get his heart set on playing the leading role, a high school boy named Henry Aldrich, for he had Eddie Bracken, who was traveling with the southern company of *Brother Rat*, in mind for the character. He did, however, allow Ezra to cast himself as Henry for the worklight reading. Subsequently, Abbott gave his suggestions to Goldsmith, which included changing the play's title to *What a Life*, and he eventually purchased the rights to produce it. Ezra, of course, assisted his boss with the final casting.

What a Life concerns the escapades of Henry Aldrich, a boy with an infinite capacity for getting into trouble. The son of a Princeton Phi Beta Kappa father, who provides what Henry refers to as his "sinking fund" so that he too may attend Princeton, young Aldrich spends the majority of his school time in the principal's office. He is expelled after his drawing of a bespectacled whale, labeled Mr. Bradley, falls into the hands of the school's principal, Mr. Bradley. Only one teacher realizes the good and the talent within him, for Henry has a kind heart and the ability to draw.

While Henry sits in the principal's office, which serves as the setting for the entire play, a teacher instructs him to continue his study of *Hamlet*. Confused by the language, he looks up to find Barbara Pearson, the pretty president of the junior class honored by her peers for writing the team yell: "Central! Be Gentle! Be Brutal! Be Central." The confused boy asks her, "What's a parle?"

BARBARA: Maybe it means pearl.
HENRY: Maybe . . . Only if it does, it doesn't make as much sense as
         just plain "parle" does.
BARBARA: Read the rest of it.
HENRY: (*Reading.*) "So frowned he once when in angry parle, He smote
         the sledded Pollacks on the ice." That certainly explains
         everything. — It must be something you keep on ice. Maybe it's
         some kind of a drink. Sure. And "parle" means parlor. They
         were sitting around in the parlor drinking these pollacks, and
         they got tight. Or maybe I better just call it a colloquial expres-
         sion. Any time you aren't sure about something, just call it a
         colloquial expression. What can they say?
BARBARA: (*Thoroughly enjoying herself.*) Isn't there a footnote?
HENRY: There are three footnotes. The darned thing is crawling with
         footnotes. (*Reading.*) "Quarto 1, Quarto 2, Folio 1." — Those
         quartos probably refer to the number of quarts they had drunk.
         Just a colloquial expression. (*His book slips, the pages close.*)
BARBARA: (*Laughing.*) Stop!
HENRY: (*Rises and gets book.*) There's a footnote on that footnote.
         (*Opens book and reads at once.*) "Let not the royal bed of Den-
         mark be a couch for luxury and damned incest—" No! (*He is
         sincerely embarrassed.*) That isn't where I was reading. (*Sits.*)
         And I'll bet that if I had written that, they would have thrown
         me out of this school.
BARBARA: (*Laughing.*) Stop! I'm dying!
HENRY: You're not dying any harder than I am. You know why Hamlet
         killed himself? He was afraid there might be another act! He
         couldn't take it.

This episode convinces Barbara that Henry's wit is that of a good humorist.
Throughout the play, she continues to believe in Henry, although the
circumstantial evidence seems to prove otherwise. When Barbara accepts
his invitation to go to the junior prom and his mother promises him money
if he passes his history examination, he blithely copies another student's
answers. Suspended from school, he invents a dying uncle in Denver as an
excuse for backing out of his date with Barbara. Later, the band teacher
falsely accuses him of stealing the school's musical instruments and hock-
ing them at a nearby pawn shop. Demonstrating a talent for head-on colli-
sions, always ingenious, never crafty, always there with an answer, though
never the right one, brash, and rattled, Henry grows into that rare thing
on the stage, a person. He finally does manage to get to the prom although
he has to borrow the carfare from his date.

At the time Goldsmith penned *What a Life*, he was a bespectacled
man in his late thirties who looked more like a business executive for a
large corporation than a man of the theater. But he had had theatrical ambitions since his days at Moses Brown High School in Providence, Rhode
Island. One year after an illustrious high school acting career, Goldsmith

enrolled at the American Academy of Dramatic Arts. His graduation coincided with the Actors' Equity Association's strike of 1919, but even that omen could not dissuade him from looking for work on the stage. Despite his positive attitude, his venture into the world of professional theater quickly ended in bitter disappointment. Needing to make a living, he obtained a position under the guise of "Happy" Goldsmith with the Interstate Dairyman's Association in Philadelphia. His job was to lecture to high school students in various New England states on the relation of nutrition to athletics. This later provided him good source material for his play.

Goldsmith was also a consummate writer who had achieved only modest success until a friend suggested that he write on the topic he knew best, high schools. In the early stages of creating *What a Life*, he feared teachers and school administrators might consider Central High and Henry Aldrich a caricature rather than an accurate portrayal of school life. But most people with whom he spoke claimed that Henry's affairs were rather tame compared to their own amazing true stories. In a *New York Times'* article entitled "Lecturer into Playwright," a reporter quoted him as having said,

> None of the characters in the play are modeled on any single individual, but nearly all are composites of teachers and students I have known. I think I have met hundreds of Henry Aldriches during the course of my travels. One boy, for instance, was working for a meatpacking house after his graduation from high school when he found out quite accidentally that he could sell the drawings that he had done in his spare time. No one was more surprised than he, unless it was the teachers and parents who had done their best to discourage his efforts.

After Abbott optioned the play, Goldsmith continued with his lecture engagements, which provided him with the opportunity to act as an extraordinary advance agent for *What a Life*. He usually found occasion to mention the play at some point during his talks with teachers and students, who constituted a significant part of the show's primary target audience.

When it came to casting *What a Life*, it was Ezra's responsibility to select scene excerpts; he invariably chose ones including Henry Aldrich. The casting process typically lasted from two to three weeks, and in that time every actor who auditioned for any role was forced to read opposite Ezra playing Henry. But still Abbott had his heart and mind set on having Eddie Bracken play the lead. In fact, around the office it became known that Abbott had slated Ezra to play Bill, Henry's friend, alongside Bracken. And so the pragmatic young actor prepared himself for the probability of receiving the smaller role. He had no intention of quitting his job or even letting this momentary disappointment upset him, for he knew the Abbott office was the best place in town for him to receive employment on a regular basis. Ezra also had his mind set on becoming a director, and he knew of no better teacher than Abbott.

Although Ezra and Eddie had met only a short time before, they became fast friends. And although they competed for similar roles, there was little sense of conflict between them. Ezra, in fact, had played a key role in introducing Eddie into the Abbott organization as Mistol Bottome in the touring production of *Brother Rat*, his first legitimate professional role. Abbott so liked Bracken that he later promoted him to play the lead in *Brother Rat*. "I would have to say that Garson Kanin and Ezra Stone directed me in *Brother Rat*, not just one but both of them," Bracken later said. "Ezra helped me thoroughly without any thought of who was going to be better, . . . That's what I loved about Ezra. He is the most unselfish man I've ever met." Soon all the arrangements had been made for Bracken to leave the southern tour and come to New York to play his first lead on Broadway. Abbott as much as told him that the audition was a mere formality.

Eddie Bracken arrived on the train from Richmond, Virginia, on a Friday, the last day of casting. After lunch, he walked into the Ethel Barrymore Theatre where everyone greeted him warmly. Observing the remaining actors scheduled to audition, he sat in the auditorium waiting for his turn to read. After the last person finished, Abbott said, "Eddie, why don't you get up. You've had the script down there in Virginia with you." He then suggested that Ezra go onto the stage and read Bill opposite Eddie's Henry. Actually, Bracken had several strikes against him during this audition. First, he knew little about characterization. Although he had played other roles as a child, he had really only played himself, a brash, New York type of comic character. It had worked in *Brother Rat*, so he assumed Abbott wanted that for Henry. His line readings sounded like a tough kid from the Bronx, as he said things like "H'ya Mudda." Of course, this was completely wrong, and Bracken later admitted that by failing in this role, he learned how to develop a character of someone unlike himself. Second, Bracken had never graduated from high school; in fact, his teachers had held him back five times. For that reason, he lacked good reading skills and had trouble pronouncing large, multisyllabic words. Third, Goldsmith had envisioned Henry as a thin, lanky, Midwestern adolescent. Although Ezra physically certainly did not fit the playwright's ideal, Eddie, an ethnic city type with dark brown, wavy hair, no more looked the part than his rival.

Ezra, on the other hand, had been reading the role of Henry for Abbott and Goldsmith for the last two weeks. He later allowed that he had probably worn a groove in their ears, spoiling Bracken's chances. After hearing Eddie read Henry, Abbott unexpectedly requested to see and hear Ezra read the part one final time. Ezra knew this meant he had a chance — he was "a contender," to borrow a line from Budd Schulberg's *On the*

Waterfront. Abbott then instructed both actors to "Come up to the office in a couple of hours and you'll know who starts rehearsals on Monday as Henry."

Meanwhile, Ezra and Eddie went to a Turkish bath in the Dixie Hotel on West 42nd Street and quite literally sweated it out together. When they returned to the office, Janet Cohn, a leading literary agent from New York's prestigious Brandt & Brandt Agency, which represented Goldsmith, handed Ezra a red rose, which she had borrowed from a vase located on the desk of Celia Linder, Abbott's longtime secretary. This signified his victory. Abbott, being kind to Eddie, gave him two options: he could go back on the road and continue with *Brother Rat* or accept the role of Bill in *What a Life*. Eddie chose to accept the smaller role in the original New York company, a role that would force him to learn the art of characterization.

Despite the decision, Ezra and Eddie remained friends. Coming from a poor family, Eddie had great respect for Ezra and viewed him as a person from a higher social class. His father had once told him, "Always remember that if you're in the gutter, you can look up and somebody will help you," and Eddie perceived Ezra as one who could do that. Ezra sometimes invited Eddie to visit him at 148 Columbia Heights in Brooklyn. Eddie marveled at Ezra's double-decker bed, his trains, his pipes, his guns, a myriad of interesting things that he had never known. Eddie saw his friend as a genius who willingly shared his belongings and his knowledge.

Ezra in turn had great respect and admiration for Eddie. Against Abbott's first inclination but with the support from Ezra and Edie Van Cleve, Eddie later took the role of Henry in the *What a Life* road company and made a success of it, receiving wonderful notices in almost every town he played. Upon returning to New York, a radio station invited both performers for an interview. Before Eddie could cut him off, Ezra began telling the reporter, "Eddie Bracken deserves this role. It's not mine. It belongs to him." Eddie thought, "Gee, why would he say that?" He was still putting Ezra on a pedestal.

Many of Ezra's friends believed that he, despite his confident exterior, had deep insecurities about his abilities. They knew him to be deeply compassionate and sensitive, but they thought he downplayed his own achievements to such an extent that he deprived himself of most of the gratification one would normally expect a person in his position to enjoy. He was compulsively modest.

Like many of Ezra's friends, Bracken now believes Ezra's insecurities may have stemmed from his relationship with his father. Following one Philadelphia performance as Henry in an Abbott touring production of *What a Life*, Eddie emerged from the theater to find Sol Feinstone, whom he had met in New York, waiting for him. Feinstone said, "Mr. Bracken, I loved the performance. I want to tell you that you are so much better than

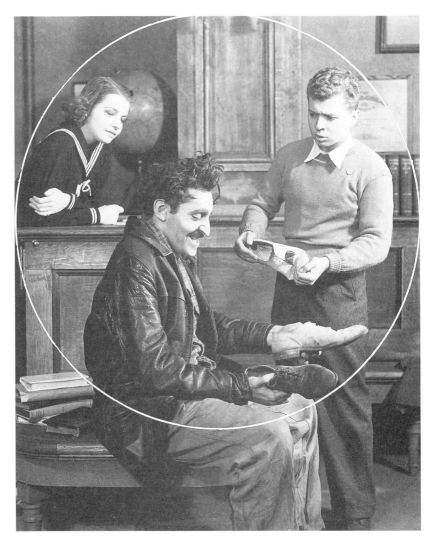

Ezra Stone as Henry Aldrich in Clifford Goldsmith's *What a Life* (1938) with Betty Field and Danny Ock.

my son." Eddie stood aghast; he could not believe what he had heard. Feinstone was a brutally honest man, and if he had said that to his son, it could have broken Ezra's heart. It could have caused him to lose confidence in himself. "I'm afraid that maybe that's what did happen," Bracken concluded, "because in no way was I better than Ezra."

Ezra's insecurities, however, seemed to disappear when matters of integrity arose or when he stepped onto the stage, and his boss and friends had supreme confidence in his talents. In a congratulatory letter written just after Abbott had cast *What a Life*, Van Cleve wrote, "Throughout the last two years you have more than gratified every belief I have in you. Mr. Abbott said only the other day, 'Ezra is an extraordinarily gifted and sensitive person.'" In his later life, however, Ezra was apt to remark that people placed too much faith in his abilities; his friends, however, were proud of him and were sad that he did not delight in his own accomplishments.

What a Life opened on Wednesday, April 13, 1938, at the Biltmore Theatre to a wildly enthusiastic audience. Just prior to this production, Abbott had produced and directed three successive failures: *Angels Island* (1937), *Brown Sugar* (1937), and *All That Glitters* (1938). *What a Life* thus represented his return to Broadway prominence. As was typical of Abbott's successful productions, he had a splendid acting company. Besides Stone and Bracken, Betty Field as the charming Barbara, Vaughn Glaser as the somber and slightly sardonic principal, Arthur Pierson as the understanding Mister Nelson, James Corner as Henry's enemy, Butterfly McQueen as the hopeful Mary, and Van Cleve as Miss Pike provided strong support. The critics were unanimous in their praise. Grenville Vernon went so far as to declare it one of Abbott's best productions to date.

For Ezra Stone, *What a Life* represented the zenith of his acting achievements; at age twenty, he had reached maturity as a Broadway performer. This was his show, his moment in the spotlight, and he made the most of it. The kudos and accolades thrown in his direction were overwhelming. E. Mawby Green of *Theatre World* described his performance as "remarkably droll and unbelievably delightful." Edith J. R. Isaacs of *Theatre Arts Monthly* wrote, he "gives you every nuance of his muddled and friendly nature. His is a first-class performance of a fully observed, skillfully drawn, amusing character." Brooks Atkinson referred to him as the "comic inspiration of the evening. . . . Scowling, plotting, explaining, protesting and suffering inwardly, Mr. Stone plays a long part without letting any of it grow commonplace." But perhaps the grandest ovation came from Vernon, who wrote,

> Mr. Abbott has cast the play impeccably, and in Ezra Stone he has found a young actor who is unique, a sort of American Roland Young. Mr. Stone is said to be twenty. He looks fifteen. The dead-pan of his face lit up by an occasional twisted smile, which seems to come out and disappear of its own sweet will, the baffled puzzlement with himself and his surroundings, his earnest affection for his girl, his complete and utter seriousness make his performance one of the most original of the season. It is his play and he makes it a joy.

Most assuredly, the audience agreed with the critics' reactions, and Ezra Stone as Henry Aldrich arguably became one of Broadway's most lovable heroes ever.

But as much as the reviewers enjoyed the characters, they found the plot rather weak. Many of them described it as ordinary, simple, and unskillful. Naturally, many critics compared it to *Brother Rat*, but most of them found it lacked the dexterity and craftsmanship of its illustrious "cousin." Remarks such as these upset the playwright Goldsmith, making his celebration of a hit Broadway show somewhat bittersweet. His frustration was visible in a letter to Ezra several days after the show's opening. "Naturally, I am delighted over the unanimous reviews you have been receiving and assure you that if you are ever in another show of mine, I'll try my best to give it a plot."

But *What a Life* overcame this weakness through its funny incidents, its dialogue, its atmosphere, and Henry. Henry was a real character and far from a simple one; he was hugely amusing, human, and poignant. Vernon, who obviously enjoyed the play a great deal, said, "I don't know who Clifford Goldsmith is, but he has created a figure worthy to stand beside any of the adolescents of Booth Tarkington. He is a delight and ought to appear in future plays." Others obviously agreed with Vernon's assertion, as the Broadway premiere marked the beginning of a fifteen year run for Henry Aldrich.

Beginning with *What a Life*, Henry's cracked voice, which squeaked from his lips during moments of crisis and made the boy sound as if he were in perpetual puberty, became his most recognizable character trait. Not long after Ezra made his debut as Henry on stage, a host of imitators, particularly on radio, appeared. Two distinct stories emerged as to the origins of this familiar squeak. Bracken recently said, "I was the one who thought of putting in the cracked voice. I used it for the first time." Bracken maintained that Ezra had persuaded him to visit various high schools in preparation for his role in the play. "Ezra asked me if he could use it. I said, 'Ezra, I wanna give you a little secret. I don't own that voice. Every kid in that high school used that cracked voice.'"

But Ezra insisted he had begun experimenting with this vocal peculiarity the summer following his graduation from the AADA when he and Hoff took their group to perform in the Catskill Mountains. In one of their one-act plays, *Thank You, Doctor*, Ezra played a Western Union boy who delivered a telegram to a doctor's waiting room. When he entered the office, the hysteria began as the nurse, mistaking him for a patient, sent him in to see the doctor, who then proceeded to examine the boy. In this role Ezra discovered that by cracking his voice in fear and hysteria he received laughs from the audience. Therefore, he kept this technical gimmick in mind for future reference. During *Brother Rat*, he used the squeaking voice sparingly at points of high tension when the elder cadets hazed or questioned him. The audience typically responded with laughter and applause, so Ezra again kept the trait in his repertoire of vocal effects.

Ezra thought back to a classmate from Oak Lane as a model for the cracked voice. Charles Moos, who later attended Harvard and then law school at the University of Pennsylvania, was undoubtedly the brightest student in the class. When a teacher posed a question, he typically thrust his hand high in the air ahead of the other students. In his excitement, he squealed out the answer, triggering a flurry of giggles from his peers. In a recent letter Moos wrote, "This is attributable to the fact that with the onset of puberty my new voice, more or less in the baritone register, would unpredictably produce a squeak. . . . I was aware of it. . . ." Although most pubescent boys go through the same hormonal changes, Ezra particularly remembered his classmates' reaction to Moos, and he deftly recreated the sound for the pleasure of his theater and later his radio audiences.

Ezra had used the gimmick sparingly during rehearsals of *What a Life*, but he began to insert it more frequently during his performances. Three weeks into the run, Abbott came backstage after a show and scolded his rambunctious young actor. "That's not the way we rehearsed it. You're going crazy with it and cracking your voice too much," he said. So Ezra obediently pulled back. Some time after this, Charles Jehlinger came to see a matinee. Following the performance, the old man came backstage as he always did. He had little to say except, "I think it is time we had lunch together, Ezra." When Jehli told his pupil to meet him at the Astor Hotel, Ezra knew he was in for another temperance lecture.

Ezra went prepared to take it with the thick skin of a nineteen-year-old actor with his name above the play. "I couldn't eat a bite," he later wrote. "Food didn't go down and tears couldn't be held back." From Jehli's lips Ezra heard accusations followed by insults. "You're smug; you're false and you're resorting to cheap and common tricks," the old man jeered. He went on to inform the young man that his portrayal was shallow and superficial and that he was accepting money from audiences under false pretenses. He was jeopardizing the employment of his fellow actors, and, worst of all, he was in the wrong field of endeavor.

Following this verbal challenge, Ezra reevaluated his performance. He worked on it; he studied anew, but it did not improve much. Despite admonishment from two of the most influential men in his theatrical career, Ezra began to rely on his vocal gymnastics with more regularity later in the run of the stage play and after the Aldriches had moved to radio. He knew he could get a laugh with his voice even from weak jokes. Consequently, the popularity of the radio program boosted the stage play's ticket sales. For this new audience, who had grown accustomed to and expected to hear that squeaking voice, Ezra used the cracked voice even where Abbott had specifically instructed him to omit it.

Since his youth, Ezra had always had a problem with excessive belching. Sometime during this period, he consulted a physician about his problem. After the doctor ruled out gastritis, he asked Ezra to show him how he cracked his voice. The doctor noticed that in order to relax his vocal folds, Ezra swallowed a small amount of air before speaking. "When you swallow air," he explained, "it's got to get out somehow. You've got two options. Lucky for you, it escapes through your mouth."

As a George Abbott production, *What a Life* appealed first to the considerable number of reliable New York theater patrons, a group that in the 1930s represented a substantial cross section of the community. Long before the creation of the present TKTS Booths, cut-rate tickets became a valuable method to market unsold admissions. The largest half-price outlet in New York was located in the basement of Gray's Drugstore on 44th Street and Broadway. The room consisted of a large open floor with big sales counters just in front of large changeable boards on which the ticket sellers posted shows with vacancies. Hours before curtain, theater faithfuls patiently waited, hoping a show they had not yet seen would appear on the board. Every time the board changed, the crowd converged around the desk, for the theaters typically sent only a small block of unsold tickets. Of course, this predated any computerized system, so the hard ticket traveled from the theater's box office to Gray's Drugstore, where it was sold to the customer, who then returned to the original box office with the token in hand. If a show could draw these loyal patrons, it could sometimes run for quite some time even if it had not received critical acclaim. Plays that featured a big-name star, or that had a popular director or producer, commanded a certain respect and homage from these regular theatergoers. Fortunately, the critical reviews together with Abbott's name assured *What a Life* of a healthy following.

What a Life's appeal extended beyond the conventional Broadway audience, for its universal qualities enchanted a broader group of people. Apparently the characters mirrored many of their own former classmates and teachers. In an anonymous letter written on February 15, 1939, an adult woman reflected on her enjoyment in seeing the production.

> Mother and I both enjoyed the show immensely, particularly "Henry." Ezra Stone played the role so realistically that it brought back memories of my own school days. To me, the years spent in high school were about the happiest of my life. . . .

As indicated in the following fan mail, the play also struck a chord with a new younger generation of theater patrons, who regularly attended the show in organized groups. A young lady from New York City wrote,

> I have seen your play *What a Life* and I want to say that you were the typical high school fella. My high school girls club (just organized) decided

to see a play and we chose your play because we thought it represented us. We certainly were with you when you spoke about *Hamlet.* Honest, that book caused us all trouble as you can imagine.

A sixteen-year-old girl from Sayville, New York, said she had attended

> with the rest of my school club. Out of the twenty who went I was the only one who had never seen the city or a play but somehow I felt as if I had known you all my life for you were so real and understanding. . . . You are my first real celebrity that I have ever seen. . . . Perhaps you can imagine my feelings at seeing New York and your name in lights. . . . I want to thank you and the entire cast for the happiest day of my life . . . nothing will ever take the place in my memory of that rose-colored curtain going up on that grand play *What a Life* or that little speech you made after the play.

Ezra insisted that his portrayal of Henry Aldrich on Broadway didn't make him a celebrity or alter people's perception of him. He later said, "If it had been the start of a full-fledged acting career of leading roles on Broadway, it perhaps would have been a different story. But Henry Aldrich was a one-shot; lightning struck once and never again." His later exposure on national radio certainly enhanced his social status, but his fan mail also seemed to indicate a healthy following for his work on stage.

On June 9, 1938, before the Aldriches made their radio debut, Ezra's father had written his son a letter addressing the subject of fame.

> I hope you realize by this time that success and popularity bring with it [*sic*] added responsibility and the demand for increased consideration for one's fellows. . . . As an example and paradoxical as it may seem, I personally am apt to be more critical of your faults now that you need my protection less. Conversely, you should I feel make sacrifices more readily now than before. To please me and ultimately for your own good I wish you would: Firstly, be more modest in your incidental expenses and thus take a larger proportion of your earnings. You know of course, that money as such never had any attraction to me but it irritates me to suspect that your habits are becoming wasteful and hence unsocial. Secondly, in regards to your diet I ask you for my sake, to make a conscious and consistent effort to check at once the increase in your weight and shortly afterward to begin to reduce very gradually to, say 135. You need not deny yourself anything provided you eat in moderation. As to exercise, I believe a short, brisk walk daily is more beneficial than irregular "gym." If you care to, talk it over with mother and in any event do not assume a resentful attitude. You are asked to take care of yourself and to please those who love you most. Daddy.

Not only does this letter further illustrate the relationship between father and son, but it indicates that Feinstone interpreted his son's new position within society as being that of a celebrity.

4. New York's Busiest Little Man

Although the majority of Ezra's formal training had prepared him for a career in legitimate theater, radio played an integral part in his development as a performer. From 1923 to 1927, Ezra's first public performances occurred on a children's variety program. Beginning in 1932, he worked alongside the Brozas on Horn and Hardart's *Children's Hour*. As an academy student in 1934 and 1935, he could not maintain regular outside employment, but he managed to enhance his meager allowance with radio appearances on *Young America* as part of the *Tasty Yeast Program* on the NBC Red Network. At that time, he also performed with Garson Kanin and Martin Gable on their half-hour biblical program. But Ezra had never been heard nationwide. Regional broadcasts served only to augment his theatrical training and income.

In the second half of the decade, the National Broadcasting Company's (NBC) *Rudy Vallee Hour* reigned as radio's top variety program. The show broadcast from Radio City Music Hall's Studio 8H, built originally for Toscanini and the NBC Philharmonic Orchestra and subsequently made famous as the home of television's *Saturday Night Live*. Other variety shows, such as *The Jack Benny Show*, *The Eddie Cantor Show*, and *The Fred Allen Show*, featured a stock company of stooges or characters performing comic routines with the stars; only for a change of pace were vocalists or other acts added. But *The Rudy Vallee Hour*, as well as its chief competitor, *The Kate Smith Hour*, originated the guest star concept, which was later made famous by television's *Ed Sullivan Show*. In addition, *The Rudy Vallee Hour* regularly featured excerpts from current Broadway shows enjoying a long run or from those that had recently opened to optimistic reviews. Of course, any Broadway production regarded an appearance on a major radio show as a golden opportunity that was even better for business than buying a full-page ad in the *New York Times*.

Stars such as Rudy Vallee took partial responsibility for the overall format of their variety programs, but an advertising agency serving the sponsor made most of the production decisions. Unlike today's shows, which were endorsed by several clients cooperatively, radio programs of that

period were typically sponsored by one of two giant food companies—
General Foods, Inc., or Standard Brands. The latter was the sponsor of *The
Rudy Vallee Hour*. In early July of 1938, J. Walter Thompson, the advertising agency representing Standard Brands, invited George Abbott and
Clifford Goldsmith to present a scene on their radio program. Ezra jokingly
remarked, "When they ran out of top Broadway shows running in 1938, we
did our first guest shot."

It was an exciting moment for Ezra as he stood in the wings of Studio
8H listening to Graham MacNamee, Rudy Vallee's announcer, read the
lineup for the program that evening. The twenty-year-old performer's heart
pounded as he heard names like Dinah Shore and Joe Penner, a successful
vaudevillian who had converted to radio comedy, listed before him. Mac-
Namee concluded by saying, "And from the Broadway stage we will bring
you a scene from Clifford Goldsmith's long running hit, *What a Life*, starring Ezra Stone as Henry Aldrich." Thus, Ezra received his first national
guest star billing.

The day after their national radio debut, the advertising agency for
Standard Brands informed Goldsmith that the scene from *What a Life* had
received unanimous applause. In a surprise move, they offered to air two
original eight-minute Aldrich family sketches featuring the troublesome
boy, one in July and the other in August.

Of course, the offer flattered the cast and production team, but they
realized that Vallee featured seemingly secure running acts, such as Edgar
Bergen and Charlie McCarthy and Joe Penner about once every month.
The representatives from J. Walter Thompson had hopes that Henry Aldrich might also come to occupy a regular spot on the show, but the cast
knew radio popularity was fickle and that turnover was likely. When an act
wore out its welcome on a variety show, another act was always waiting in
the wings.

For the cast's second appearance on national radio, Goldsmith wrote
a sketch entitled "The Early Life of Henry Aldrich." The author added two
family members not present in the play: Mr. Aldrich and Mary, Henry's
sister. Lea Penman, Betty Field, and Clyde Fillmore joined Ezra in the
radio cast. The script expanded Henry's troubles outside the halls of Central High School, as Goldsmith set this entire sketch before eight o'clock
in the morning just outside the Aldriches' only bathroom. It opens with
tone-deaf Henry singing an operatic aria as his parents plead for him to
finish his morning ritual and vacate the bathroom. A few moments later,
Mary beseeches him to quit singing.

> MARY: Henry!
> HENRY: Dum dum dum dum dum —
> MARY: Henry!

(*Sound: Knock on the door*)
HENRY: Yes, Father?
MARY: It's not Father. It's me.
HENRY: (*Evidently his toothbrush is still in his mouth*) Well—get away.
MARY: Mother says to keep quiet. Aunt Harriet is trying to sleep.
HENRY: I-didn't-even-know-Aunt-Harriet-was-here.
MARY: Well, she is. She arrived in the night.
HENRY: Well, well, well—out of the nowhere—into the here! (*And that, naturally, gives him an idea for a song*) Out of the nowhere—into the here! Out of the herewhere, into the no!
MARY: Henry, do you want Aunt Harriet to hear you?
HENRY: I thought you said she was asleep.
(*And with that we hear a prolonged and deep gargling*)
MARY: Henry, hand me my vanishing cream.
HENRY: Whatdoyouwant?
MARY: Hand me my vanishing cream. It's right there on the glass shelf.
HENRY: (*His voice is once more with him*) There isn't any vanishing cream on the glass shelf. Evidently it must have vanished. . . .

Besides accusing Henry of monopolizing the bathroom, family members go on to falsely accuse the boy of losing the cord to the toaster, leaving the newly repaired lawn mower in the rain, mooching unearned money, and blowing the fuse in the electric icebox thus ruining its contents. The sketch ends with Henry presumably going to school to confront more troubles there.

The initial response from the live audience during the second program was enormous, and program officials received a flood of optimistic letters and telephone calls. Two weeks later, Henry Aldrich appeared for the third time on *The Rudy Vallee Hour*. In his introduction of the sketch, Vallee said in his nasal, down east, melodic voice,

Two weeks ago our listeners learned something of the Early Life of Henry Aldrich . . . that astonishing young man created as they say in dramatic circles . . . EZRA STONE in the George Abbott comedy success, *What a Life*. Clifford Goldsmith, author of *What a Life*, obliged and delighted us on that occasion by writing a new sketch based on the characters of his play. It was, in three little words, a quick click. So we invited Mr. Goldsmith to tell us more of the life of Henry Aldrich . . . and his answer was another sketch, called "More of the Life of Henry Aldrich." . . . Ezra Stone in "More of the Life of Henry Aldrich."

This episode found Henry in similar predicaments with his family while eating the evening meal, but, more importantly, Goldsmith introduced Henry's first sidekick, a boy originally dubbed Joe but at the last minute named Bill. Blaine Fillmore, son of Lea Penman and Clyde Fillmore, created the role. "He was a nice fellow," Ezra later wrote, "but not really an actor and certainly not a comedic one."

BILL:	(*Calling from outside*) Eh, Henry!
HENRY:	(*Yelling*) Hi, Bill! . . . That's Bill.
MR. ALDRICH:	What's the matter, doesn't that boy have any home?
HENRY:	Why?
	(*Sound: Whistle is heard again*)
MRS. ALDRICH:	Mary, go to the window and tell that young man that Henry can't come out until he has finished his dinner.
MARY:	(*Opening window*) Mother says Henry can't come out until he's through.
BILL:	(*Outside*) What's he doing?
MARY:	He's eating muffins.
HENRY:	Tell him to come on in.
MR. ALDRICH:	You tell that boy to stay out there where he belongs.
HENRY:	We've got something important to discuss about our trip.
MRS. ALDRICH:	Your trip where?
HENRY:	From New York to San Francisco.
BILL:	How much longer will Henry be?
MARY:	We don't know. This is the first food he's had since three o'clock this afternoon.

Following this appearance on the program, the Henry Aldrich sketches began to develop into a spin-off radio program. Over the years, various people have taken credit for this development. Ezra later believed that the idea to give Henry his own show may have come from a young agent from the William Morris Agency, Sam Weisbord, who later rose to the presidency of the organization. After realizing the show's long-range possibilities, he likely sold the notion to Tony Stamford, the producer and director of *The Rudy Vallee Hour*, who then for years took credit for the idea.

Henry Aldrich quickly became an extremely marketable product, and word spread that Standard Brands wanted to hire Goldsmith and the acting company for thirty-nine weeks, the full 1938–39 season. Only then did Ezra begin to comprehend the show's impact and the possibility of his becoming a national celebrity. Until then only the Times Square crowd, the New York theater patrons, and his colleagues recognized him and his recent accomplishments. But he wisely guarded his feelings about the possible effects of long-term national exposure. "It was great. I loved it," Ezra later said. "I enjoyed it, but that wasn't what I was all about. I wasn't going to turn my nose up at it, but my theater work as a director was where I wanted to concentrate my effort and energy." Besides, Ezra figured that radio would afford him the luxury of careers in two media. The radio program would typically require only nine hours per week—two hours of rehearsal the night before the performance and one entire day for airing.

As a young actor portraying a popular character like Henry Aldrich, Ezra faced the problem of potentially losing his identity in the role. He credited Rudy Vallee's style as an emcee for helping him to distinguish himself as an actor rather than as the mischievous adolescent character. Vallee was not the typical Broadway type nor the average Tin Pan Alley musician; instead, he was a rather starchy and dignified man with a degree in music from the University of Maine, the birthplace of his band. His style of introducing acts was gentlemanly. He always emphasized the actor properly over the act. Thus, in his introduction of *What a Life*, Ezra Stone's name appeared before that of Henry Aldrich. That simple credit would continue with Ezra for the remainder of his career.

With Ezra's growing popularity, Weisbord recommended to Sol Feinstone that his son hire a press agent. Ezra hired Paul Mosher, one of the top public relations officers for the Earl Ferris Agency, to handle his media promotion. It was Mosher who arranged the clause in all Ezra's subsequent radio and stage contracts requiring the credit: "Ezra Stone as . . ." Mosher was also responsible for Ezra receiving an on-the-air credit for any show he might act in or direct. Ezra felt that one publicity gimmick made him marketable throughout his career. "All the jobs I got after *What a Life*, all my directing jobs on television, came out of my being a known personality," he later said. "Not the talent, it was just the sheer weight of proper marketing of your product, you. That's the only product you have to sell."

The Kate Smith Hour, sponsored by General Foods through Young and Rubicam Advertising Agency, provided *The Rudy Vallee Hour* with its chief competition. Both shows aired at 8:00 P.M. on Thursday evenings; Vallee appeared on the NBC Red network, and Smith's program aired on WABC, the Columbia Broadcasting System (CBS) affiliate station in New York. Musically, the show was good, with Smith delivering songs in her usual dynamic style backed by Jack Miller's accomplished orchestra and Ted Streeter's chorus. Smith's appeal, plus an apparently unlimited budget for guest stars, unquestionably made the program stiff competition.

Following Henry Aldrich's outstanding success on *The Rudy Vallee Hour*, Sam Weisbord "pitched" the idea to Ted Collins, the announcer and all-around boss of *The Kate Smith Hour*, of making the Aldriches a regular act on their program. Collins approached Smith and Young and Rubicam, who then contacted Goldsmith with an offer for the rights to present his sketches throughout the 1938–39 season. Nobody knows what tilted the scale in the bidding war from the J. Walter Thompson Agency toward Young and Rubicam. Ezra figured they made a noncontractual offer to Goldsmith, who still controlled the property. If the sketches could hold high marks in the Crosley Rating System as a regular guest shot on *The Kate Smith Hour*, then General Foods more than likely verbally committed to give the author his own half-hour program at the end of the season. As creator and writer, Goldsmith received fifty-one percent controlling interest in the property. Ezra, as the star and with the help of his new press agent, negotiated for forty-nine percent ownership.

In the dressing room before a performance of *What a Life* (1939).

On September 16, 1938, CBS distributed the following press release
to all the major national magazines and New York newspapers:

> Ezra Stone, the incorrigible juvenile of the current Broadway comedy hit,
> *What a Life*, soon to reach its 200th performance, has been engaged by
> Kate Smith to play the lead in a comedy serial in her 1938–'39 series of
> variety shows starting over the Columbia network Thursday, Septem-
> ber 29. (WABC-CBS, 8:00 to 9:00 P.M. EST). . . . Although many theatri-
> cal artists have starred concurrently on the stage and before the micro-
> phone, Ezra Stone's forthcoming series will mark the first time that the
> star of a Broadway hit has adapted his special role for a radio series run-
> ning simultaneously. This type of act also represents an innovation for the
> programs of "The Songbird of the South."

It went on to say that Betty Field, Lea Penman, Clyde Fillmore, Eddie
Bracken, and other members of the cast of *What a Life* would support
Stone in the radio program. In addition to the cast of this comedy, the singing mistress-of-ceremonies planned to continue to present stars of Broadway and Hollywood in guest roles each week.

Beginning September 29, 1938, Henry Aldrich became a regular on
The Kate Smith Hour. Every Thursday promptly at 8:00 P.M., Jack Miller's
orchestra struck up such familiar fanfares as "When the Moon Comes Over
the Mountain." On cue the orchestration cut for announcer André Baruch
who said, "Calumet Baking Powder and Swans Down Cake Flour — your
two best baking friends — present *The Kate Smith Hour*." The applause sign

flashed in the audience, as the music then swelled up in another familiar tune. After a moment, Ted Collins spoke over the now softened music. "Good evening. This is Ted Collins speaking. The lights are up on 45th Street here in New York for it's time to begin another *Kate Smith Hour*. It's another big show tonight for featured with us are . . . " Along with Goldsmith's sketches, Bud Abbott and Lou Costello, who debuted with their famous "Who's on First" routine, and the mock-quiz "It Pays to Be Ignorant" made regular appearances on Smith's show that season. All three of these acts subsequently launched into their own half-hour prime-time programs. These acts, along with several appearances by John Barrymore and Smith's introduction of her celebrated "God Bless America," made for an extraordinary amount of talent.

The show typically began with several numbers featuring Kate Smith, Miller's orchestra, and a musical guest. After a final number, the orchestra faded to the Aldrich theme, and Smith introduced the sketch. A typical introduction went as follows:

> Well, we're going visiting again with those loveable folks who live next door. But this time we're stopping off at the garage that adjoins their cottage, for there we find Mr. Aldrich working on his car. Mary is watching, and Henry—well, Henry as usual, is speaking.

The scripts followed the format established on *The Rudy Vallee Hour*, centering around the Aldrich family—Sam and Alice, the parents; Mary, Henry's sister; and Henry. The biggest alteration was Goldsmith's new title, *The Aldrich Family*, which would continue throughout the show's tenure.

Throughout the season, Ezra also continued to play Henry Aldrich in Abbott's production of *What a Life*, which had moved across 47th Street from the Biltmore to the Mansfield Theatre, only two short blocks up 8th Avenue from the CBS Playhouse on 45th Street. On Thursday evenings, the stage manager of *What a Life* held the curtain until after *The Kate Smith Hour*. In order to juggle the two assignments, Ezra arrived at the Mansfield at approximately 6:00 P.M. to dress and make up for the stage play. He then walked to the radio stage to perform in the variety show. At the end of the broadcast, he quickly returned to the Mansfield for his nightly performance. After *What a Life*, he had just enough time to disrobe, wipe off his makeup, and come back to the radio stage for the West Coast repeat of *The Kate Smith Hour*, which aired at 11:30 P.M. EST.

Playing Henry Aldrich in two media, Ezra utilized the stage show to promote the radio broadcast and vice versa. One afternoon, Ezra arrived at the theater with a radio and a sign. The radio he placed in the mezzanine lounge; the sign he placed in the lobby. It read, "Those who attend the

theater on Thursday evenings are invited to come a little early and listen
to Mr. Stone and the Aldrich family on their Kate Smith radio sketch in the
rear of the mezzanine before the performance of the play." The audience
of *What a Life* found the occasion an unusual interlude.

Smith, on and off mike, was the consummate star of her radio program.
With the exception of Collins, the program's directors, and a couple of
agency people who had become her close friends, the subordinate actors
referred to the grand lady as Miss Smith. The privileged few called her
Katherine. Soon after her show began, Miss Smith inserted into her weekly
format a thank you speech to the studio audience after her show signed off.
She and Collins insisted that all guests who appeared on the show each
week should remain on stage with her. Because he needed to exit immediately after the program, Ezra positioned himself at the end of the curtain call line on stage left, the nearest route to the stage door. As Smith
made her speech and took her final bow and as the audience responded
with thunderous applause, Ezra readied himself to make a break for the
stage door. On the second week of the season, however, Smith's large,
beefy hand caught Ezra just under his jaw holding him on stage until she
had made her exit. Once in the wings, she turned on the younger actor and
said, "Ezra, no one leaves the stage before me."

Ever since his involvement in *Parade*, Ezra—influenced by Philip
Loeb—had been actively campaigning for reforms in the Actors' Equity
Association. The union, which was strengthened as a result of the actors'
strike of 1919, had by the 1930s settled down into a dignified association,
but it was controlled by right-wing conservatives. Meetings were held only
a few times each year, and many members thought the union did not adequately address the problems facing them. Although actors had contracts
and certain rights, many injustices—all of which undermined the principles of unionism and created terrible suspicions among members—
continued to plague the profession. Those who controlled the guild appeared content to slowly address these issues, while a rebel faction committed to immediate action emerged in opposition to the conservatives.

Some of these actors, including Ezra and many of his friends, began
meeting on their own as a rump steering committee at Union Church on
48th Street. From this emerged a number of leaders, but the three strongest were George Heller, Sam Jaffe, and Philip Loeb. The group, which soon
became known as the Actors' Forum, met every couple of weeks with hundreds of actors in attendance. With no dues and no structure, the committee merely served as a discussion group dedicated to redressing the actors'
grievances.

More often than not, Heller chaired the unofficial meetings; Jaffe,
although a reserved and quiet man by nature, also participated. Loeb, on
the other hand, was the consummate comedian, and he used his wit to

rouse his audiences to action. "Loeb had a wit that people would wait and wait to hear," said Eugene Frances in "The Oral History of Philip Loeb." "When Loeb finally wanted to speak, they were not only roused from indolence, but they would be amused. He was probably the wittiest man I've ever met; he was just extraordinary." To dramatize a point, Loeb often impersonated people holding equity council offices. While waiting for something to begin, he sometimes enacted entire equity meetings, impersonating every councilman. It was an exciting period, and under the leadership of these three men the group's followers soon numbered in the thousands. Equity eventually had no other choice but to recognize this insurgent committee.

Ezra idolized Loeb, and he took great pride in his participation in this group. He frequently told the story of his ability on a matinee day to amass signatures from one hundred or more equity members on any petition that Loeb, Jaffe, and Heller wanted to present to the council on the following Tuesday. For this expertise, Loeb dubbed Stone "La Petionara," a nickname inspired by the then-famous Spanish loyalist's young girl messenger, "La Passionara."

On the whole, the rebels were free and independent thinkers with no specific political agenda. They included republicans, democrats, progressives, and socialists, and a certain faction even belonged to or sympathized with the Communist Party. Naturally, this activity provoked a backlash, particularly from the archconservatives and fascist elements. It remains unclear whether Heller, Jaffe, and Loeb sympathized with the communists, but all three men, along with other rebels, eventually gained seats on the equity council. While they fought for and improved the actors' working conditions, they made many enemies who sometimes unleashed relentless attacks on their character. Since these three men also happened to be Jewish, their enemies were provided with additional ammunition.

Meanwhile, following a successful run throughout the summer of 1938, ticket sales for Abbott's production of *What a Life* declined. In order to break even, the show required a weekly minimum income—referred to as the nut—of three thousand dollars. Some weeks it reached its goal, while other weeks it fell short. Abbott therefore decided to bring down the final curtain on Saturday, October 8, only six months after the show's debut.

Ezra, who had learned the inner workings of production from his mentor and who had discovered the show's primary target audience by frequenting the box office prior to performances, devised a revolutionary plan to keep *What a Life* running on Broadway without its original entrepreneur. By this time *The Aldrich Family* had gained national exposure, so Ezra reasoned it would be a good risk to try to maintain an audience for the play. He anticipated additional publicity as the show edged toward its second season, and he expected increased audience potential with the beginning of the 1939 New York World's Fair. He devised a formula that allowed himself and the other cast members to run their own production. Stripped to its bare necessities and operating outside the Abbott system, he deduced that *What a Life* could break even on only twenty-three hundred dollars a week.

Before taking his plan to Abbott and Goldsmith, Ezra first approached the acting company. He explained that if the entire group would reduce their salaries to the equity minimum, they could establish a comfortable nest egg. At the time, Ezra received only seventy-five dollars each week for playing the leading role. This was a rather modest salary considering that Joyce Arling, who played the small role of Miss Wheeler, received one hundred seventy-five dollars weekly salary. In fact, Glaser, who portrayed Mr. Bradley, and Field, who played Henry's future prom date, both had larger contracted salaries than Ezra. But that was simply Abbott's system of rewarding his actors' loyalty in their previous work. Although financially others risked more than Ezra, the entire company agreed to accept the union scale for two weeks, hoping thereby to keep the show running.

Once he had secured this agreement, Ezra divulged the second phase of his formula: all actors would accept minimum scale in subsequent weeks unless the box office income for the previous week exceeded the nut. If during the previous week they exceeded the nut, then the following week they would take home their previously contracted salaries regardless of that week's box office income. This scheme meant they could possibly alternate between minimum and contracted salaries, but the financial reserve would be constant as long as they met or exceeded the nut. The new plan allowed no actor to renegotiate a contract. Everyone had to remain at the rate they had been paid by Abbott. As part owners of the "corporation," they could also anticipate periodic dividends from the accumulated nest egg. For instance, when Betty Field later left the company to go to Hollywood to film John Steinbeck's *Of Mice and Men*, her prorated share of the financial reserve amounted to almost nine hundred dollars.

In view of the alternative of finding another acting job in the middle of the Great Depression, the acting company enthusiastically agreed to all terms in the arrangement. On that fateful weekend of October 8, the cast, led by Ezra, officially met with Abbott and Goldsmith to discuss the future of *What a Life*. In the end, the producer and the author not only agreed to the new plan, but both men waived their royalties. For Goldsmith, the play complimented the radio program, his new income source. Abbott, on the other hand, was pleased at the prospect of proving to his actors that he appreciated their initiative. Legally, however, his name remained on the program as producer, which meant he still had ultimate control of the show. It also meant that he would have three shows running simultaneously on Broadway: *Room Service, What a Life,* and *The Boys from Syracuse,* a musical comedy he had slated to open in November of 1938. Therefore, Abbott not only supported the plan, he even donated scenery, costumes, and properties.

According to an article in the *New York Times,* when the curtain rose that Monday evening, the audience could tell no difference in the production.

> Actors were the same, lights were the same, the set was the same, clothes were the same and even the producer's name on the program was the same. But behind the scenes there was a new breath of life on Broadway. Actors were acting in their own production. Not only were they commencing a period when they must maintain their artistic standard with a vengeance, but they must learn the fine art of bringing people into the theatre.

After they worked through initial details and the show made its Broadway debut under new management, the company elected Jack Byrne, Arthur Pierson, Edith Van Cleve, and Ezra Stone to a committee to do the major portion of the planning, scheming, thinking, and worrying necessary to keep the show afloat. When Byrne, who originated the role of Mr. Ferguson, left the company, Vaughn Glaser replaced him on the committee. The committee soon became well versed in the quirks of showmanship. One of the first things the group did was to persuade Carl Fisher, Abbott's general manager and nephew—Abbott did not consider nepotism a dirty word—to leave the *What a Life* Corporation intact. This eliminated tax and insurance problems. Thanks to the help of Frank Goodman, the company's press agent and a master at the art of mass mailings and assembling groups, the show frequently sold out for many subsequent months. According to a contemporaneous report, the actors considered him one of "the greatest magicians of all time."

The *What a Life* Corporation established an aggressive advertising campaign featuring a three-for-one ticket sales promotion to back up Goodman and Stone. The company placed large tables under the stage adjoining the orchestra pit at the Mansfield Theatre, and the cast, from leads to walk-ons, addressed, folded, and licked envelopes containing announcements and coupons to be mailed to prospective customers. They used the telephone directory as their primary source for addresses. Doctors and beauty parlors showed the biggest returns. Then Goodman and Stone orchestrated an active campaign during lunch breaks at various factories and schools throughout the region. They appeared at club meetings, clambakes, and picnics. Wherever they could find an audience, Goodman made the arrangements, and Ezra delivered set speeches and told anecdotes and stories of his own high school experiences. They then distributed a handful of three-for-one coupons. "Not the greatest drama ever penned," Ezra conceded, "but I'm sure you will laugh most heartily at our modest effort. Now if each of you will bring two friends. . . ."

Because it took only a short time to make up and dress before a performance, Ezra sometimes greeted customers at the box office. He then returned backstage, reported to the cast the condition of the house, and prepared himself for that evening's performance. On some occasions, the house manager and ushers informed Ezra of particular groups, such as English and drama classes, attending that performance. Then during his curtain speech, Ezra invited them on stage to meet him and his "schoolmates" from Central High School. The kids usually accepted the offer, enjoying a chance to stand on the set and compare their own school experiences with Henry's. Of course, autographs on their playbills were in constant demand.

As *What a Life* played through the fall and into winter, Ezra and company continued their advertising blitz, promoting the show as a "clean and wholesome comedy dealing with school life in a big city." They devised special bookmarks in the form of discount cards, which they mailed to local libraries and bookstores. They also offered free tickets to local settlement houses and orphanages. In a letter to Mayor Fiorello LaGuardia, Ezra wrote,

> On behalf of *What a Life* company which is run cooperatively by members of the cast, I respectfully place at your disposal 250 orchestra seats for Saturday matinee, December 24, for youngsters of any city orphanage or any other institution you may choose. I would deem it an honor if your own children would be present as official hosts to these youngsters. . . .

This type of publicity not only promoted goodwill during the holiday season, it also created a splendid image for the show and the organization. In a subsequent letter, Marguerite Woodin, executive secretary for the Society for Seamen's Children, expressed her gratitude for the committee's thoughtfulness.

> It is with sincere appreciation that we thank you for the splendid entertainment which some of our children enjoyed on December 24th. The play was particularly suitable for the boys and girls, since most of them are now in high school. Except in a few cases, this was the first stage play they had ever attended.

The company entered the new year, and when the 1939 New York World's Fair opened, matinees were added to accommodate the influx of tourists. Every Friday the actors also presented special "Four O'clock Scholar Matinees," which successfully drew afternoon shoppers and hoards of student groups. For World's Fair visitors, they eventually added Saturday and Sunday matinees. Around the Easter holiday, the troupe performed both matinee and evening shows seven days a week. Since the company owned the production, extra work meant larger dividends.

Soon the organization functioned like a finely tuned machine. Attending one of the *What a Life* committee meetings must have been like visiting a meeting of the board of directors of General Motors. The members discussed the cost of cleaning costumes, of retouching scenery, and of magazine advertising rates. They settled matters of special rates and who should fill required speaking dates. They detailed the progress of understudy rehearsals, problems of cast discipline and illness, and problems of ventilating and heating the theater. The actors were concerned with the doorman's cough, the promotion manager's results, and, most importantly, the time when dividends were to be declared. During their existence, they declared dividend distributions more than half a dozen times, each usually equaling three weeks' salary.

By the time *What a Life* reached its one-year anniversary, it had become Broadway's oldest comedy and second oldest play and was chosen by Burns Mantle as one of the ten best plays of 1938. All along, Abbott, although not as intimately connected with the show as before, kept close tabs on its growth and progress. The cast of *What a Life* affectionately became known as the Abbott Beavers, a name which derived from Abbott's league softball team, the Abbott Rabbits. According to an anonymous article in the *New York Herald*, to celebrate the show's first anniversary, the Abbott office closed operation one Friday "so that the producer's employees might make an informal motion picture" to be shown at a party sponsored by Abbott on April 14, 1939. They dubbed the film, *When the Cat's Away*, referring to their antics during Abbott's recent departure to Florida. On the night of the party, one of the younger understudies presented the following unpublished poem, which aptly described the relationship between the cast of *What a Life* and Ezra Stone and between the Beavers and the Abbott corporation.

Oh, What a Life:
    And still we are undaunted;
So long we wanted work, and now we've got just what we wanted.
Now we're the younger players that you see in "What A Life"
    With Ezra Stone as Henry Aldrich.

Back-stage is full of brother-love,—you slice it with a knife
    With Ezra Stone as Henry Aldrich.
We all are understudies, we try to do our best,
    With Miss Van Cleve all over us like gravy on a vest
So far no actor's even had a rumble in his chest
    With Ezra Stone as Henry Aldrich.

Co-operative acting seems to throw us for a loss
    With Ezra Stone as Henry Aldrich.
The trouble with this wacky job, you never know who's boss:
    With Ezra Stone as Henry Aldrich.
At each Committee Meeting they criticize each one;
Performances are analyzed, — they have a lot of fun.

Then one by one they come and tell us how it should be done;
    With Ezra Stone — as Henry Aldrich.
With advertising stickers we have plastered up the town;
    With Ezra Stone — as Henry Aldrich.

We stick 'em up as rapidly as they can tear 'em down;
    With Ezra Stone — as Henry Aldrich.
We find they bring the business; — We've got a show to sell
They're stuck on Fords and Chevrolets, and Packard cars as well;
They're even in the Ladies Room in ev'ry big hotel;
    With Ezra Stone — as Henry Aldrich.

Hurray for our committee, they have money in the bank;
    With Ezra Stone — as Henry Aldrich.
A bow to Mr. Goodman too, whose Christian name is Frank;
    With Ezra Stone — as Henry Aldrich.
O Long we've seen our billing, it's got beneath our skin
Just try to find a paper that his picture isn't in;
Poor Ezra works so hard, I do believe he's getting thin:
    With Ezra Stone — as Henry Aldrich.

Now Mr. Abbott's back in town, — His shoes are full of sand.
    With Ezra Stone — as Henry Aldrich.
He came to see our show — we had to laugh — he had to stand;
    With Ezra Stone — as Henry Aldrich.
He counted up the house and then he gurgled softly "Oh,
    What is it drags the people in to see this little show?
Do you suppose "The Primrose Path" could get your over-flow?"
    With Ezra Stone — as Henry Aldrich.

At night when we are tucked in bed, we're haunted in our sleep
    With Ezra Stone — as Henry Aldrich.
Because we see a three-sheet on the back of ev'ry sheep:
    "With Ezra Stone — as Henry Aldrich."
One night we went out steeping, and drank up seven kegs;
We staggered to a restaurant on weak and wobbly legs;
We told the waiter, when he asked: "How will you have your eggs?"
    With Ezra Stone — as Henry Aldrich."
OH WHAT A LIFE!

This poem underscores the dedication of all members of the corporation. The revolutionary arrangement worked, and Ezra Stone "as Henry Aldrich" was clearly the inspiration behind the operation.

Although the World's Fair greatly increased the potential audience for the show, attendance began to sag in late April. According to Abel Greene and Joe Laurie, Jr., in their book *Showbiz from Vaude to Video*, New York theaters, which expected a tremendous boom in business as a result of the fair, were dismayed by results of the first few months. They wrote, "Tourists weren't arriving in the expected numbers. Most came with thin wallets, staying at the Fair all day and returning to their hotels too tired to do anything but rest their feet or sleep." The Abbott office, which still had control over the show's fate, sent closing notices to the company as early as May 22. But because of last-moment improvements in ticket sales, Abbott reversed his decision to close the show week by week throughout the month of June. The closing notices, penned by Carl Fisher, became a familiar joke to the cast and crew. One read,

> Dear Cast: You will never guess what this letter is about. It is not to tell you that we are going to run until Labor Day, but rather to inform you that the run of *What a Life* will close on Saturday, June 24, at the Mansfield Theatre. I don't really believe it myself, but now we're covered. Best regards.

The show, however, struggled along until July 8, when Milton Stiefel, owner of the established Straw Hat Theatre, contracted to present *What a Life* in the Bronx, Brighton Beach, and Atlantic City. Several of the cast members, including Ezra, performed in three separate summer stock engagements: Marble Head, Massachusetts; Ivorytown, Connecticut; and closed in Fairfield, Connecticut, in August of 1939. *What a Life* came to rest after playing close to eight hundred performances, including over five hundred on Broadway.

What a Life instilled magic in its audiences until the end of its run. Toward the end of the summer, the players many times faced sparse crowds, sitting in scattered clusters throughout the auditorium. Before the curtain was raised, many people muttered and fussed that perhaps they had made an unwise decision to attend. "Actors never do their best for a handful of people, and I'm afraid we'll have a pretty dull afternoon," one woman said as she counted the 150 patrons scattered around the orchestra. At the show's conclusion, however, this same woman reportedly said, "I'm going to bring my husband and my two boys. They'll love it — simply love it. It's a crying shame this house isn't packed."

Their response to that situation was precisely what separated Ezra and his associates from other companies. Playing to a handful of spectators, who perhaps produced only one-third the normal volume of laughs, applause, and appreciation, they continued to give maximum effort. "Never before have I seen a small house acting with the enthusiasm that your audience did the other afternoon," wrote Maureen McKernan, a reporter for the *New York Post*, in a letter to Ezra. "Myself — I whooped and laughed and

Ezra Stone manages eight jobs and gets by on only five hours sleep (1938).

got a lump in my throat repeatedly. The girl with me decided she would bring her boy Saturday as a reward for a week of good grades in school."

Ezra and the entire cast of *What a Life* had withstood the test of time. They had disproved Abbott's assertion that an actor in a long running show inevitably loses all spontaneity because of the monotony. Primarily through Ezra's inspiration, the actors surmounted this obstacle by keeping their performances fresh and inspired, not merely routine. The audiences may have dwindled, but Ezra at least had a sincere desire to make each performance better than the previous one. Perhaps his dedication stemmed from his leading role, or perhaps it came as a result of his investment in the corporation. But he had clearly reached a new level of professionalism.

In early fall of 1938, Ezra played for the third time simultaneously multiple roles on Broadway, this time as understudy for two prominent comedians in Abbott's upcoming musical comedy. Lorenz Hart, who had strong protective feelings for his brother, Teddy, had brought to Richard Rodgers and George Abbott an idea for a play that would serve as a vehicle for his brother. Taking the story from Shakespeare's *The Comedy of Errors*, he suggested they adapt the material for a contemporary musical comedy. Originally, Lorenz Hart was to provide the lyrics, Rodgers the music, and all three men, including Abbott, were to collaborate on the book. Before they could meet, however, Abbott had penned the first draft of a script that blended well with Rodgers' and Hart's musical composition. Abbott entitled the new play, *The Boys from Syracuse.* Abbott, as producer and director, engaged Jo Mielziner to design the scenery, Irene Sharaff for the costumes, and George Balanchine for the choreography. He then took Eddie Albert out of *Room Service* to play the romantic lead, Antipholus of Syracuse. Jimmy Savo and Teddy Hart were contracted to portray the two Dromios.

The *Boys from Syracuse* had started rehearsals at the Alvin Theatre the first week of October, only a few days before the actors of *What a Life* took control of their production. As Abbott's casting and production assistant, Ezra had already taken an active role in the preparation of the new show. And because Ezra was perhaps the only actor in New York who could pass for either Savo's or Hart's twin, Abbott assigned him another responsibility to his already hectic schedule, namely to understudy both Dromios. Ezra, as one will recall, had previously served as Savo's understudy in the Theatre Guild production of *Parade* and twice worked on the second team under Hart in the Abbott productions of *Three Men on a Horse* and *Room Service.*

As was customary for an understudy, Ezra attended all rehearsals and watched the development of both Dromios as Savo and Hart created them. Because the text continually changed and evolved, he, like other stand-ins, did not commit the script to memory. Not until Abbott froze the show and they opened to favorable New York reviews did Ezra and his fellow substitutes begin serious rehearsals.

In the early days of a run, understudies rehearsed a couple of days each week, typically supervised by the stage manager, or in the case of an Abbott production, by Van Cleve or Stone. Just as the original cast members had done, the substitutes began with scripts in hand and simulated the choreographed movements. Having sat through past rehearsals, most of the actors learned quickly, and they soon weaned themselves from the scripts. As understudies, it was their responsibility to portray the character as created by the actor and frozen by the director. In effect, they not only had to learn the same text but also had to learn the original actor's timing and rhythms so as not to disrupt the established flow of the action. Only actors taken on as permanent replacements had the luxury of endowing the role with their own interpretation. This, of course, still depended on the original director's or stage manager's approval.

When *The Boys from Syracuse* opened on November 23, Ezra remained backstage at the Alvin Theatre until a few minutes before curtain, then rushed over to the Mansfield for his performance in *What a Life.* That night he returned to the Alvin in time for the final curtain, but of course too late to have the pleasure of seeing the finished product play to an audience. Norman Tokar, Ezra's understudy in *What a Life*, was ready to play school-boy Henry Aldrich any night. He had the extra exciting thought that not only would he get a chance to portray the troubled boy if Ezra called in sick, but he would also have a chance to play the role if something happened to either Savo or Hart.

The stage managers at each theater coordinated the maneuver by telephone. Every night, at half an hour prior to curtain, Ezra reported to the Mansfield's stage manager who in turn called the stage manager at the Alvin. Thus, both men knew how to reach Ezra and each other if necessary. If either Savo or Hart could not perform, Ezra's primary responsibility was to *The Boys from Syracuse*, which represented a much greater box office draw. As time passed, however, Ezra never had to play either Dromio in front of an audience, and he never required an understudy to fill in for him as Henry Aldrich. Although he could deliver a letter perfect performance on demand, he actually saw a full performance of the musical comedy only a few times, one of those times being a benefit show for the Actor's Fund. Ezra had to pay his own admittance.

Even before *The Boys from Syracuse* had opened, Paul Mosher, Ezra's press agent, began promoting his client as one of the most versatile and aggressive theater artists in the city. Mosher's syndicated cartoon panel and other stratagems obviously captured the attention of several reporters, who actively pursued interviews with the actor dubbed "Broadway's Busiest" and "Broadway Dynamo." Ezra, however, took the attention thrust upon him in stride. Robert Francis of the *Brooklyn Eagle* reported that although Ezra maintained a frantic business schedule, he remained a quiet, sedate, and rather unassuming man when not on stage or behind a microphone. As Francis put it, "He [Ezra] has youth, bubbling enthusiasm, and above all a sincerely objective interest in people and things." As Abbott's casting director, for example, Ezra often interviewed people much older than himself. Even with them, however, he had developed patience and a sympathy that enabled him to unearth players with whom a more cantankerous executive would not have bothered. "I made a habit of sending thank you cards to each actor I interviewed or auditioned—whether they were hired or not—to show them I appreciated their help in the casting process," he later wrote. Ezra maintained his innocence and did not develop the characteristics so often found in people holding commanding positions. After listening to a flurry of questions posed by Dan Collins of the *New York World-Telegram* concerning his hectic schedule, Ezra slumped in a chair with his feet dangling over the sides, chewed the end of his pipe, grinned, and answered the questions in an easy manner. He even looked mildly surprised by the attention he was receiving. He did not consider himself unusually energetic.

Ezra maintained his busy schedule not through superhuman feats of endurance but rather through an uncanny sense of time management. He later said in an interview,

It wasn't that difficult really. The legit shows I was in during that period ran eight performances per week. My radio show was usually one day per week, a Thursday. My teaching at the American Academy of Dramatic Arts varied around three mornings a week, maybe two hours. As for my work in the Abbott office, I was really my own boss as far as scheduling my time. It wasn't an eight hour a day work job. I'd show up a little before noon on all days except matinee days and my radio day. I'd do the mail and touch base with Mister Abbott to see if he had any special assignment for me. I set up my own interviews to my own schedule. The cooperative business I dealt with only two or three days a week in the schools, the factories, etc. . . . . After *The Boys from Syracuse* opened, I attended all understudy rehearsals once a week in the afternoons.

But Ezra did admit he typically operated on five hours of sleep each night. Six hours he considered a luxury. The energetic young man might have heard of the five-day and forty-hour workweek, but he rarely enjoyed the luxury of free time.

5. Starring Ezra
Stone as Henry Aldrich

Following a thirty-nine week regular season, which usually ran from October until the middle of June, a radio program in the late 1930s typically rebroadcast previously aired shows throughout the thirteen-week summer season, or the agency booked another tryout program as a temporary replacement. Those rebroadcasting previous performances used recordings that had been made on large acetate discs known as electrical transcripts or e.t.'s. This undertaking was expensive, and many programs therefore did not have this alternative.

After *The Aldrich Family*'s full regular season on *The Kate Smith Hour*, General Foods and Young and Rubicam offered the show the replacement slot for Jack Benny on Sundays during the summer of 1939. If the show held high ratings throughout the thirteen weeks, General Foods would sponsor their own prime-time show beginning in the 1939–40 regular season. Benny, then the king of radio, hosted the nation's most popular comedy program. Therefore, acquiring his large and loyal audience ensured *The Aldrich Family* healthy ratings for its debut as a half-hour, prime-time domestic situation comedy.

Soon after the 1938–39 season had ended, Ezra and Charles Moos, his high school friend on whom he had modeled Henry's voice, arranged a vacation in the south. The two young men planned to drive to New Orleans and then to Miami in Ezra's car—a black Ford convertible sedan—which he owned without his father's consent or knowledge. The convertible, which Ezra dubbed "Black Bastard," had formerly belonged to Mayor Jimmy Walker's official New York City greeter, Grover Whalen. John Most, one of Ezra's three best friends from the academy, agreed to take out the title in his name. Although this represented Ezra's first vacation, he was uncertain as to how long it would last. The Young and Rubicam agency was trying to arrange for him to appear as a guest on the last *Jack Benny Show* of the season, which was to air the week before *The Aldrich Family*'s debut. With this eventuality in mind, Ezra and Charles coordinated their trip with Western Union and with Paul Mosher.

When Ezra and Charles arrived in New Orleans, they checked into

Ezra and Charles Moos on vacation in Miami, Florida, 1940. Photo courtesy of
Charles Moos Collection.

the first bed-and-breakfast they found on the outskirts of the city. They
called Western Union for any messages and gave them their temporary address. However, in their rush to visit the French Quarter, they forgot to
make a note of the address of their lodging for themselves. After much
carousing, they wandered around the quaint back alleys near Bourbon
Street pondering their dilemma.

      Sometime early in the morning, they overheard a drunken young man,
who leaned against a lamp post, saying, "Fuck the American Academy of
Dramatic Arts." At first Ezra figured his fun-loving press agent had staged
this stunt, paying this man to follow and protect them. But the fellow kept
mumbling something about how the academy had "screwed him." "If you
want to be an actor, that's the last goddamn place to go," he roared. Intrigued, the men decided to sober up their new companion, after which
they learned that he had actually attended the academy and had not been
invited back for his senior year. In return for their kindness, the New Orleans native led them to a telephone, so they could call Western Union for
the address of their lodging.

      The next day, NBC arranged for Ezra to be interviewed by New Or-
leans' leading talk show host, who later showed them the sights of the city.

He was a popular local personality, and young fans recognized the host wherever the three went and requested autographs. He said to the kids, "There's the guy you ought to get an autograph from. He's a radio star." The children, of course, did not recognize Ezra. One of the young autograph seekers, however, happened to work for Western Union. "Is that Ezra Stone?" he inquired. "Our office has been looking all over town for you." The boy then told Ezra to call the William Morris office. Ezra did so and learned that he was in fact to appear on Jack Benny's last show of the season.

Upon his arrival in Los Angeles at the NBC studio, Ezra was instantly taken by Benny's gentle and professional manner. He recalls that Benny treated the other members of his permanent company — Mary Livingstone, his wife, Phil Harris, Dennis Day, and Don Wilson — as he would his children; however, he handled his sidekick servant, "Rochester," whose real name was Eddie Anderson, with less respect. During a rehearsal, Ezra overheard Benny chastising Anderson for his lack of motivation. "Come on! Let's go to work Rochester! You're always late and holding us up." Although Benny claimed that he loved Anderson and was devoted to him, regarding him as one of the show's greatest assets, in his book, *Sunday Nights at Seven*, he wrote, "In real life, Rochester often worried me because he was rarely on time for line readings, rehearsals and the broadcast itself. I'm a nail-biter and a pessimist by temperament and Rochester's tardy habits did not calm my nervous system."

To most people, including Ezra, Benny was a kind and generous man, and the young actor learned a great deal about editing and respect for other performers in the short time he spent with him. With a staff of six or seven top Hollywood writers, Benny's guests were certain to receive ample material of high quality. In Ezra's case, Benny made certain his comic setups were true to the character of Henry Aldrich and within Ezra's range as a performer. In the actual broadcast, Benny graced *The Aldrich Family* with a marvelous send-off.

The final episode of *The Jack Benny Show* of the 1938–39 season, which aired on June 25, was divided into three parts, with the last portion devoted to *The Aldrich Family*.

> WILSON: Incidentally, Jack, who's taking over our summer show? Has it been settled yet?
>
> JACK: Yes, Don, the Aldrich Family is gonna move in for three months. . . . As a matter of fact, young Henry Aldrich is dropping in here in just a little while, and I want you all to be very nice to him. . . . He'll probably be scared stiff in front of a microphone.
>
> WILSON: Scared in front of a microphone? . . . Why Henry Aldrich is a veteran in radio. . . .
>
> JACK: Funny? . . . does he do comedy?

Jack Benny's replacement, summer 1939.

PHIL: Haven't you ever heard him, Jackson?... Why that kid's a riot... he's terrific.

JACK: He is?... And he's young, eh?

PHIL: Yeah... you want to watch out for that boy.

MARY: Remember the old saying... MAKE WAY FOR TOMORROW!

JACK: (*Mad*) Well if he thinks he's coming out here and steal my... (Oh, I'm not worried)... But then... (Oh, no!)

MARY: Oh *yes*... Well... suppose at the end of the summer, Henry Aldrich goes to our sponsor, and says... "LOOK I DID ALL RIGHT ON THE SUMMER SHOW... WHY MAKE A CHANGE?"

JACK: *WHAT?*

MARY: "WHY NOT KEEP THE ALDRICH FAMILY?" "WHY LET GO OF A GOOD THING?"

JACK: (*CARRIED AWAY BY THEM NOW*) "*YEAH, WHAT DO YOU NEED WITH BENNY?*" ... why the little double crosser!... I'LL PUNCH THAT ALDRICH KID RIGHT IN THE NOSE!

WILSON: Now Jack, don't get excited... The kid doesn't mean any harm.

JACK: Then why is he trying to put me out of work?... especially at my age!... Oooooh, my back...

EZRA: Hello Mr. Benny, I'm Henry Aldrich...
JACK: Well young man, you can very nicely get right out of this Studio.
EZRA: Get out of this Studio?... Why our sponsor sent me here to —
JACK: I DON'T CARE WHAT OUR SPONSOR DID... YOU DON'T START WORKING ON THIS PROGRAM UNTIL NEXT WEEK... SO SCRAM!
EZRA: But I flew all the way here from New York, just to be on your show tonight.
JACK: I DON'T CARE IF YOU DID... GET OUT!...
EZRA: *(VOICE BREAKING) WHAT'S GOIN' ON HERE?*
JACK: You know what's going on... I'll teach you to take my job away... Look at him standing there... IF YOU'RE SO DARN FUNNY, ALDRICH, WHY DON'T YOU GO AHEAD AND TELL A JOKE... GO AHEAD, MAKE *ME* LAUGH!

The permanent company of actors let this continue only for a short while before assuring the host that Ezra had no intentions of taking over his job. Benny then reconciled with the younger actor and gave him a few tips on how to succeed as his replacement. He suggested that *The Aldrich Family* become a dramatic show, incorporating a little poetry reading. He then recommended the show change its format to an adventure serial filled with suspense and action. "For instance, you can be lost in the jungle . . . savages and wild animals will be after you . . . you know, make a real thriller out of it," the veteran comedian said. But in the end, Benny wished *The Aldrich Family* the best of luck, recognized Ezra by name as the actor portraying Henry — further fortifying his personal identity — and signed off for the summer.

Throughout the next fourteen years on radio,

MRS. ALDRICH: *(Calling)* Hen-ry! Henry Aldrich!
HENRY: Coming, Mother!

opened almost every episode of what was to become the country's most popular situation comedy about teenagers. To its millions of weekly listeners, these words became a national cliché, a rallying cry signaling fans to gather around the radio. In much the same way that "Hi-Yo Silver! Away!" represented the catchphrase for *The Lone Ranger*, "Coming Mother!" became *The Aldrich Family*'s opening signature.

Prior to its summer debut, the lead-in to *The Aldrich Family* had nothing to give it real distinction. It had simply been a repeated comedy routine set within the framework of the larger program. Before the show was to begin as Jack Benny's replacement, however, both Goldsmith and the producer realized the need for an opening catchphrase that was different and yet easy to remember. In a previous episode, Goldsmith had experimented with:

MRS. ALDRICH: (*Calling*) . . . Henry Aldrich.
HENRY: (*Off*) Yes, Mother.

This beginning, however, lacked flair and pizzazz. Ezra later said the show's opening signature was devised by a "very talented, eccentric radio producer and director, Bob Welsh, who went on to do great work in films." But even after the producers had discovered the phrase, there remained the question of which parent would call for Ezra.

Apparently, Goldsmith initially believed the opening line should be assigned to Mr. Aldrich. Therefore, the call appearing in the debut script read:

MR. ALDRICH: (*Calling*) Henry! Hen-ry Aldrich!
HENRY: Coming, Father!

But the phrase did not seem to work, and at the last moment, "Mother" replaced "Father." This wavering back and forth between the two parents went on throughout the summer. In the episode of July 30 "Coming, Father!" remained in the script and apparently stayed in the broadcast. By summer's end, however, "Coming, Mother!" became the program's official calling card.

On July 2, 1939, at 7:00 P.M. EST, Jack Miller's orchestra struck up the familiar tune accompanying "J-E-LL-O," Benny's longtime program sponsor *The Aldrich Family* inherited for the summer. For the first time listeners then heard Henry's rallying croak. André Baruch, the show's first announcer, then said,

> Jell–O — presents — THE ALDRICH FAMILY — starring Ezra Stone as Henry Aldrich, written for us each week by Clifford Goldsmith, whose long running Broadway hit is now playing at the Mansfield Theatre here in New York. . . . The Aldrich Family is the story of the minor but important growing pains of a typical American family. There are Mrs. Aldrich, Mr. Aldrich, their son, Henry, and their daughter, Mary. Both are in their teens! The scene tonight opens. . . .

On this evening *The Aldrich Family,* became the predecessor of most domestic situation comedies on radio and TV. Goldsmith and this show led to the emergence of Aaron Ruben, producer and head writer of *The Andy Griffith Show,* Ed Jurist, producer and head writer of *The Flying Nun,* Phil Sharp, one of the head writers of *I Love Lucy,* and Norman Tokar, who became a fine TV director and then went on to direct feature films for Disney. Even such contemporary situation comedies as *The Cosby Show, Designing Women, Murphy Brown,* and *Seinfeld* have their roots in radio's *The Aldrich Family.* But the show had a more immediate effect on several other radio programs of that period, especially on *A Date with Judy*, which chronicled the teenage tribulations of Judy Foster and Oogie, her boyfriend. *Archie Andrews*, based on Bob Montana's comic strip, and *Harold Teen* also adopted Goldsmith's pattern along with his subject matter. *Leave It to Beaver*, *The Patty Duke Show*, and *Ozzie and Harriet* represent only a few of the early TV programs that followed Goldsmith's recipe.

Goldsmith was entirely responsible for the new format. He found a groove of plot construction that was extremely tight and so new to the medium that it became axiomatic. In fact, to be accepted by the American public, later situation comedies dutifully followed the pattern established by Goldsmith. Above all, no matter how honest the actor's characterization was, the writer could include no joke for the sake of comedy alone. The humor had to spring from the character and from the situation. The sketches were not monologues, like those featured by George Burns and Gracie Allen. They were not farfetched comic and variety sketches like those used by Jack Benny, whose show was essentially an elongated vaudeville show with familiar people. His scripts were so fantastic and improbable that the plots were impossible to believe. And no *Jack Benny Show* was complete until everyone had gathered in Benny's living room to tie up loose ends.

Goldsmith's construction allowed for a main plot involving the leading character and one or two subplots involving the other characters, the latter generally becoming intertwined with the main plot by the end of the episode. Each of these plots had to have a logical beginning, middle, and ending that fit into the time frame of twenty-three and one-half minutes, the actual time allotted to a thirty-minute program. Thus, Goldsmith's scripts were essentially short one-act plays utilizing familiar characters. *One Man's Family*, a top-rated radio program which predated Goldsmith's show, had many of these same traits, but it was a neverending serial without a defined beginning, middle, and ending.

The Aldrich Family continued as Jack Benny's replacement through Sunday, October 1, when Baruch reported Benny's return.

> But . . . *what about Henry Aldrich?* You know, Henry is fast becoming one of the most famous young men in the country! . . . you *won't* have to say goodbye to Henry Aldrich! For The Aldrich Family will *continue* with their own half-hour program, brought to you during the coming season by JELL-O's fastest growing new dessert.

The new program was to begin in most parts of the country on Tuesday, October 10, 1939, at 8:00 P.M. EST, on the NBC Blue Radio Network. Henry Aldrich had become a solid hit.

Ezra maintained in interviews that as good as *The Aldrich Family* was as a half-hour program, a great deal of its initial success was due to the timing of two things. As discussed, the show received Benny's endorsement

and inherited a tremendous audience. Just as important, however, was
that at the beginning of the 1939–40 season, General Foods had assigned
the show its most exciting new product on the market. Already the talk of
the country because of the ribbing it had taken on Benny's radio program,
Jell-O gelatin powder grew so famous that it became the generic name for
all gelatin desserts. "The mountains of unsold Jell-O disappeared. Even the
warehouses ran out of supplies. People liked it. They kept buying it," wrote
Benny in his book. "The more we kidded it, the more they bought. The
Jell-O campaign was the greatest success story for radio as a selling
medium."

With the debut of *The Aldrich Family*, however, Jell-O unleashed its
newest product — Jell-O Pudding. As Harry Von Zell, the show's second announcer, put it,

> Jell-O Chocolate . . . Butterscotch . . . and Vanilla Pudding . . . three of
> the smoothest, best-tasting desserts that your family ever sat down to. For
> Jell-O Puddings are *different*. They have the rich goodness of old-
> fashioned HOMEMADE Puddings . . . the kind you used to cook and stir
> and *fuss* over for half an hour or more. But Jell-O Puddings are quick . . .
> they're EASY . . . they're prepared in a few minutes time, and there's
> nothing to go wrong. And they *taste* simply *swell*.

In a later interview with Larry King, Ezra said, "It was such a wonderful
and new revolutionary product that people used to tune in to our show just
to find out which local markets were going to open to get the Jell-O Pud-
dings." Ezra believed the product helped sell the program rather than the
other way around. General Foods simply could not manufacture and ship
the pudding to the markets fast enough to keep pace with consumers'
demands. Soon the commercial jingle sang by Henry and Homer became
almost as famous as Henry's opening croak.

> Oh, the big red letters stand for the Jell-O family; Oh, the big red letters
> stand for the Jell-O family; That's Jell-O! Yum-yum-yum! Jell-O Pudding!
> Yum-yum-yum! Jell-O Tap-i-oca pudding, yes sir-eee!

The Aldrich Family immediately became radio's top comedy series,
easily outdistancing *Easy Aces, Blondie, L'il Abner, Lum and Abner*, and the
perennial favorite *Amos 'n' Andy*. By its third full season, *The Aldrich Family*
had reached a market rating of over thirty points, which meant that during
a typical weekly broadcast over thirty percent of all families listening to
radio in the United States tuned in this program. In other words, over thirty
million devoted fans listened to this show every week.

Many factors contributed to the tremendous success of *The Aldrich
Family*. Because it had no predecessors with similar formats, it was a fresh

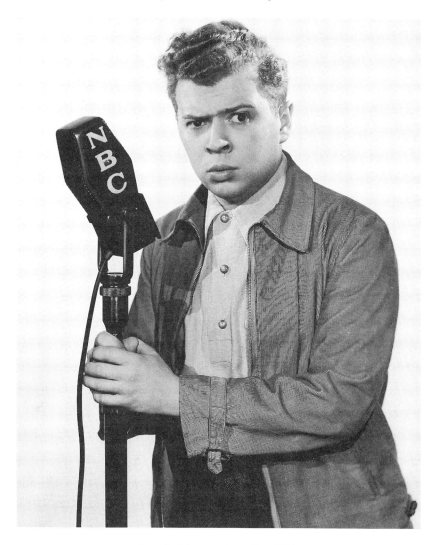

A typical boy at the mike, 1938.

and unique concept. The American middle-class family also identified with Henry Aldrich and his family. Gene Leitner, a radio expert, wrote, "It seemed to me like Goldsmith looked into my house and other houses across America and wrote what he observed." For the younger children as well as the teen culture, Henry Aldrich represented the only person they knew who was constantly in more trouble than they. The introduction to the program utilized this perceived identification. The following prologue by Von Zell was typical:

A Christmas present we'd all appreciate would be the ability to turn back the calendar to our high school days, for somehow none of the years before or since have quite the same charm. The next best thing to actually re-living that period is to know Henry Aldrich, for Henry is a typical American boy — a youngster who'll take you back to your teens.

This introduction not only targeted preteens and high schoolers but also set the scene in which adults could relive bygone days when little matters seemed all-important — a time before the pains and headaches of the adult world interfered. *The Aldrich Family* gave society a chance to reenter that wonderful fantasy world of a youth that probably never existed.

Goldsmith based much of the show's humor on the old comedy of errors, mistaken identity, "Who's on First," and other popular comic techniques of the day. Through his mechanical design, he intended to evoke laughter from the audience at least three times every minute. An example of this technique can be seen in a scene between Henry, his family, and Dizzy, as they decide upon a suitable Halloween costume for Henry.

DIZZY:	They've got a horse there they'll rent for Six Dollars.
HENRY:	A horse?
DIZZY:	Sure, we'll go as a horse!
HENRY:	I don't think any girl would want to dance with a horse, Dizzy.
MRS. ALDRICH:	Well, whether they would or not, we're not spending any Six Dollars on a costume.
DIZZY:	I'll pay Three-fifty, Mrs. Aldrich — If Henry'll let me be the front end.
MRS. ALDRICH:	It seems to me we ought to be able to fix up a very nice costume right here at home.
DIZZY:	In the way of a horse, Mrs. Aldrich? . . .
MRS. ALDRICH:	Sam, I know the very thing . . . Do you remember that costume you wore when we went to that dance just after we were married?
MR. ALDRICH:	I do.
HENRY:	What is it?
MRS. ALDRICH:	George Washington.
HENRY:	George Washington! George Washington! Mother, do you think I want to go to a Halloween party as George Washington?
MRS. ALDRICH:	I certainly don't see why you couldn't . . .
DIZZY:	Between ourselves, Mrs. Aldrich, I think Henry would look better as a horse . . .
MARY:	(*Approaching*) Here it is, Henry. Look, Henry, it's darling . . .
MRS. ALDRICH:	Dear, you look just exactly the way your father did that night he wore that to the ball.
MR. ALDRICH:	(*Startled*) I looked like that?
DIZZY:	To me he looks quite a little like a horse.

Goldsmith certainly wrote poignant and heart-filled emotional scenes; but if the audience was not laughing, the playwright and cast did not consider the broadcast successful. Ezra later said, "True, the laughs had to come out of the situation, but, brother, they had to come or we were in trouble. But, boy, if we could get them rolling with a situation, we'd play it for all it was worth."

To help establish its popularity, *The Aldrich Family* used the universality of the teenage culture because every adult had gone through this stage of life. Certainly, things had changed since their own teenage years, and yet in a sense they had not. Most importantly, there was Henry, a boy like Huck Finn, Tom Sawyer, and Penrod Scofield, who became more than a fictional character because in what he did and said he mirrored real boys of the time. And as with most boys his age, trouble always seemed to follow Henry closely. Von Zell's announcement after the broadcast's middle commercial was entirely apt: "Getting back to the troubles of Henry Aldrich." Not adventures or escapades; no, the boy always found ways to get into trouble. In his book *The Great Radio Comedians*, Jim Harmon gives the following examples: Henry dropped his father's suit in a newly paved street still fresh with hot tar en route to the dry cleaners, and he tried to make the football team by practicing yoga and sprained his back. For Goldsmith, each of Henry's trials and tribulations was only a starting point; he then embellished them with snowballing complications. Henry made a crisis out of the simple act of going to the store. One episode, for example, began with the boy tying up the family telephone, and within the next twenty-three and one-half minutes he somehow managed to entangle every phone in Centerville with calls coming into the Aldrich home for everything from taxis to plumbers.

Harmon points out that despite the boy's shortcomings, his family, friends, and teachers liked Henry. He inspired unyielding dedication in his best friend, Dizzy Stevens, and later in Homer Brown. Although they had a near-perfect daughter in Mary, Henry's parents always seemed to favor the boy. His teachers recognized his many problems, but they all seemed willing to help the troubled adolescent. Despite all that help and goodwill, Henry eternally seemed to get himself entrapped in some humiliating situation, usually because of his utter refusal to do the logical thing or to tell the truth about his boyish blunders. For example, he would not admit to either of two girls he had invited to the prom that through simple, human emotion on a moonlit spring night he had invited one girl too many. He would not admit to his even more inept friend, Homer, that he, Henry, knew no more about handling women than Homer did, and that his advice to Homer was less than useless when Homer wanted to correct his girlfriend's misconception that he had proposed marriage.

For Goldsmith, *The Aldrich Family* was the turning point of his career, making him a rags-to-riches playwright. From the night of *What a Life's* Broadway debut, when Goldsmith's wife, Kay, took their last five dollars to buy cuff links for her husband's evening attire, to his enormous radio contract with NBC, Goldsmith became the industry's best paid writer, earning three thousand dollars for each first-run episode. On his Aldrich salary, Goldsmith reportedly paid as much income tax in one day as he had once earned lecturing for an entire week.

After finding financial security, the Goldsmiths moved to a modern, gray stone farmhouse on Johnny's Way in Paoli, Pennsylvania, where the playwright converted a quaint, comfortable old milk house in the back yard into his writing room. There he wrote most of his Henry Aldrich material, drawing much of it from observations of his son, Barclay, and stepsons, Peter and Thayer. The boys occasionally charged him with plagiarism. In addition to his personal experiences and simple imagination, Goldsmith also drew on a steady flow of childhood anecdotes from enraptured fans.

Writing did not come easy for Goldsmith, and perhaps that was just as well. Given so familiar a pattern as small-town family life, a more facile author might have fallen back on clichés, a common practice of writers in his field. How Goldsmith avoided them, how he imbued the old experiences and situations with new life, became the wonder of the so-called Radio Row. The answer seemed to lie in an understanding heart and the conscience of a good craftsman. Of Goldsmith, John K. Hutchens of the *New York Times* wrote,

> . . . no other program that comes to mind is more consistently excellent, of its kind, than this one. There it is, week in, week out, artfully composed, brightly written, rich with comic invention, and, above all, with the warm stuff of life in it. That, of course, is what matters most. It could be less humanly appealing than it is, and it would still be a pretty good show, as some of its imitators have been. The added touch of reality with which Mr. Goldsmith endows it, makes it a really fine one. . . .

Goldsmith's characters never became stock in either writing or playing. Being clearly fond of the characters and the actors for whom he wrote, Goldsmith was never derisive or condescending, and his players brought assurance to their tasks for they enjoyed and believed in the writer.

Every Wednesday, Goldsmith left his farmhouse in Paoli and boarded the commuter train bound for New York, where he stayed till Friday afternoon to work at the NBC broadcasting studio. From there he rehearsed with the cast and did necessary rewrites on that week's and the next week's program. At any given time he was reportedly developing three different Aldrich episodes. The playwright continued this hectic schedule throughout the first three seasons, writing every episode himself and maintaining a gentle balance between outright comedy and the bittersweet problems

Rehearsing an A-script with Katherine Raht and House Jameson.

of growing up. In subsequent years, a staff of writers including Sam Taylor, Norman Tokar, Frank Tarloff, Ed Jurist, Patricia Joudry, Aaron Ruben, and Phil Sharp took over for Goldsmith, and the farce became much broader.

Goldsmith and his writing staff had a nearly ideal cast to perform their scripts. Besides Ezra, there was the head of the Aldrich clan, Sam, originated by Tom Shirley, who lasted only a couple of episodes. An unknown actor who survived only one performance replaced Shirley. Finally, House Jameson, who came from the stage to radio in 1935 and had created many notable roles in both media, gave stability to the role. He not only sounded the part of the wise and kindly father, but the distinguished man with prematurely white hair also looked the role.

Lea Penman, a fine character actress, originated the role of Henry's mother on stage with *What a Life* and continued to play her in the early stages of the radio program. Penman's style, however, did not fit the image the producer and writer wished to portray on the series. Possessing good theater speech with British overtones, she played Mrs. Aldrich as Goldsmith had originally intended her: an outspoken, upper-class woman living in a small town. Somewhere along the way, though, Goldsmith realized the parents could not stay aloof and upper-crust in a wholesome, family-oriented show, and so Penman was let go.

The Aldrich Family — House Jameson, Kaye Raht, Ann Lincoln (?) and Ezra Stone.

Soon after the series began, Katherine Raht, a kindly and more motherly character actress, formerly a teacher in Chattanooga, replaced Penman. Raht and Jameson played their roles as sensitive and understanding parents to perfection. Throughout his life, Ezra regarded Jameson with the utmost love and respect. "House was always on time and didn't engage in distracting chit-chat in rehearsals," Ezra said. "He was always gracious and

With both mothers—Ezra with Kaye Raht and Rose Feinstone.

extremely helpful to single-shot actors. He took direction swiftly and surely, never leaving the microphone if his character remained in the scene — even if Sam had no more lines."

With superb timing, he always made eye contact with the other actors while on the air and stood ready to praise the good work of others. As a result, he and Raht remained with the program for over a decade. Jameson even portrayed the kindly father when *The Aldrich Family* made the leap to television in the early 1950s.

Betty Field, who originated the role of Barbara Pierson in the play and later portrayed the role in the movie version of *What a Life*, initially played Mary on the radio series. But because of other commitments, Field soon left the cast. Of the company, Gene Leitner wrote,

> I think the cast was picked perfectly. . . . With each voice you could surely relate to someone in your family, and EZRA, especially sounded like someone each of us knew. . . . I honestly do not think anyone else could have portrayed the characters more than those chosen for the parts. In a way, though, they were typed-cast (vocally), because when we heard the voices from *The Aldrich Family* on other shows, we could only see in our "mind's eye" Henry, Sam, Alice, or Mary Aldrich or Homer Brown. We could only see them as "The Aldrich Family."

Goldsmith certainly did not invent the concept of the sidekick, but Henry's buddies had a different function from others of their kind. Harmon believed that in the more heroic adventure shows, the laughable sidekick typically carried the humor. In the thirties and forties, the leading man always seemed concerned with his image and thus remained true to stereotype. The hero would never crack a smile, much less tell a joke or participate in a seemingly meaningless adventure. But Henry Aldrich and his pals were different.

Bill, played by Eddie Bracken, was Henry's first buddy in the play, but it was a smaller part that Goldsmith believed would not translate well into a larger role for the series. He soon realized, however, that Henry needed a companion—someone to share his dreams, his desires, his adventures. Henry also needed someone less intelligent and more gullible than himself, a person who would add another dimension to the adolescent male character. The playwright invented Dizzy Stevens and hired Bracken to create the role, which was an instantaneous hit. But when Bracken left the cast in March of 1940 to go to California to fulfill a film contract with Paramount, Goldsmith decided that rather than replacing Bracken with an actor with similar vocal qualities, he would create another companion for Henry. And so Homer Brown became Henry's best friend throughout the remainder of the show's run on radio and television.

Although some years older than high-school age, Jackie Kelk looked youthful enough to enroll in classes. Previously on radio, using a slightly lower and less comic voice, he had created the roles of young Terry on *Terry and the Pirates* and cub reporter Jimmy Olson on *Superman*. With what seemed like all the other young actors in the city, Kelk auditioned and won the role of Homer, playing him with a distinctive nasal twang. Young and Rubicam scheduled Kelk to join the cast on March 12, 1940. In a recent letter, Kelk wrote, "On the day of the first show I was on I had a conflict at the time of the dress rehearsal, and they almost let me go before I even started." Kelk portrayed Henry's inept friend to perfection, and the two characters blended well together. The following classic exchange typifies the relationship between the boys.

AGNES: Boy, Homer, the minute I heard, I hadda call you and thank you!
HOMER: Heard *what*, Agnes?
AGNES: What you're getting me for our anniversary present.
HOMER: You know?
AGNES: Uh huh!
HOMER: Gee, everybody knows what I'm getting you but me! What *am* I getting you?
AGNES: I don't think I oughta tell you, it'll spoil the surprise!
HOMER: Listen, Agnes, when I give you a present, *you're* supposed to be surprised, not *me*!

AGNES: Oh. Well, I'll tell you what, Homer. You come on over. I want a
          see your face . . . when you give me that engagement ring. . .
          (LATER)
HOMER: It's terrible, Henry, just *terrible!*
HENRY: Why not look at it this way, Homer: engagements have their ad-
          vantages, too.
HOMER: Yeah? Name one.
HENRY: Well, they . . . well, you . . . there must be *some* advantages.
          Otherwise, why would so many people do it?
HOMER: *Name* one. Just one!
HENRY: Well . . . *(AN IDEA)* for instance, when you're engaged, you
          don't have to spend so much money on the girl.
HOMER: Oh, yeah? What about the engagement ring? That alone will
          keep me broke for the next two years! . . . I never thought of
          Agnes as something to get engaged to . . . Engaged! Henry, Mr.
          Bradley will throw me out of school!
HENRY: See! I *told* you there were advantages to being engaged!!

Kelk and the rest of the cast worked well together, but the chemistry
between him and Ezra was particularly apparent. "I am reminded of this
every time I listen to tapes of the old shows," Kelk wrote. "Ezra was a consummate pro, and none of the actors who played Henry after him had the
timing and assurance he had in the part."

Radio actors, unlike legitimate stage and motion picture performers,
rely wholly on sound, and their performance is based exclusively on the
power and expressiveness of their voices. In a radio play, the audience cannot see movement, gesture, or physical expression; these merely exist in
the listeners' minds. "The radio gives them many clues and suggestions;
doors are slammed, papers rattled, shots fired, and lips smacked, but the
human voice is the principal medium of communication," wrote Garff B.
Wilson in his book, *Three Hundred Years of American Drama and Theatre.*
"Actors discovered anew that emotion could be stirred and attitudes and
states of mind could be revealed by nuances of tone and variation in vocal
quality." Therefore, performers who excelled in vocal expressiveness, either
comic or serious, became stars of the radio and commanded a following as
great as that of the popular film idols.

Because of his extraordinary vocal gymnastics, Ezra became a national
celebrity in the character of Henry Aldrich. Ezra unquestionably possessed
a vocal dexterity rarely found in even the most polished performers, and
his appeal as Henry came from his adroit ability to familiarize the dialogue,
not merely from his seeming facility to crack his voice at will.

Ezra maintained that selling a character vocally was not as difficult as
stage acting primarily because of three factors: the writers, who set the
scenes and delivered wonderful dialogue; the superb artistry of the sound
engineer, who ultimately created the illusion of life through physical and
electronic means; and the power of the audience's imagination. Through

the magic of Ezra's voice, each listener created a mental picture of Henry. Most people probably pictured the boy as tall, skinny, and freckled with a head of blond hair. Ezra in reality was rather short, had brown, wavy hair, and fought a continuing battle to reduce his weight.

In a 1982 interview with Thomas H. Arthur of *Dramatics*, Ezra said, "It was a fascinating job. It was very in and current, and if you were working in radio, it was like you were an astronaut today." Indeed, Ezra gained immediate celebrity status and was highly sought after by many radio variety and talk shows of that period. Fans wanted to meet the man behind that intriguing voice. Between 1938 and 1941, he appeared on *The Eddie Cantor Show*, *The Fred Allen Show*, *The Jack Benny Show*, *CBS Workshop*, and *The Edgar Bergen Show* to name a few. On some of the shows he merely talked with the host, and on other programs he performed various characters in sketches. For Corwin's program, for example, Ezra portrayed young men, who may or may not have possessed qualities similar to Henry's. On *The Eddie Cantor Show*, he appeared as Ezra Stone but always maintained the characteristics of Henry. While introducing her guest on *Nellie Revell Presents*, a show that featured interviews with radio stars, the hostess vocally painted the picture of a man resembling a swooning teenage girl's dream date.

> So many have inquired what this young man looks like, well he is 5 ft. 4 in. tall and weighs about 145 lbs. He has brown eyes and dark red hair. And girls, it is very wavy. The kind of wave you and I couldn't get if we sat under one of those machines for three days. Something should be done about men having that kind of hair.

As indicated by the many boxes of fan mail he received from listeners across the country, Ezra became a matinee idol to many young ladies, a friend and colleague to countless young men, and an adopted son to a host of mothers. The following excerpts exemplify the letters he received. A young lady from Rhode Island wrote,

> I am one of your most ardent fans and haven't missed a Henry Aldrich broadcast since it came on the air. I am "sweet sixteen," five feet three inches tall, weigh one hundred twelve pounds, am a brunette and have blue eyes. . . . I would like to personally correspond with you.

A male college student wrote,

> Your weekly portrayal of Henry Aldrich has been one of my favorite pleasures during the past year. As a student of dramatics at the University of Iowa, I have always admired your versatility on the stage. In fact, I have selected you as my ideal.

A mother with teenage children of her own warned,

> With all of this success, you will get much backslapping and all that goes with it, and you seem so wholesome and worthwhile that I *do hope it won't turn to your head*. In other words Ezra, "Stay as sweet as you are." You will never regret it.

Perhaps the letter that best summed up America's love affair with Ezra and his creation came from a young lady in New York City. She wrote, "I have an article saying 'Henry Aldrich (Ezra Stone) crept into the hearts of America and America refused to let him go.' I hope they never let him go."

Because the live broadcasts required many complicated maneuvers and coordination among actors, announcer, sound engineer, and orchestra, many fans often asked about rehearsals. But surprisingly, rehearsals and performances occupied only nine hours each week. Over the years, *The Aldrich Family* broadcasts were produced in various studios including Studio 8G in Radio City Music Hall and two converted legitimate theaters. During its first year, however, the show came out of the ballroom of the Barbizon Hotel.

For rehearsals the initial gathering usually convened at the studio around seven o'clock on Wednesday evenings for a one hour reading of what the cast referred to as the B-script for the following week's program. This gave Goldsmith an opportunity to hear his script read aloud; major modifications would then be worked on at his home office in Pennsylvania. Next, the cast read the revised A-script, which was to air the following evening. For this reading, the actors positioned themselves in front of their respective microphones—without the aid of sound effects—while Goldsmith and the other writers sat in the control room and noted potential changes. Around 9:00 P.M. the cast departed, leaving the writers to make appropriate alterations.

The following morning at nine, the company again gathered in the studio to begin rehearsing the A-script, which was essentially the text to be used for that evening's performance. They began with a table reading, which gave the playwright another chance to correct awkward dialogue or make necessary cuts. Following this, the actors went "on mike," and the director staged the show scene by scene, incorporating sound effects. If the episode was not technically complicated, the cast usually found time to run through the entire show before lunch. For a more difficult broadcast, the actors ran through the show after lunch. After that the director gave the cast a half-hour break while the writers again edited the script. The director in the meantime rehearsed the musical bridges, which occurred at the show's opening and between commercials and scenes. At this time, he also rehearsed the announcer and ran through the commercials, which sometimes included actors singing various jingles. At approximately 3:30 P.M., the actors began dress rehearsal, which incorporated all production elements. After this, the cast received another round of cuts before breaking for dinner.

To relax before a show, Ezra frequently went to a gymnasium near Radio City to exercise and get a massage. Having little appetite prior to performing, he simply ate some fruit or drank a little juice. He arrived back at the studio around seven-thirty to get dressed and peruse any last-minute script changes. Fifteen minutes before air time, the ushers admitted the studio audience, and the announcer prepared the audience by explaining the format and what was expected of them. Ezra, as the star of the show, then entered the stage and spoke with the audience for a few minutes. The full cast followed closely behind him, and each took his or her place for the live broadcast.

When the program began, the studio audience performed as if it was in a theater for a stage production. "Our show was a hybrid, a combination of radio and stage," Ezra later said. "We always had a studio audience, so as theatre trained actors and performers, we were really playing to a live audience, and the radio listening audience was eavesdropping." The actors energized their performances by responding to the live audience. They also did visual takes after a punch line and extended their reactions by other visual means. Occasionally, in response to an especially funny line, the studio audience laughed so long and intensely, it threatened to confuse the radio listeners. The performers, however, tried never to engage in anything not immediately and eminently clear to a radio audience. But if the line or situation received a strong reaction from the spectators in the studio, the performers naturally assumed the radio audience would laugh along with them.

The importance of the live studio audience was never more clearly demonstrated than when Young and Rubicam and General Foods eliminated it. For a brief period there was a certain discontent at the agency concerning the appropriateness of hearing live laughter emanating from the Aldrich family living room; consequently, the actors had to perform in a small studio without an audience. Needless to say, it was a disaster, and the sponsors soon realized their mistake. From that moment on, spectators continued to be an integral part of the production.

Radio provided the entire country with simultaneous exposure to an event; therefore, the media had tremendous power to influence the American public, to shape the mores of society, and to provide a morale boost during a depression and a world war. As a performer at that time, however, Ezra had little idea of radio's immense power. "It's only in these later years when I've been absolutely astounded and amazed that there could still be recognition of my name," Ezra recently said. "People may not know why, but the name is familiar to them. They either say, 'Are you the actor who played Henry Aldrich?' or 'That's a familiar name, why is that?'" Years later, while working in Hollywood, a waiter, looking at Ezra's credit card said, "Ezra Stone, that's a famous name. An actor. He's dead now you know." "This is over forty years later," he said only a few years ago. "That to me is amazing."

Certainly, he and his colleagues had some idea of their impact on society, for they used this knowledge as leverage for their contracts with employers. And, of course, fans seeking autographs, various theatrical galas or events, studio audiences, press coverage in newspapers and magazines, invitations to luncheons, benefits, auctions, and political campaigns naturally made the actors aware of their celebrity status and their rather unique position in society.

Following their initial performance of an episode, the actors dispersed and later returned to the studio to reenact the same program for the west coast. The repeat broadcast did not begin until 11:30 P.M. EST, so finding a studio audience sometimes posed a difficult problem, especially if foul weather restricted travel. With a smaller live audience, the laughs did not interrupt the flow of the action as frequently or as long as in the earlier performance; therefore, Goldsmith often had two versions of the same script ready to perform. Often, cuts that had been made in the dress rehearsal of the first performance were reinserted into the repeat show. Ezra maintained that such changes did not hurt their presentation. "It was like a second night performance," he said. "We now knew for sure where the laughs were, and we'd go for them."

The live radio broadcasts presented the same excitement and potential dangers of live stage productions, since mistakes by actors and technical errors had to be covered without breaking the illusion of the character or story. The typical radio actor worked with a script in hand, dropping expired pages onto the floor. Ezra had a problem acting with a script, so he devised a stand to hold his papers. With this device, he placed all the unread pages on the right side. As the action continued to the next page, he merely flipped the page to the other side, thus freeing himself as an actor and at the same time making the scene more real for the studio audience. For example, if the script required Henry to run, Ezra worked his body as if he were actually running. He felt he had to free his hands of the script in order to give an accurate portrayal. Even in his later life, when Ezra held audition workshops for young actors, this was the root of his system for cold readings. His key phrase was "neutralize the text": Get it out of your hands whenever and wherever you can, so you can turn over as much of your physical energy as possible to the character.

Ezra's clever idea of turning pages on a stand was, however, not without its problems. For example, during one remote broadcast from Rochester, he requested and received a music stand. As luck would have it, the old stand lacked a few bolts, which led to a severe wobble. Though he had asked for a replacement, he found himself dealing with the broken stand during the broadcast. During a physical moment in one scene, Ezra's hand tipped over the music stand. The people in the audience gasped as they saw pages fluttering to the floor. Fellow actors rushed to his side silently offering to share their own scripts. Realizing the severity of the situation, however, Ezra immediately grabbed the right side of the stand to catch the unread pages. As a result of that harrowing experience, he designed a special script stand, complete with a sliding pointer to keep his place on the script page, an ashtray, pencil holders, a slot to hold his wristwatch, a place for his cigars and pipe, a small lockable compartment in the four-legged base to stash his valuables and sometimes flasks of liquid "pick-me-ups."

During the heyday of *The Aldrich Family*, Ezra's life as a performer was moving along quickly and everything seemed to be going his way. Nevertheless, one of his biggest disappointments was his failure to break into the movie industry. In a 1939 interview with a student reporter, Ezra proclaimed that movies were a better medium than the Broadway stage. And like many New York actors he kept a close eye on the film industry in Hollywood. As early as 1937, after receiving rave reviews for his participation in *Brother Rat*, he had expressed his desire to take part in the movie, which was scheduled for that same year. To pacify his concerns, Garson Kanin had written a letter to young Stone addressing his ambitions.

> I don't believe you need have any fears about the BROTHER RAT picture. I think Mr. Abbott is completely satisfied to have you and no-one else if you don't grow out of it. But just keep smoking those black stogies and you'll stay the right size, always, I know.

Meanwhile, Abbott had told Warner Bros. studios that Ezra was not available without asking the actor first. Abbott sometimes took it upon himself to make career decisions for his protégés, and he thought Ezra's future as a director would be better served in New York. When the movie was released, Ezra's name did not appear in the credits.

In September 1938 Paramount Pictures purchased the film rights for *What a Life* from Abbott and Goldsmith for fifty thousand dollars, and again Ezra hoped to break into the movies. In Manhattan, Paramount screen-tested him together with Betty Field for the leading role. She was hired. Much to Ezra's dismay, Ted Reed, the motion picture's director, and Paramount selected Jackie Cooper to portray Henry. Cooper apparently possessed the physical attributes they sought in the character, and the company felt his name represented more drawing power at the box office. When

Ezra with Bob Hope promoting his role in Paramount's *Those Were the Days,* 1940.

shooting began in February 1939 Ezra had a difficult time suppressing his bitterness. A reporter wrote, "He is also nothing loath to admit that he is not in the movies 'because they don't want me.'" After Paramount released *What a Life*, Ezra gained some satisfaction when he learned that Cooper did not receive the unanimous high marks he had enjoyed in the role. "Jack and I later became good friends," Ezra later said. While playing together at the Bucks County Playhouse, Cooper even helped Ezra remodel the silos on the Stones' newly purchased Stone Meadows Farm.

As Paramount had hoped in the early 1940s, sequels spun off the first motion picture, but executives clearly began to have second thoughts about who would play Henry in subsequent films. They hoped to secure Jimmy Lydon but had trouble making a contractual agreement. Meanwhile, Paramount arranged to produce a low-budget film about college life in 1904 entitled *At Good Old Siwash* and released as *Those Were the Days*, which had been concocted by scriptwriter Don Hartman and director Ted Reed from ingredients supplied by George Fitch's once famous stories of "old Siwash."

Opening on a wedding anniversary in 1939, the film shifts quickly back to the characters' collegiate days of thirty-five years ago. There, at Siwash

College, a particularly fresh freshman is pledged to a fraternity, gets into jams, falls in love with the daughter of a judge who has put him on probation, lands in jail, and inspires a riot on the part of the student body to bring about his release. The film starred William Holden, Bonita Granville, Judith Barrett, and Vaughan Glaser.

By hiring Ezra to costar as Holden's loyal roommate and a Beta Omega Pi fraternity pledge who falls in love with Barrett, Paramount would be covered in case the Lydon contract fell through. Besides having Ezra available to stand in as Henry Aldrich, the studio also realized that *Those Were the Days* would receive free weekly publicity during each introduction of *The Aldrich Family* radio series; therefore, the company had nothing to lose from this arrangement.

Paramount agreed to pay Ezra three thousand dollars each week, a large sum of money for an actor with no film experience. They also conceded to cover the cost of relocating the entire Aldrich cast to Hollywood during the ten week shoot and to give Ezra each Thursday off to rehearse and perform in the radio program. At the same time, Holden, the film's star, received only seventy-five dollars a week. *The Aldrich Family* rehearsals and weekly performance from California were confusing to the actors since they had to air at 5:00 P.M. on the West Coast in order for the East Coast to hear the broadcast at 8:00. For the later broadcast, they recorded the early performance on acetate discs. Since Ezra had only Thursdays free from the movie studio, Goldsmith and the cast did the initial reading for the following week's script right after the recorded rebroadcast of the present episode. This gave the writer a week to rework the script, and it left the radio cast with much free time to enjoy the California sights. Ezra, however, reported back to Paramount at seven o'clock the next morning to resume work on the film. "It was so topsy-turvy from the routine I had been used to, that I was very confused," he said.

On the first Thursday on which *The Aldrich Family* was to air from California, rehearsals began at 8:30 A.M. The cast and crew worked hard the entire day in order to present a polished performance at 5:00. After the broadcast, Ezra decided to forgo dinner and return to his suite at Ravenswood — a hotel owned by Mae West in which Paramount provided rooms for the entire cast — to take a shower and a nap before returning to NBC to rehearse the next week's episode. When he arrived at Ravenswood, he turned on the radio in the living room portion of the suite, took a shower, set the alarm for 8:00, and lay down to rest. Just before the alarm rang, however, he was awakened by the sound of Jack Miller's theme song, written especially for him and labeled "The Stone Opening," blaring from the radio. Half dazed, he jumped out of bed and burst into a full gallop down the hall of the suite. He thought to himself, "My God! I'm on the air!" Stark naked, he flung open the hotel room door, but he was saved by the sound

William Holden, Bonita Granville and Ezra Stone in *Those Were the Days* with Judith Barrett, Vaughan Glaser, William Frawley and Lucien Littlefield. Directed by Ted Reed (A Paramount Picture, 1940).

of his own voice. Only then did the overworked actor realize that he was listening to the recorded broadcast.

Upon release, *Those Were the Days* received favorable reviews. Of Ezra's film debut, Kenneth McCaleb of the *New York Mirror* wrote, "This brilliant young man of stage and radio may now add filmdom's laurels to his habitually quizzical brow." Realizing his client's desire to continue working in film, the head of the William Morris Agency in Los Angeles, Johnny Hyde, relentlessly worked to negotiate a picture contract for Ezra. With his work in radio, his association with Abbott, and now his affiliation with Paramount, Hyde felt Ezra was extremely marketable as Broadway's wonder boy. During one of Ezra's free days, Hyde arranged for him to meet Louis B. Mayer of Metro-Goldwyn-Mayer (MGM).

On the appointed day, Hyde picked up the young actor and drove him to Culver City and into the Irving Thalberg Building at MGM studios. The reception room outside Mayer's office was extremely busy that day. Little did the two men realize that *Gone with the Wind* had just premiered in Atlanta the night before and the press was anxiously awaiting interviews with the company's top man. It was not the most opportune time to meet

Mayer concerning a potential career, but the appointment had been made, and Ezra was there.

Stone and Hyde waited for some time in the reception area before being ushered in to meet Mayer. Once inside, the younger man felt as if he were being presented to Joseph Stalin. The office was unbelievably large, and Mayer's huge white oval desk sat at the far end of the room. The silver-haired mogul sat behind the desk in a white leather chair that rose high above his head. His conversation with Ezra lasted but a moment, only a few words, and the press agent did most of the talking. "You know, Mr. Mayer, Ezra's tops on Broadway now," Hyde said as he listed Ezra's credits. "And he would certainly be right for the MGM entertainment family. He's eligible for the draft, but as soon as that's over, I'm sure he would be a valuable addition to your family." Mayer said very little. He did not question or argue but simply nodded his head. About the only thing the powerful man said was, "He reminds me a lot of Irving."

"You're in," Hyde excitedly told the young actor when they exited the office. "You want a contract with Mayer, you got it. If he compared you to Irving Thalberg, that means it's a yes! He's impressed with you!" Much to his dismay, however, Ezra never heard from MGM after he had left Mayer's office. Following his work on *Those Were the Days*, he returned to New York, his career with Paramount over. The picture, incidentally, was a box office flop. Afterward, Ezra frequently referred to this episode of his life in his warm-up speech to *The Aldrich Family* studio audiences, "I made this picture for Paramount, *Those Were the Days*, but Paramount decided to hold the picture and release me."

His failure to enter the motion picture industry obviously hurt the young man's pride, especially considering that many of his friends had successfully made the transition. When later asked why Paramount and MGM had rejected Ezra, Eddie Bracken, who starred in many films, said, "Stupidity in California, it's as simple as that. I mean if you play a part on Broadway, you expect to play it in the pictures. . . . But the Hollywood people were producing it. They were going to cast it their way." Garson Kanin, who also scored many hits in Hollywood, wrote,

> The ways of Hollywood are strange indeed—a mystery which I do not propose to *attempt* to solve! We could list literally dozens of cases where the Hollywood Brains Trust committed boner after boner especially with regard to casting. The thought of engaging the same actor or actress who has scored a great success in a Broadway play for the film version was rare. It was then considered—much more than it is now—two separate worlds. There was Hollywood and there was Broadway. Films, by and large, were made in Hollywood, not, as they are today, everywhere in the world! To bring an actor or actress from New York to Hollywood was quite expensive. I remember in my early days in Hollywood, whenever I would

suggest a New York actor there was objection. They would say, "We'd have to bring him out, keep him here. That'll make him too expensive. We can get a much less expensive actor here."

Ezra, like many actors based in New York, was temporarily trapped on the East Coast, but he remained on the top as a radio actor, and he continued to produce quality work on Broadway although he stepped off the stage and into the director's chair.

6. *The Stage Director*

. . . a beautiful song is hardly a song unless there is someone to hear it. I have, I confess, developed through the years a Pygmalion complex: I have wanted to mold the young. Teachers and preachers have the same disease. Luckily for me, I had a captive audience for my advice and theories.

George Abbott, *Mister Abbott*

George Abbott's own unappreciated years made him compassionate toward others following the same path, and he began to champion deserving actors. But in the case of Ezra Stone, Abbott took on the role of mentor, and, consciously or unconsciously, the master of farce groomed a young director. Ezra stood in awe of his teacher and observed his work habits, his manners, and his technique with comedy as both a producer and a director. "In this commercial theatre, we have several fine directors and we also have several fine producers, but there is no man who excels in both to the extent that Abbott does," the young man told a reporter in 1938. Ezra learned a great deal from his mentor, and throughout his own career as a stage director reporters and critics almost always compared him to Abbott. Although he developed his own methodology in handling a theatrical production, he was a direct descendant and a disciple of Abbott and his system.

The plays Abbott presented were sometimes labeled trivial and superficial, a simple escape for the tired businessman with little concern for things of the spirit. But his productions always epitomized good theater. In one way or another they usually presented the old story of boy meets girl, and the boy always got the girl. He produced and directed plays dealing with the foibles of American life, avoiding graver problems and the vices. "No one, not even George S. Kaufman, has a keener knowledge of the wisecrack, or is master of a more headlong pace," wrote Grenville Vernon of the *Commonweal*. "He feels and expresses what foreigners assert is the American spirit, and which is certainly the spirit of New York." He asked no hidden questions and never permitted his playwrights, actors, or audiences to do so.

Ezra quickly grasped his mentor's style of directing, and he believed the trademarks of an Abbott farce began with truth. To direct a successful farce, no matter how extreme the elements, he surmised the audience had to believe the characters, the dialogue, and the situation. Only after the conflict and forthright situation were established did Abbott allow the madcap adventure to begin.

Ezra also characterized Abbott's productions as possessing a lively pace and great variety. If one asked the average New York theater patron during the thirties and forties to name the one outstanding attribute of Abbott's direction, he or she would have probably named speed. With Abbott, however, speed did not mean moving and speaking at a quicker than normal rate. Speed meant variety, the illusion of speed, and he achieved this objective through his construction and writing of plays as well as through the physical staging. Abbott abhorred what he called "stage-waits." He compelled his actors to pick up their cues, forcing their characters' brains to function as fast as the human mind does in real life. He also frequently used overlapping dialogue, for he believed that, too, was human nature and at the same time moved the plot along.

Abbott's farces possessed impeccable comic "cleanliness." He provided actors with clear and distinct pieces of business, which simultaneously helped the dialogue to move at a rapid rate. When it came time to deliver a punch line or to set up a joke, Abbott's actors were directed to deliver the line in crystal-clear fashion with no distractions. Performers moving or drawing attention to themselves on either side of the focused actor were severely chastised. "Teddy (Hart), stand still! Don't move a muscle until you hear the audience laugh," Ezra reported to have frequently heard.

As an editor, Abbott had no equal. George S. Kaufman possessed a superb wit, perhaps superior to Abbott's, but in Ezra's view Kaufman did not have Abbott's disciplined ability to cut all unnecessary dialogue and movement. Abbott also used this editorial technique when he directed musicals, cutting entire numbers that either delayed the action or lacked the force and power of other songs. He found ways to advance the plot by indication or by trusting the audience to make the chronological jump, often allowing the audience to solve the dramatic or comedic conflict during the intermission. He might say, "We'll bring down the curtain here." Ezra and his cohorts then replied, "Oh yeah, well, when are you going to tie a bow on that or resolve that conflict?" "Oh, the audience will do that themselves during the break. We'll get them involved during the next set of circumstances." Thus, he often cut out seemingly important exposition in order to give other lines more dramatic impact.

From the beginning of his association with Abbott, Ezra had expressed an interest in the production phase of theater, and he had gained his initial directing experience by assisting Abbott with putting together the road companies of *Room Service* and *What a Life*. Since Abbott usually was already busy with new projects, his production team had the opportunity to try to reproduce his staging for the road companies. Ezra was only assigned to duplicate his boss' direction for one entire road production, *What a Life*. With the help of such stage managers as Bobby Griffith, who later teamed up with Hal Prince, Ezra also gained valuable directing experience by coaching understudies for several Broadway productions.

Ezra's future as a director was clouded, however, since Abbott had always either directed or codirected all his productions. It seemed unlikely that Ezra would ever find important directing opportunities within the present system. Nevertheless, when Abbott unfurled his first show of the 1939–40 season at the Biltmore Theatre on September 27, his associates were shocked to learn that Abbott's only alliance with the enterprise was as producer. Apparently dumbfounded, a *New York Times* reporter, reliably or otherwise, wrote,

> . . . an erudite linotype operator in the shop of the New York Theatre Program Company interrupted himself on his compositorial task once he had set the words "George Abbott presents 'See My Lawyer' by Richard Maibaum and Harry Clork," and queried of a supervisor whether some mistake had not been made on the next line of copy, which read: "Directed by Ezra Stone."

Any deviation from so firmly established a custom probably would have caused some surprise around the Manhattan streets. The idea of the veteran handing over the reins of one of his shows to a fledgling, who had only recently reached voting age, provoked astonishment. Ezra had directed student productions, short playlets in the Catskills, and obviously had assisted Abbott, but he had never directed a full-length play, not to mention a Broadway production.

In retrospect it appears that Abbott's decision to allow his young assistant to direct *See My Lawyer* was based on three reasons. First, Abbott had accepted the task of producing and directing the new Richard Rodgers and Lorenz Hart musical, *Too Many Girls*, an elaborate spectacle starring Eddie Bracken and Desi Arnaz and scheduled to open in New Haven, Connecticut, the day before *See My Lawyer* was to debut on Broadway. Second, Abbott had always made it a habit to encourage young, talented professionals. Finally, Ezra Stone had discovered and cultivated Clork's and Maibaum's script. Richard Maibaum, incidentally, later enjoyed great success as the author of many of the James Bond films. As an executive at Paramount, he was also partially responsible for Ezra being hired as a costar in *Those Were the Days*.

While he was working as one of Abbott's play readers, Ezra had stumbled upon *See My Lawyer*, a play based on the life of an eccentric millionaire of the period, Tommy Manville, who owned the Manville Asbestos Company. Manville, a playboy, had married and divorced six or seven wives, but he always arranged a financial settlement before the cases reached court. Evidently, his last wife demanded more money than the millionaire wished to pay, so he let the case go to trial. Unhappy with his present attorney, he apparently placed full-page ads in all the major New York newspapers that read, "I want a lawyer. Tommy Manville." No explanation followed, only a telephone number. Maibaum and Clork, upon reading the ad, figured this true story had potential as a plot for a farce.

When Ezra took the script to Abbott and recommended it for possible production, he fully expected his boss to instruct him to arrange a worklight reading. But to his surprise Abbott returned it and said, "That's a funny script. It needs work, and it needs top people to pull it off. I think I'll do it." He calculated that this play could potentially run only one full season; therefore, it needed to open at approximately the same time as *Too Many Girls*. "I can't do both," he explained. "So I've decided to let you direct it, Ezra." He instructed Ezra to begin work with the playwrights and to meet with Carl Fisher, his business manager, to establish a budget.

Both Maibaum and Clork lived in Hollywood, so Ezra had no way to meet with the playwrights to work on script revisions. Therefore, he, like his mentor, began editing the manuscript without their consent. When Ezra gave Maibaum the revised script, the playwright half jokingly said, "I hardly recognized it as the original." He did not protest beyond that. "I don't remember structurally what I did in the rewrite," Ezra later said. "I know that I added a lot more jokes and action." One example of his contribution was a joke about the infamous protracted strike at the Brass Rail Restaurant on 7th Avenue.

During the time when Ezra was rewriting the script, the daughter of a close friend of the family visited the Feinstones in Brooklyn. Ezra, being close to her age, dutifully escorted her around the city and took her to lunch at the Brass Rail. He carried with him a two-dollar bill and a twenty-dollar bill. They ate a quick lunch, which came to less than two dollars, but he gave the cashier his twenty to cover the check. Although he received nothing but pocket change in return, he did not realize the mistake until he had passed through the restaurant's revolving door. He immediately reentered the building to confront the cashier, but the employee and restaurant management denied the error. Ezra retaliated by having Irving Frankel — a role played by Norman Tokar and later taken over by Ezra — report on the adventures of the lawyer's eccentric client, Carlin.

> IRVING: 1:10: Walked up Sixth Avenue . . . bought one dozen dark sunglasses . . . second-hand tennis racket six feet of rope and registered at three employment agencies.
> ARTHUR: He did O.K. on Sixth Avenue.
> IRVING: 1:30: Entered Brass Rail and had lunch. 2:00 o'clock, came out and picketed the joint. . .

Ezra's punch line was later quoted by Walter Winchell and became a Broadway catchphrase.

Abbott had warned Ezra that the script would need a strong cast to make it work with at least modest success. For Arthur Lee, the leading male character, Abbott first thought of Sam Levene, but he had obligations elsewhere. Abbott then toyed with the idea of casting a new actor named Danny Kaye, who was making a hit at the Martinique Club; however, Milton Berle suddenly became available, and he and Abbott met to discuss the possibilities. Berle recalled the incident in his autobiography:

> I was in his office in half an hour. I got right to the point. "You're doing a play called *See My Lawyer*. Nothing would please me more than to be in it under your direction." And I told him the character I thought I could play. Mr. Abbott . . . looked startled. "Do you realize that no one will be starred over the title?" "That's okay with me." . . . Abbott leaned over his desk at me. "Do you have any idea what the part pays?" I brushed that aside. "Whatever it pays will be fine by me." . . . Now what I really wanted was a chance to show I could do something straight rather than just stand-up clowning. So I went into the show . . . for $200 a week. Only I didn't get George Abbott as my director. He produced, and turned the direction over to a kid still in his twenties, Ezra Stone.

Regardless of his feelings about having a first-time director in charge of his first straight part in the legitimate theater, Berle joined the cast. Ezra later said, "I knew he wanted to do the show. And this was the only way on this property that it was going to happen. Milton was always a wiseacre, and his mother was a pain in the ass. He wanted to do this."

One of Ezra's biggest concerns in directing Berle, a vaudevillian, was to make him interact with the other actors rather than pose for the audience. Happily, when the cast went into rehearsals Ezra found Berle to be cooperative and receptive to his ideas. "Milton is an exceptional talent, always was. It was his ego that was so overbearing," Ezra recalled. "That was part of his signature, but he possessed a will to discover the key to legitimate acting." And when he received good notices from the critics, the comedian apparently forgot all animosity. The *Sun's* "Conning Tower" columnist later wrote, "Ezra Stone has made an acting pearl out of the brash Milton Berle."

Ezra and his cast, which included Teddy Hart, Millard Mitchell, Gary Merrill, Mary Rolfe, Norman Tokar, and Berle, went into rehearsals in early September 1939 at the Biltmore Theatre. As a young director, Ezra certainly tried to use everything he had learned from his mentor. "If I did anything that Abbott might not have done, it probably was the over-invention of business," he said. "Abbott would have had the end product even leaner than I achieved. Because let's face it, it was like whiskey to the Indians; if

I sensed a comedy situation, I would milk it for all it was worth." As inexperienced as Ezra was, Abbott interfered little with his rehearsals. It was after the fifth day of preparation, after Ezra had blocked the entire play and the actors had memorized the first act, before Abbott broke away from *Too Many Girls* to critique his young protégé's work.

On the sixth day of rehearsal, the cast of *See My Lawyer* ran through the entire show for Abbott and Stone. After the rehearsal, the elder man held the cast for notes, which was his normal way of keeping all problems in the open. Before the cast assembled, however, he suggested that Ezra release the young actress playing Blossom Le Verne, a Mae West type. Abbott never fired anyone publicly; this he did privately when only Ezra, Carl Fisher, and Charlie Harris, the company manager, were present. Abbott then gave notes to the rest of the cast, and after that rehearsal, he left Ezra completely in charge.

Typically, an Abbott production of a nonmusical rehearsed three weeks although equity allowed four. The company usually ran through the entire show on Monday of the fourth week. All the other Abbott casts were invited to attend this performance just as they had previously been invited to the worklight reading. Abbott did this so he could get a sample audience reaction to the show. This was such an intimate group of people, however, that much of the response came from friends laughing at friends rather than at characters or situations. Therefore, this did not always give a true picture of a paying audience's reaction.

That Wednesday, Ezra and his troupe boarded the company train departing the city. Abbott allowed straight plays only one week of out-of-town tryouts before returning to Broadway. Musicals got two weeks. Each show closed out of town on a Saturday night and transferred back to Manhattan on Sunday. Monday and Tuesday evenings were reserved for invited guests, who helped the cast prepare for opening night. Almost all Abbott shows opened on a Wednesday evening in order to avoid conflicts with the critics and to receive reviews prior to the weekend. If the show flopped, he closed it after Saturday's performance. *See My Lawyer* followed this typical routine, and after three weeks of rehearsals, the cast headed for an out-of-town test in Baltimore.

On the vaudeville, cabaret, and theater circuit, Sandra (Sophie) "Queenie" Berle was known to attend all her son's performances. He represented her "meal ticket," and she followed him everywhere, offering advice and passing judgment on his every move. During his performances, however, Berle believed she provided an important function. Knowing his routines completely, she sat in the audience and cued the laughs. Night after night she laughed a beat ahead of the audience so as to stimulate them to follow.

During *See My Lawyer*'s tryout week in Baltimore, Ezra, who had been warned of Queenie, decided he must keep her out of the audience.

This week was to be devoted to tightening the performance and making intelligent script additions or deletions. He thought her phony laughter would trigger false audience reactions and make it difficult for him to get a true response to the show. Meanwhile, Ezra had discovered that Queenie was a terrific poker player; in fact, it was almost an addiction with her. When the company moved into the Maryland Theatre and set up for the performance, he told the stage property master, "Every show when you guys set up your poker table under the stage, I want you to invite Queenie Berle to that game." He even authorized the company manager to provide the stage crew each night during the tryout with twenty-five dollars to lose to the notorious spectator. This ploy kept Queenie busy during rehearsals and performances, and the show matured nicely during its stay in Baltimore.

When *See My Lawyer* opened on Wednesday, September 27, Ezra, at age twenty-one, undoubtedly became Broadway's youngest director. According to several reports, the opening night audience enjoyed his creation immensely; the critics, however, had mixed feelings about the show and its young director. Most of them agreed that it was not one of Abbott's best productions and thought the plot became lost in a mishmash of silly actions and dialogue. "It does reach occasional peaks of merriment, and its absurdities are too obvious to command even fleeting belief," wrote Sidney B. Wipple of the *New York World-Telegram*. "It contains many opportunities for laughter, but most of these consist of local allusions to the New York system of jurisprudence, or of topical wit having nothing to do with the plot and very little to do with the character." Some of the harshest critics went so far as to call it second-rate, but this label was usually applied in comparisons to Abbott's previous productions.

Perhaps Ezra as a young director had tried too hard, and he undoubtedly lacked Abbott's mental discipline for editing out unnecessary action and dialogue. Perhaps at this point in his career he simply did not fully understand how to implement Abbott's concept of truth and believability. Brooks Atkinson indicated that Ezra's direction resulted in well-intended but uneven performances. He wrote, "Some of the harassed confusion of that high school student (Henry Aldrich) passes over into this hard driven performance."

Most of the same reviewers who criticized Ezra's overinventiveness and the script's impertinent dialogue, however, also praised the effort of the youthful director. "When it is funny, *See My Lawyer* can be very funny indeed," wrote John Mason Brown of the *New York Post*. "Only an ingrate could claim to have found no pleasure in the giddier stretches. . . ." Most critics agreed that Ezra had inherited an engaging dizziness of pace from his mentor and that he seemed an able lieutenant under Abbott's command. Richard Watts, Jr., of the *New York Herald Tribune* perhaps threw Ezra the biggest bouquet when he wrote,

. . . it bears all the marks of the old master's handiwork. That is to say, of course, that it is brittle, ingenious and rapidly paced, that it is more striking in its speed and its inventive stage business than in its writing and that it contains at least one comic reference to a lavatory. Perhaps its chief achievement is that it employs that strenuous vaudeville and radio comic, Milton Berle, in the leading role and keeps him pleasantly subdued. I think that this feat in itself marks young Mr. Stone as a director of some talent and force.

See My Lawyer held the stage for 224 performances. Berle left the cast before the end of the run, and Paul Stewart, Orson Welles' right-hand-man and actor in *Citizen Kane*, stepped into the role. When Abbott witnessed a performance, however, he decided to close the show in a few weeks. Stewart's comic skills simply did not compare to Berle's impeccable wit. Meanwhile, Ezra, who had already replaced Norman Tokar in the role of Irving Frankel, stepped into the leading role of Arthur Lee for the remainder of the show's Broadway tenure.

Even before *See My Lawyer* closed, the Jewish Relief Committee in Manhattan approached Ezra to codirect another Broadway production. The show also represented the second American production of a group of Viennese actors, singers, dancers, and writers, who had only recently fled their country now occupied by Hitler's regime. Known as the Kleinkunstbûhne (Little Art Theater) in Vienna, this ambitious group of young performers, who believed the theater to be more than a business venture, had begun operation in 1933. Sensing the catastrophe that would befall Europe, these actors raised their voices in the hope that their pointed ridicule and satire would destroy the adversary. The censor could not silence them, and for five years the Kleinkunstbûhne played continuously. Eventually, their parodies of Hitler and his cohorts imperiled their lives. In 1938 the political situation worsened, and the German army took over Austria. The group's stages were closed and its sets burned.

Most of the troupe escaped to the United States, where they immediately began the re-formation of their company. While earning a living working in shops and households, the performers learned English in their spare time. Their writers adapted old scripts and formatted new ones, and the troupe began rehearsing an unfinanced production. In June 1939, with the help of a group of theatrical people headed by George S. Kaufman, they presented in the Music Box Theatre their first American show, *From Vienna.*

Even after the presentation of their first production, this company, now called the American Viennese Group, had a difficult time making the cultural transition, though the Refugee Relief Committee supported them both psychologically and financially. As they began to feel more comfortable in their new country and as the plight of the refugees became more publicized, however, the company turned to improved material and pre-pared to present a second production entitled *Reunion in New York*.

Sympathetic to their cultural and political cause, Ezra agreed to work on *Reunion in New York*. Although he had nothing to gain financially—he volunteered his time—this play represented an important point in his directorial career. Not only was this his second Broadway directing credit, but it marked his initial break from George Abbott, who, in all fairness, was never possessive of his actors or production teams. In fact, he often en-couraged his people to explore outside career opportunities.

Of his rehearsals with the American Viennese Group, Ezra later said, "They were all bilingual, so communication was no problem. No problem stylistically. . . . A very talented group." Within the organization, however, there existed a great deal of infighting, as actors scrambled for the best musical numbers and parts in sketches. Letters and memorandums written between Ezra and company members also seemed to indicate that a trou-blesome communication gap plagued them. For example, tardiness and absenteeism continuously disrupted rehearsals. Ezra had set up a tight schedule; therefore, when he called a rehearsal he expected everyone to be on time and ready to work.

Although she always had an excuse, Vilma Kurer, one of the com-pany's leading actresses, incessantly wasted Ezra's time. In a letter she wrote, "I'm sorry to bather [bother] you again in a letter. I heard you left the rehearsal because I wasn't there. I had to go to the lawyers because I was summoned for $35, and had to make an appointment." Kurer, in fact, seemed to be the root of many of Ezra's rehearsal problems, and the direc-tor later chastised her for her lack of discipline in front of the other cast members. Naturally, Kurer perceived his outburst as unwarranted. "I don't want you to be nasty to me in front of all our people and would appreciate it very much, if you'd not be that way anymore," she wrote in another letter. "And if you want to change 'Shooting Gallery' and let somebody else do my part, why didn't you tell me before?" Kurer and the other temperamental performers, however, did not comprise all of Ezra's troubles.

During the weeks of rehearsals, a tremendous artistic and managerial struggle erupted between Ezra and Herbert Berghof, the original director of this Viennese "coffee house" group. When U.S. financial backers had originally agreed to produce the show, they demanded that Berghof co-direct with an American. Although Berghof conceded to this arrangement, he resented Ezra's position as having the final word in all artistic matters. "He was very neurotic about it," Ezra later claimed.

As they worked their way through difficult rehearsals, Ezra felt the brunt of his colleague's bitterness. Berghof, on the other hand, seemed to think that Ezra was taking a condescending view toward his criticism. On February 18, 1940, only three days before the opening, the confrontation reached its peak when Ezra, apparently responding to a note from Berghof, vented his frustrations in a letter. He wrote,

> Let *me* come right to the point. These weeks that I have spent with the Viennese Theatre Group have been the most trying I have ever experienced. I hope it will be a long time before I again have to battle with so many different temperaments, conflicting forces and intrigues. I wished I could have withdrawn several weeks ago and God how I wish I could do so now. But I won't! And nothing will make me. . . . I promised to do a job and I will. . . . My own creative ability I have always doubted but my ability to get along with the people with whom I must work, up to now, I have never doubted. So to-night you have made me feel doubly unhappy. You have shown me that I have, in your opinion, failed as an artist and even as a diplomat (God's lowest form of life). I am sorry. . . .

Ezra was not alone in his opinion. Almost a month before sending his explosive letter to Berghof, he had invited his friend, Kyle Crichton, to observe and critique a run-through of the show. Crichton, also a reporter, wrote, "After seeing that group of 'professionals' at the run-through the other day I certainly don't want to get mixed up with them."

Years later, however, Berghof directed Ezra and his wife, Sara, in the Bucks County Playhouse production of *The Middle of the Night*. "It was a warm reunion," Ezra recently said. "He even let me sit on a sofa down front peeling an apple in one long continuous peel. I had few lines but managed to steal the scene." The audience apparently loved it as the peel became a bracelet reaching up to his elbow.

Despite some original artistic differences, when *Reunion in New York* opened on February 21, 1940, the cast and Berghof hastened to give Ezra words of appreciation. Composer and writer Werner Michel, speaking for the entire group, wrote, ". . . my hopes you really aren't mad about anyone of us. Everybody would feel very badly about it. . . . you have done a grand job and without you we would never have had a show." Fortunately, the ill feelings did not handicap the final product, and critics gave the play much more favorable marks than they had Ezra's first directorial project.

Reunion in New York marked Ezra's first attempt at staging environmental preshow activity to establish the appropriate mood. Treating the entire theater as if it were part of a Viennese beer garden, he had some of the ladies in the cast stroll down the aisles peddling pretzels and candy sticks. Waiters came on stage to arrange the tables for the evening's clientele, while musicians and singers haphazardly gathered to tune their instruments and warm their voices, and accordion players wandered throughout the theater enchanting the audience with their folk tunes. This activity began precisely at 8:15 and lasted thirty minutes. With it Ezra wished to establish a sceneless atmosphere, which meant he wanted the play to appear as if the events on stage were occurring spontaneously. He also directed a slow thirty-minute fade of the house lights to black, which again made it difficult to tell when the preshow ended and the production began. The show consisted of grotesque solo dances, a satire on modern art, a burlesque of chorus girl manners, monologues, and songs such as "They Made Me a Surrealist" and "I'm Surreally in Love with You." Much of the evening's humor, however, derived from several blackout sketches, which followed the formula of typical revue sketches of that period. Within a framework of a ten-minute playlet, the writer of these sketches established a comic situation, then constructed the vignette entirely for the blackout line. For example, in "English in Six Easy Lessons" a male foreigner landed in America with only his book of common English phrases to aid his communication. The scene, written by Lothar Metzl and Werner Michel presumably began on Ellis Island.

LORENZ: America—I feel safe in America because I've bought the "Little Yankee," English in six easy lessons, a pocket conversation guide for everyone . . .
OFFICER: Next! Are those your things?
LORENZ: Moment, moment. (*RUSTLING OF PAPER IS HEARD*) How do you do . . .
OFFICER: How do you do?
LORENZ: Ladies and Gentlemen. Isn't it a lovely morning, afternoon, evening, night?
OFFICER: (*BEWILDERED*) What?
LORENZ: Thank you very much. I feel not so good, fine, rotten. . . .

However, after Lorenz is thrown out of customs, a hotel, a restaurant, and slapped by a pretty girl for his miscommunication, he is rewarded for his troubles.

LORENZ: I walked through the streets practicing out of my phrase-book. (*STREET SOUNDS*) What is the time by your watch? What time have you? What time do you think it is? What is the time by your watch, what time . . .
A MAN: There are a good many answers possible. By my watch it is exactly 1,2,3,4 o'clock. It is 5,6,7 minutes past or after. It's a quarter past, it's half past, it's 25, 20, 10, 5, 2 minutes to 2. It's 7 o'clock.
LORENZ: Gentleman, you are the first mister who understand me.
A MAN: Is that so?
LORENZ: You know this book?
A MAN: Know it? I wrote it! (*BLACKOUT*)

Reunion in New York received warm reviews that applauded the Viennese players for capturing American humor while maintaining their foreign personalities. Most of the critics agreed that the new revue radiated with captivating and touching material. Only a few felt that the numbers and sketches were dull and uninspired. Brooks Atkinson was one who enjoyed the group's effort and he threw a large bouquet in their direction when he wrote, "As an example of the light touch in entertainment it is warming and delightful, for these singers, dancers and comedians know how to translate capricious ideas into unassuming gaiety." Nevertheless, the show never found a consistent audience and closed after only a couple of months.

Following his association with the American Viennese Group, Ezra was involved with two successive Broadway flops, first as a director and then as an actor. In late spring of 1940, Clifford Hayman brought a play to Ezra entitled *Your Loving Son* and written by Abby Merchant. Working independently from Abbott, Ezra agreed both to direct the tryout production and to portray the leading role, Joshua Winslow. Before moving on to Broadway, Hayman secured a deal with the Cambridge Summer Theatre in Cambridge, Massachusetts, to present the play in the Brattle Theatre. *Your Loving Son*, with Jessie Royce Landis, Judson Laird, and Rex Williams, opened after a brief two-week rehearsal period and ran only one week. As far as Ezra was concerned, the production failed. But Hayman, a tenacious young man, somehow arranged for Jay Richard Kennedy, in association with Alfred Bloomingdale and Joseph F. Loewi, to produce the play as a Broadway production, starring Frankie Thomas, Jr., under the direction of Arthur Cirgum. As Ezra had expected, however, it closed after three performances at the Little Theatre.

Perhaps Ezra's greatest failing as an actor outside the security of the Abbott system was his lack of good judgment in selecting scripts. Ezra later maintained, "Quality vehicles were not offered to me." Resting on the laurels of his work as Broadway's youngest director and as a national celebrity in the role of Henry Aldrich, he should have had many opportunities. But perhaps because of his size and juvenile appearance, he received only one firm offer in the fall of 1940.

Horse Fever, a comedy by Eugene Conrad and Zac and Ruby Gabel, was a perfect example of the kind of play Ezra should have refused. But Ezra agreed to play the lead in the show for two reasons. First, he wanted to remain active and hoped, as with *See My Lawyer*, to make it through the Broadway season with this show. Second, he felt a sense of obligation and debt to the show's producer, Alex Yokel, who had earlier allowed him to leave *Three Men on a Horse* without rancor or malice to join George Abbott and *Brother Rat*.

Horse Fever, however, violated Abbott's number one requisite for a farce—truth. The farcical elements had no basis in reality. Instead the entire play was a series of sight gags, such as a stool that automatically emerged from the wall beside the telephone stand when someone picked up the receiver or a desk drawer that opened automatically every time someone pulled the cord to turn on the electric light. Although ridiculous and entertaining, these gags had little to do with the narrative. Many critics echoed Atkinson's analysis, "When the curtain finally comes down you have an impression of having laughed frequently during the evening, as you laugh at a briskly written radio skit, but you have not much to laugh over in remembrance." Although Ezra received no negative criticism of his performance, most commentators cited him as *Horse Fever*'s chief victim. The show flopped, playing only a few months at the Mansfield Theatre.

If *Horse Fever* did nothing to enhance Ezra's career, it did allow him to meet the woman he would eventually marry. Sara Seegar, who played Milly in this failed production, had spoken her first words on stage in the London company of *Three Men on a Horse*. Yokel reportedly gave her the role because she had told him the truth about her inexperience after he heard her read. She remained in London to appear with featured billing in *Post Road*, *They Came by Night*, *The Bowery Touch*, and in a half-dozen motion pictures. When the German air raids on London began in early spring of 1939, she returned to New York and began searching for work on the American stage. As she made the rounds, Davy Burns, her boyfriend at the time who had played the Sam Levene role in the London production of *Three Men*, escorted Sara to Abbott's office, where she was properly screened by Ezra, the assistant casting director. At the time, neither seemed overly impressed with the other.

During *Horse Fever*, however, Ezra and Sara formed a relationship that would endure throughout the next half century. Ezra jokingly said, "The show was so lousy, we looked good to each other by comparison. . . . But truthfully, I was just attracted to her intelligence and her sense of humor. We had similar interests and fell in love." But the bond they had in the wings and outside the theater did not always carry over onto the stage. "I do not terribly much enjoy working with Ezra as a performer," Sara later said in a *Dramatics*' interview. "I didn't, I should say that. When we were young I didn't, because he loved to play tricks. All actors play tricks, and he was full of tricks."

As a young performer, Ezra occasionally took shortcuts rather than do his work as an actor. By his own admission, he was an extremely poor study. Radio had spoiled him, and he had a difficult time memorizing text. "So he would have things pasted on furniture here and there," Sara said. "I did not approve of that."

Sara, on the other hand, had a photographic memory. Once, while riding the New Jersey Transit from Trenton to New York City, she memorized her dialogue for a half-hour TV production of "The Egg and I," which she subsequently rehearsed and aired that same day. Nevertheless, she felt Ezra had a tremendous imagination as a director, and the two were in total agreement on all basics of the theater, on what was good and what constituted excellence in their field.

Their relationship, however, was off and on for the first couple of years. The Feinstones initially opposed the alliance because of two factors: Sara was several years older than their son, and her cultural background was vastly different from Ezra's upbringing. Sara, the youngest of four girls, had spent her adolescence in Greentown, a small rural community in Indiana; Ezra, of course, had spent his boyhood years in Philadelphia and New York. Religion was never a factor in their opposition. The Feinstones were proud of their Jewish heritage but never religious. Although Sara had grown up in the Methodist Church, she likewise did not have strong religious convictions. Later in his life, Ezra also believed that his sister, Miriam, had always had a strong dislike of Sara, but he remembered Miriam admitting that Sara had more brains than any of his previous girlfriends. Despite these few minor conflicts, Ezra and Sara's mutual attractions grew strong over the next two years.

Over the years, Sara and the Feinstones grew very close. "My mother was 'Rosebud' to Sara, and my father became her mentor in business matters," Ezra later said. Sara, not Ezra, handled family business matters. "My father later made her executor of the trust funds he established for our kids." Feinstone often said, "Sara has the best 'Yiddish kop' in the family . . . after mine." And in personal matters, he often took Sara's side over Ezra's.

On September 1, 1939, Ezra, like most Americans, watched in horror as World War II erupted in Europe when the Germans invaded Poland. During the blitzkrieg, President Franklin D. Roosevelt asked for huge appropriations to mechanize the army, create a massive air force, and build a two-ocean navy, one that could meet both German and Japanese threats. In June 1940, Congress introduced and passed a bill calling for compulsory military service. In September, after months of debate marked by bitter opposition from all over the nation, Congress passed the nation's first peacetime draft law.

Keeping abreast of the current political developments, Ezra realized the probability of receiving his draft notice in the near future. Feinstone, however, in an attempt to rescue his son from direct military confrontation and to have his communication skills effectively used, arranged through a friend of the family for his son to meet the commanding general of the Second Corps area on Governor's Island. The meeting with Irving J. Phillipson, the only Jewish major general in the United States Army at that time, took place before Ezra had received his official draft notice. During the course of the meeting, Ezra secured a guarantee that allowed him to remain with the cast of *The Aldrich Family*. Naturally he would have to quit his other jobs. His $1,250 weekly salary would go to the Army Emergency Relief, a nonprofit organization not administered by the military. In return,

General Phillipson guaranteed Ezra that he would have each Thursday free and would be stationed close enough to Manhattan to drive in for rehearsals and performances.

According to Ezra, Phillipson could justify his decision to grant him special privileges because he intended to use Ezra's expertise to establish or expand the morale offices in each of the thirty-two posts, camps, and stations of the Second Corps area. Troop morale was an important concept for the general, and he thought Ezra's participation in the radio series could also play an important role in this respect. In the words of Norman Copeland in his book *Psychology and the Soldier,*

> Morale is the most powerful weapon known to man; more powerful than the biggest gun; more powerful than the most devastating bomb. Again and again it has been the means of turning defeat into victory. An Army is never beaten until it knows it is beaten, for defeat is an attitude of mind and not a physical condition.

Therefore, when Ezra received his draft notice on July 14, 1941, he went through the induction ritual and thirteen weeks of basic training knowing he would be stationed in the New York area to begin working with Phillipson and to continue his work on radio.

When *The Aldrich Family* broadcast its first show of the new season on August 21, 1941, Private Ezra Stone, who now performed in uniform, returned as America's favorite teenager, Henry Aldrich. By arrangement with the authorities, his army duties did not alter his radio rehearsal schedule. An hour and a half of rehearsal on Wednesday evening was followed by three hours on Thursday morning, two more in the afternoon and a final hour and a half in the evening. As usual the first broadcast aired at 8:00 P.M., and the repeat was broadcast three and one-half hours later. Ezra then returned to base in time to report for duty the following morning. He regularly worked on the post on Saturdays and Sundays to make up for his absence each Thursday.

The Aldrich Family fulfilled its morale function and became one of the most popular programs with United States Army personnel. From the beginning of America's active involvement in the war, the comedy series immediately became one of those transmitted by shortwave radio to the armed forces overseas. During the 1941–42 season, the show maintained a rating of over thirty-one percent of the American market. During this short time, the program also became popular among Europeans; in spring of 1942, soldiers on Britain's Bermuda base command voted it their favorite program. During the same period, the show won an award from the Women's National Radio Committee as the best radio drama. Not many shows were able to please so varied an audience.

When asked later what changes were made in the program in response to the war, Jack Kelk, who continued to play Homer Brown, wrote, "None that I can remember, the situations and characters just kept on going, . . . like Peter Pan." But just as the Office of War Information had wished, the program did enlist in the war effort. Although episodes did not directly relate to the war, they dealt with issues facing all Americans. Peripherally, many broadcasts dealt with war themes. For instance, they depicted the Aldriches rationing their gas, carpooling, and collecting rubber to aid the Allied effort. The episode on July 1, 1943, dealt entirely with transportation difficulties in wartime, hinting at least that Americans should limit their travel over the holidays. In the broadcast on September 23, 1943, Mary tried to join the WACs (Women's Army Corps). When her letter arrived, however, Henry became confused and filled out the form intended for Mary. After discovering his error, he thought he had joined the WACs. The program on March 16, 1944, dealt entirely with the war effort as Henry became involved in his usual comical situation while working on a scrap waste paper drive.

The Aldrich Family, like all shows of its genre, did sanitize the blood-letting to a certain degree by never revealing the negative side of the war. In the program's defense, however, it has to be pointed out that it had never looked at any issue more than just superficially. "That negative stuff about the war wouldn't have been for our series at all," Ezra later said. That was not the objective of this type of show, which existed for the sole purpose of entertaining the masses—including the troops.

For the first time in the program's history, *The Aldrich Family* did not go into summer repeats at the end of the 1941–42 season, and Ezra's association with the show temporarily came to an end when, on August 12, army officials renewed the enforcement of regulations against soldiers carrying on civilian activities. The announcement came as a shock to the cast, as *The Aldrich Family* was scheduled to begin its new season the next evening at 8:30 on the NBC Red Network. For a while it seemed that army officials would rescind their decision because the program had already been advertised. Just prior to the broadcast, however, a spokesman for Young and Rubicam announced that a replacement for Ezra Stone would appear for as long as he was in the service.

Ezra's arrangement with the army was not altogether unusual; for example, boxer Joe Louis and entertainer Tony Martin were similarly allowed to carry on civilian duties. The denial of permission for Ezra came after a rash of applications by prominent celebrities for special concessions so they could be in the service and still appear on the air under commercial sponsorship. The army concluded that awarding special provisions for only a few entertainers was unfair to countless performers who had enlisted or been drafted without these allowances. Officials also believed that such arrangements defeated any morale values inherent in the programs, because friends and parents of those doing a regular soldier's duty might resent executive approval of these so-called cushy jobs. "These charges kept hitting us, not just those of us who were extensively engaged with civilian activities," Ezra later said of the accusations. "But that attitude was very much in evidence for all of us in Entertainment Divisions in the army. We heard it from the other men and the press and officers in camps where we were based when touring. It was very demoralizing." In one sense, these charges were true because entertainers in uniform often did not fight in the front lines. The decision, however, graphically demonstrated the narrow-mindedness with which most high-ranking army personnel viewed the importance of troop entertainment and morale.

Troubled by feeling that the work to which he had been assigned was useless, Ezra turned to one of his mentors, Charles Jehlinger, for help and advice. To Ezra, soldier shows and army morale often seemed terribly unimportant in the overall "big picture." The ridicule and administrative difficulties to which soldiers were subjected were often difficult to withstand. Jehlinger, knowing very little of the army way, gave Ezra new courage and spurred him on to accomplishments during his four and a half years of service, of which he was extremely proud. Ezra later wrote,

> I am sure his confidence in the worth and need of our work was transmitted through me to a large and important percentage of the some thousand men with whom I came in contact on the various projects to which I had been assigned. To this day I have a wonderful mental picture of Charles Jehlinger when he came to visit our *This Is the Army* unit and witnessed a retreat formation parade and review. Before him passed some 350 men, many of them his students. He stood on the sidelines of the parade ground, small and unobtrusive, but, as each platoon passed, they executed an eyes-right in his direction and for his benefit. I often wondered what he thought during those moments, but never had the courage to ask him, but I remember vividly as I gave the order to my platoon for eyes-right and my gaze caught the steel glint of Jehli's across the parade ground, that here was my symbol, my reason for being in uniform, here was my patriotic fervor.

For Goldsmith, Young and Rubicam, and General Foods, twenty-three-year-old Norman Tokar, who had played an extra in *What a Life* and who had created Willy, one of Henry's buddies, on the radio series, seemed the logical replacement in the role of Henry. Goldsmith had been the young man's mentor, and as a writer of many of the episodes, Tokar intimately understood the character. In addition, he had the ability to mimic Ezra's vocal characterization. He played the cracked-voiced, irresponsible adolescent throughout the 1942–43 season, a period in which the program remained the nation's number one comedy drama. But Ezra's first replacement barely squeaked out the season before the Army Signal Corps called him to active duty in July 1943.

Young and Rubicam then began a nationwide search for a new and draftproof Henry. By the highest press agent count, over seven hundred aspirants auditioned for the role. Finally, the contest narrowed to one Chicago and two Hollywood actors. During the early days of September 1943, the winner of the most coveted juvenile role in radio was announced: Dickie Jones, a sixteen-year-old, brown-haired, hazel-eyed Hollywood veteran with more than ten years of film experience.

Unlike Tokar, who tried to copy Ezra's original creation, Jones consciously attempted to create a new Henry. Although expressions such as "Who, I, Mother?" and "Oh gee whiz" remained part of the Aldrich heir's vocabulary, Jones apparently made an unwise character decision to rid Henry of his most distinguishable trait: the cracked voice. During the 1943–44 season, *The Aldrich Family*'s market rating fell to just over twenty-six percent, a six point drop from the previous season. By the end of the 1944–45 season, its rating fell to sixteen percent. This downfall meant that *The Aldrich Family* had lost over half its weekly listening audience since Ezra's reign as Henry. It could be that the later scripts simply did not have the magic of Goldsmith's original episodes, or perhaps the downturn was simply a natural development in the life of a situation comedy; however, many people believed the key to the show's loss of popularity was Ezra's absence. Kelk, for one, surmised that subsequent actors lacked Ezra's impeccable timing and consistent characterization of the troubled youth. "*The Aldrich Family*, unfortunately, was a 'casualty of WWII,' when Ezra entered the service," wrote Gene Leitner in a letter. "Without him, people started to 'tune-out' *The Aldrich Family*, because the other actors who replaced him—even though they were good—were not 'Our Henry,' Ezra Stone." In July 1945 Jones received his draft notice, and Raymond Ives became Henry the fourth.

The turnover among actors portraying Henry brought that role in line with the others. According to John Dunning in *Tune In Yesterday: The Ultimate Encyclopedia of Old-Time Radio*, *The Aldrich Family* had one of the highest actor turnover rates in the business. With the exception of Kelk, who remained with the show for most of its life, every part was recast many times. By 1943, not one member of the original cast remained. According to one slightly exaggerated report, the program had gone through five fathers, four mothers, and at least a dozen Marys. Ezra later joked, "I was both Henry the First and Henry the Fifth."

7. The Feud

As a soldier in the United States Army, Ezra utilized the knowledge he had gained as Abbott's casting director and production assistant and continued to refine his skills as an administrator and stage director. He entered the service with the clear assignment to create morale offices in all thirty-two army posts, camps, and stations located in the Second Corps area. General Phillipson expected Ezra to organize those posts and to secure talent as young men went through the induction process. Specifically, he was to assign at least one technician, a performer, and a musician to permanent duty on each location. Since Camp Upton, located just outside Manhattan, served as the army's major induction center, it was agreed that he could best perform his duty from there.

Soon after his own induction, Ezra devised a system with the classification officers at Upton and Fort Dix in New Jersey, whereby those officers would hold musicians, actors, singers, dancers, writers, technicians, and any other show business professionals on temporary assignment. The officers then transferred the new recruit's records to Ezra and his staff. These men then evaluated the soldiers and sent the selected artists to any base that needed their particular talents. Not only did this method allow Ezra and his company to retain specific talent, but it also provided them with a list of men available for future projects. Those selected were then placed in special service or morale units, which operated somewhat independently at various bases. The size of each unit was proportional to the size of the post to which it was assigned.

Ezra soon discovered, however, that staging entertainments was among the lesser duties of the morale staff. Decorating recreation rooms, landscaping, digging ditches, trucking and laying topsoil, house painting, and moving pianos and furniture occupied a great deal of their time. They also published a weekly newspaper, organized athletics events, had alert squad drills three mornings each week, and in their spare time performed variety programs at what was known as the Opry House at Camp Upton. In the beginning, the men performed impromptu, supplementing their numbers with whatever talent they could spot in the audience. There was plenty of room for improvement.

The Opry House had been a ten-car garage until five months before, when the morale officer, Captain A. H. Rankin, who had formerly worked as a cartoonist for the *Brooklyn Daily Eagle*, had it renovated into a theater seating four hundred with standing room for two hundred more. Inane carriage wheels were grafted onto the outside of the building. The interior decor, however, became much more appropriate for theatrical performances when *Esquire* artist Jaro Fabry was inducted and detained at Upton long enough to paint a set of beaverboard murals of large-breasted Floradora girls and seductive can-can dancers in a delightfully sophisticated Gay Nineties style.

At Camp Upton, Ezra's morale unit—referred to as the Opry House Players—included Alan Manson, Phil Truex, Mike Wardell, Jose Di Donato, Alan Anderson, son of playwright Maxwell Anderson, Ross Elliot, Zinn Arthur, Dick Browning, Dick Bernie, and Ralph Nelson. In addition, there were Peter Feller, the lone technician and designer, Milton Rosenstock, a clarinetist from Julliard and a symphony orchestra leader, Tom McDonnell, formerly an executive with Young and Rubicam, Pinkie Mitchell, who had appeared on radio's *The Children's Hour* with Ezra, Broadway actor Ty Perry, and Gary Merrill, who had worked under Ezra in *See My Lawyer*. Although the performances may not have been "fine art," each of these men believed that such shows were a psychological necessity to take a recruit's mind off the life he had to leave behind and to render him amenable to training.

Their goal was to present theatrical productions of the highest possible quality for the young men about to enter the war. In theory, the entertainment would also serve as a means of imbuing the selected men with pride in, and understanding of, their superior officers and the military system.

On the first anniversary celebration of Camp Upton's organization day, the Opry House Players presented their premiere original show, a musical revue entitled *My Year*. Written by Tom McDonnell, Ralph Nelson, and Ezra Stone, the show burlesqued the commanding officers and the birth of the camp. According to Ezra in his book *Coming, Major!*, "The book, lyrics, and music for the revue were written and produced in four days at a cost of $9.00, $3.00 for the table (which we later sold back to the second-hand store for $2.00) and $6.00 for photographic lantern slides of camp buildings."

Although Captain Rankin feared the burlesque went too far and would perhaps have a negative effect on those higher in command, the musical was a rousing success. Thereafter, each new group of inductees witnessed a performance of the show. The unit later performed *My Year* at a morale conference to demonstrate the kind of constructive camp entertainment that soldiers could create and produce themselves at a relatively low cost.

Although *My Year* seemed a far cry from the Abbott musicals Ezra had known only a short time ago, it represented to him the beginning of something more important. After this initial achievement, Ezra, who sought better material, directed a highly successful tristate camp tour of *Brother Rat*.

The production so impressed General Phillipson that he, two civilians, and four army morale specialists held a conference to formulate a plan for centralizing show units on each post by administering them from headquarters on Governor's Island. This new theater section, dubbed the Fighting Entertainment Unit, included Stone, Rosenstock, Wardell, Anderson, and Feller from the Opry House Players. In addition, Dave Breger, a former cartoonist for the *Saturday Evening Post*, Nelson Barclift, a gifted modern dancer, Louis Simon, a former production assistant to Max Reinhardt and the ex-executive secretary for the Actors' Equity Association, Sidney "Jiggy" Robin, a Tin Pan Alley composer, and Pulitzer Prize–winning playwright Sidney Kingsley also joined central command.

Throughout this period, Ezra continued to develop as a director by staging musical revues and comedies. One of his unit's projects was a musical entitled *Six Jerks in a Jeep*, which could be staged anywhere without scenery. Robin wrote the music and lyrics; Ezra's girlfriend, Sara Seegar, suggested the title. The show required only four or five musicians and an untrained natural comic who could be found in any barracks. The show premiered in the shower stall of a latrine at Fort Hamilton. Captain Maurice Evans later borrowed this idea and sent out touring units of what he referred to as *Five Jerks in a Jeep* in the South Pacific. A film entitled *Five Jills in a Jeep* was also later released.

At Camp Upton's Opry House, Ezra also directed and played Erwin in *Three Men on a Horse*. On opening night, Kay Douglas Feller, the female lead, became ill, and Sara, who had understudied the role in England, performed the part, using her remarkable memorization skills, after only an hour and a half of rehearsal.

Ezra then directed *We're Ready*, a miniature musical revue he had developed with McDonnell and Nelson.

About this time, Irving Berlin, the rags-to-riches composer, approached General Phillipson and offered to write an all-soldier show for the army, an echo of his World War I all-soldier hit musical, *Yip! Yip! Yaphank*. Although Berlin lacked formal education and could neither read nor write music, by 1942 he had written over one thousand songs including many number one hits such as "Alexander's Ragtime Band," "Cheek to Cheek," and "God Bless America," a song popularized by Kate Smith which threatened to overthrow "The Star-Spangled Banner" as America's national anthem.

In August of 1918, Broadway's Century Theatre had come alive with

Berlin's *Yip! Yip! Yaphank*. Perhaps a bit too sentimental in its treatment of war, the show nevertheless possessed a patriotic spirit and introduced the world to such songs as "Mandy," "Ladies of the Chorus," and "Oh! How I Hate to Get Up in the Morning." In various interviews, Berlin said that he realized that World War II would pose a longer and more difficult struggle for American troops. For this reason, he said, he intended to make his new musical tougher, less sentimental. It seemed an impossible task, but he said that he wanted to avoid "flag-waving."

When the show opened on Broadway several months later, under the title *This Is the Army*, it was a polished effort. The script began with a soldier minstrel act, then quickly moved into a vaudeville act that allowed the cast to sing, juggle, tumble, and crack jokes. Berlin's first-act numbers included a fast-paced Russian dance, a Harlem sketch, featuring black performers singing "That's What the Well-Dressed Man in Harlem Will Wear," and a lusty finale that turned the navy loose on army soil. The second half of the script bounced to life with a sketch and song about leaving one's heart at the stage door canteen. A rousing tribute to the Air Corps entitled "Head in the Clouds" and a fast, vivacious extravaganza ballet called "A Soldier's Dream" followed. To hardly anyone's dismay, Berlin broke his promise to avoid sentimentality when he and a group of his old comrades from the First World War then entered the stage in their dough-boy uniforms and reprised "Oh! How I Hate to Get Up in the Morning," from *Yip! Yip! Yaphank*.

Months earlier, however, after the famous composer had initially approached him with the idea of composing an army musical, General Phillipson had excitedly sent Private Stone orders to go to Mr. Berlin's New York office for an interview and to discuss the feasibility of the project.

Berlin believed the show must have at least one hundred soldier performers on stage, and he wanted Ezra's views on how they could select and assemble them. Following this meeting, Ezra took Berlin to Camp Upton to see a performance of *We're Ready*.

Berlin had also considered Garson Kanin to direct the new musical extravaganza, but he chose Ezra because he sensed leadership and creative potential. Ezra also maintained a unique position of having talented theater people staffing all posts, camps, and stations in the Second Corps area.

Laurence Bergreen in his biography of Irving Berlin, *As Thousands Cheer*, wrote, ". . . the songwriter did his best to inspire him with a sense of mission. 'I got the full blast of his charm, very enthusiastic, very warm, very gracious. I was really snowed by him.'" Bergreen continued with, "Berlin was particularly impressed that Stone had already been assigned to identify potential talent among the inductees and could remove them at will from the combat divisions." Because of the immense head count, Berlin regarded this point as very important. The musical eventually required more than one hundred soldiers in greasepaint, a fifty-piece band, stagehands, box office personnel, treasurers, wardrobe, makeup artists, designers, press agents, song pluggers, arrangers, and an advance cadre — in all over three hundred men.

Shortly after this, Ezra received a summons from Mayor Fiorello LaGuardia to direct a marine, army, navy, and Coast Guard show that was to play one performance on Monday, April 27, 1942, at 11:00 P.M. at the Metropolitan Opera House. To be called *Salvo: "Entertaining the Entertainers,"* the show was intended as a gesture of gratitude from these service branches to the many U.S.O. performers and the ladies of the Army Women Volunteer Corps. With their three-part program that included "New York City's Tribute to the Armed Forces," "Naval Maneuvers," and "The Army's Surprise Attack Against the Blues," they would turn the tables on the mostly professional entertainers, who would participate only as audience members. Thanks to the theater section in the Special Services Office at headquarters, the show was a rousing success.

At the time, however, Berlin had reservations about Ezra's involvement and the whole idea of *Salvo*. Berlin feared it would take the edge off his new musical and even "steal some of his thunder." But Ezra convinced him that it was only a one-night stand and that he could use this show to spot potential talent for the larger project.

In the weeks before the rehearsals for *This Is the Army*, later dubbed *TITA*, Ezra spent much of his off-duty time in Berlin's dark, walnut-paneled office at 52nd Street and 7th Avenue. At each session the songwriter came up with new ideas, snatches of lyrics, and stage business. "He acted them out for me," Ezra remembered, "playing all the parts and singing all the songs," as he sat at one of his three famous gearshift pianos, which he referred to as his "Buicks." This special instrument transposed his basic F-sharp melodies into other keys. Berlin never touched the white keys, as they had the vital function of serving to hold his burning cigarettes. He was at that time a chain-smoker. So tarnished were some of the keys, that they had little resemblance to the originals.

Berlin's talents as a salesman equaled his genius as a composer and lyricist. At one point in the organizational process, word came from Phillipson's office that his superiors in Washington, D.C., wished to hear a progress report.

Asking Berlin to audition his wares to untrained ears came as somewhat of a surprise. Berlin, however, had written flops in the past, and the army wanted to have no association with failures. Although this made Berlin terribly nervous, he consented to perform for the military brass. Ezra arranged to have one of the "Buicks" trucked to General Phillipson's office, where Berlin was to perform a one-man version of the completed songs from *TITA* while Ezra was to stand by his side describing the scenes.

While driving in from Camp Upton to Governor's Island, Berlin switched the entire show, number by number, from army to navy — just in case the army brass turned him down. After hearing a few numbers, however, Phillipson eagerly requested more, not knowing that Berlin had played all he had written. Undaunted, the composer began improvising tunes and ad-libbing lyrics. Ezra was probably the only person in the room who realized that Berlin was creating the material as he went along. The army officials liked what they heard, and Mr. Berlin and now Staff Sergeant Stone went back to their chores.

All the work Ezra and his crew had accomplished in the theater section, which had moved from Governor's Island to 90 Church Street, was wonderful preparation for *TITA*. The technical staff at headquarters easily took to the task of organizing men, equipment, and rehearsal and performance space for Berlin's show.

Ezra and two clerks immediately began transferring approximately one hundred soldiers to Camp Upton. They attempted to use men who had previously worked with them, and Ezra requisitioned several outstanding acts he had spotted during his two tours of various camps. Still, they needed over two hundred more theater artists and technicians, and they had the entire army from which to draw. How to find the cream of the crop among that talent was a problem.

Ezra devised a questionnaire that, by special orders from Washington, had to be printed in every post, camp, and station newspaper across the country. Theatrical unions also provided Ezra with the names of their members in the service, and questionnaires went directly to them. The actors, musicians, and other artists and technicians filled in the forms with information about professional and educational background and physical description. "The trick was that they did not have to be returned via army channels but could be forwarded directly by each man to me at our *TITA* detachment office at Upton," Ezra explained. "No local C.O. or S.S.O. could stonewall it or my orders for transfer of the selected soldiers to our unit."

Neither Ezra nor Berlin had ever cast a show by mail order, but under the circumstances they had no alternative.

After five or six weeks, Berlin had completed various smaller projects and turned his full attention to the musical. Ezra, in the meantime, had begun to assemble the necessary men, so the next logical step was to arrange for office and sleeping quarters at Camp Upton. On the base there existed a series of CCC barracks, originally WWI army barracks, located in an isolated area known affectionately as "Dusty Acres." Barrack number

T-11 was located close to the post headquarters, where Ezra received his orders and mail; therefore, they decided that this barrack was best suited to house Berlin, Ezra, and his production staff.

T-11 consisted of a dayroom with a big fieldstone fireplace at one end and a long corridor with individual noncom rooms on each side. The latrine and shower room, with a large coal stove to heat the water, was at the opposite end of the hallway.

The largest of the small rooms along the passageway became the official *TITA* headquarters. Ezra arranged for Berlin to sleep in the largest noncom room. Milton "Rosie" Rosenstock shared a room with a copyist, who worked on the music. Johnny Koenig and his drafting board stayed in one room, where all subsequent scenic designs originated. Alan Anderson and Peter Feller, the master carpenter, shared an office space, and Ezra had one of the smaller rooms to sleep in. The men took out a wall between two small rooms and converted the larger space into an office for Ezra and two clerks.

While the company awaited the transfer of the selected performers, the composer continued to work on the music while Ezra's writing staff — Richard Burdick, James MacColl, and Jimmy Shirl — worked on the smaller dialogue portions of the script. Berlin often worked through the night banging away on his gearshift piano, which Ezra had ordered moved into a dayroom.

On one particular evening, while Ezra tried to relax in his room, he listened to Berlin for hours repeating the same musical phrases from "Puttin' on the Ritz." Following these lengthy evening sessions, the composer usually slept late, but on this particular morning, he woke up rather early. He said to Ezra, who had been up for some time, "As soon as it opens, get me my publishing house office. Get me Helmy on the phone." Ezra knew right away that the Irving Berlin Music Company opened at ten o'clock and that Helmy Kresa worked as his music secretary. "I've got the number for the colored boys," as he called them. "I finished it this morning."

As instructed, Ezra rang Helmy precisely at ten. The phone in T-11, however, was located in the clerk's office around the corner from the dayroom, and the cord did not reach the piano. Therefore, Ezra held the receiver around the door while Berlin yelled instructions and played the song into the receiver. When the composer had finished, Ezra confirmed that Helmy had clearly heard the music and thus concluded the conversation. After lunch that day, Helmy returned a phone call to T-11 and played the number for his boss, who immediately made corrections or changes.

Thus Ezra quickly learned Berlin's unorthodox and untrained method of music composition.

During these early stages, Berlin and Ezra became relatively close. "I would pick Berlin up at his house on East 63rd off 5th Avenue, and we'd drive all the way out to Upton on a Sunday night," Ezra said. "We worked in our little CCC barracks Monday through Friday afternoon, and I'd drive him back to his house." Sometimes when Ezra arrived at Berlin's home on Sunday, the composer invited him upstairs to hear a number he had written over the weekend. On one occasion, Berlin wanted to meet Sara, so he took the couple through Chinatown's back alleys where he had once worked as a singing waiter at Nigger Mike's.

Because Berlin had been stationed at Camp Upton during World War I, he knew the area. Berlin hated army food, so every night he and Ezra left the post and went to various local restaurants for dinner and drinks. Berlin loved martinis, and they had to be made a specific way. "The numbers of times I'd watch him go back to the bar with the bartender to teach him how to make a suitable martini," Ezra recalled. "We became very close."

But all the while Ezra noticed in Berlin an uptight and paradoxical personality; the composer always seemed on the defensive. On one particular Sunday evening as they drove from Berlin's house to Camp Upton, two incidents occurred that confirmed Ezra's suspicions. While driving, Berlin refused to let Ezra play the radio. On this night, however, as Ezra waited in the car for Berlin to return from the rest room, he tuned in a local station.

As Berlin walked toward the car, he heard Ezra singing along with George Gershwin's song, "Mine." Before he could stop himself, Ezra said, "That's my favorite song." Berlin then asked why he liked it. Ezra thought for a moment, then explained, "Well, I guess because of the countermelody and lyrics; it has two melodies and two sets of lyrics, and it's unique." "It's an old trick," the songwriter retorted. "I've done it years before Gershwin had ever thought of it." Incidentally, after the war Ezra noted that Berlin's last great song, "You're Just in Love," from the musical *Call Me Madam*, produced and directed by George Abbott and starring young Russell Nype and Ethel Merman, maintained two melodies and two lyrics.

To break the monotony of the long trip back to camp, the two men often stopped for a hamburger and a beer at Huntington Inn in Huntington, Long Island. On this particular Sunday as they pulled away from the inn, Berlin said, "Ezra, I want your opinion. I've finished the lyrics to "I Left My Heart at the Stage Door Canteen." Ezra certainly knew that Berlin had been working on a ballad for the canteen number, which was to be introduced during the minstrel show in the first half hour and then reprised during the opening of the second act. "Let me sing it to you," he said. Berlin loved to sing his own songs. He began, "I left my heart at the stage door canteen. I left it there with a girl named Irene. I . . . ." He stopped. "Irene?

What do you think of that name for the girl?" "Well, I'm prejudiced, Mr. Berlin," responded Ezra, "because one of my favorite school class companions was a girl named Irene." "What was her last name," he asked? "Godowski," said Ezra. She was the daughter of Leah Liebewitz and Leopold Godowski, an eminent concert pianist. Berlin thought a moment, then asked, "Russian Jews?" "I guess so," said Ezra. "Well, that's what I thought, the name's too foreign. It's not American enough, so I'll change it to Eileen."

The next morning, when a clerk delivered the mail to Ezra in *TITA* headquarters, he opened an envelope containing a lead-sheet of music. Ezra could not read music, but he plainly saw the title — "I Left My Heart at the Stage Door Canteen" — and the lyrics, which mentioned a girl named Irene.

As Ezra came out of his office, he saw Berlin at the end of the hall coming out of his room. "Stop!" yelled the composer. "I don't want to see it. You obviously got some mail which contained some music. Call Matt Behrman, my lawyer, and he'll give you the language of a form letter that you're to send to anybody who submits material." The letter — to be signed and returned by Ezra — was a disclaimer stating that Mr. Berlin never looked at unsolicited material. At the time, Ezra did not question the order, but he clearly noted the rather conspicuous similarities.

Their first head-to-head confrontation came when Berlin decided to use the same opening that he had written for *Yaphank*. The scene called for 110 white minstrels wearing blackface, to which Ezra, Rosie, and Johnny Koenig objected. True, Berlin was a genius at delivering what the public would buy at any given time, and the jingoistic tone of *Yaphank*, with its superpatriotic approach was right and proper for that period, but to Ezra and his staff the blackfaced minstrels seemed outmoded and racist.

"The sinful stereotype factor and tastelessness did not sway him," Ezra wrote in an editorial comment. "I finally won the battle only because I convinced him that I'd never have the time to get all those guys out of the blackface paint for the rest of the show. It was bad enough having the dancers in blackface for the 'Mandy' number, which was also in *Yaphank*."

Ezra and his staff were also disturbed by some of the racial slurs found in several of the other numbers.

Ezra later persuaded Berlin to cut "That Russian Winter," "Aryans Under the Skin," and "We're Ladies of the Chorus" from the show in preview performances — not because of content but because the show was running a half-hour too long. He was not able to influence the racist lyrics in "That's What the Well-Dressed Man in Harlem Will Wear." "In their main sequence the zoot-suited black soldiers, made up as for a minstrel show, strut through a stereotypical Harlem set with 'Dixie's' beauty show and the 'Orchid Club' gin mill," wrote Clayton R. Koppes and Gregory D. Black in their article, "Blacks, Loyalty, and Motion-Picture Propaganda in World War II." They report,

> One man mimics playing a cello while a woman wearing an absurd costume with a garter above the knee and a big flower on a hat performs a crudely suggestive dance. Since this is an all-male revue, the soldiers dress in drag when women are needed. White GIs don the garb of Little Bo Peep and southern belles; black soldiers are done up as whores and tramps. The blacks break into the inevitable tap dance and, displaying a stereotypical sense of rhythm, dance circles around the white hoofers — figuratively, of course, for *TITA* is as segregated as the real army of democracy.

After rehearsing at Camp Upton for a month, the company of *TITA* moved into the city for the final month. According to Richard S. Burdick's autobiography, the men were decentralized and lived in simple accommodations—their per diem pay being only $2.75. But they were generally content, for "no one was shooting at us." "Rehearsals were held at three separate locations, and we drilled in the Armory at Sixty-first Street and Tenth Avenue and in an adjoining empty lot," wrote Burdick. "Sometimes we would have parade drill down Tenth Avenue and civilians lining the sidewalks would applaud as we passed by in formation; men stood at attention and women were seen to dab their eyes with hankies." It did not take long, however, for spectators to realize that these men were not on their way to board a troopship but merely marching to rehearsal.

For Ezra and Berlin, however, conflicts began to escalate. The show was scheduled to open on July 4, 1942, and many times the deadline seemed impossible to meet.

"He was a worrywart, always figured out the worst things that could happen," Ezra recalled. The director had chosen Rosenstock, a former assistant conductor of the Brooklyn Symphony Orchestra who had conducted all the musical revues for Ezra at Camp Upton, to be the musical director and conductor of the *TITA* orchestra. Although Rosie and his group were the first unit ready for performance, Berlin began to doubt his abilities.

Subsequently Berlin decided that Rosenstock had neither the experience nor the talent to conduct his score. The composer then asked his old friend, Frank Tours, to fly in from California to observe the operation. Naturally upset, Ezra kept this maneuver a secret from Rosie. When Tours heard the orchestra, however, he informed Berlin that Rosenstock knew more about music than he did and that he could not improve on an already fine piece of work. Tours returned to Los Angeles that same day.

That simple episode marked the beginning of a series of major confrontations that would eventually divide the loyalties of the cast between the composer and the director.

Sometime during the early creative process, Berlin had decided that Ezra, a self-confessed nonsinger, must have a song in the production. At the time Staff Sergeant Stone and Captain "Dixie" French, the commanding officer of the theater section at 90 Church St., were bickering. French, who had Broadway theater experience as a company manager but had never done anything creative, continuously expressed opinions concerning Ezra's artistic decisions. Ezra was defensive about his choices, which made him in French's eyes a nonconformist who refused to obey military orders.

Although their struggle was an inside joke, Berlin believed he could turn the ongoing mutual disenchantment into a funny musical number called "My Captain and Me Are Buddies." Ezra rehearsed the number, but it simply did not work. No one in rehearsal laughed at the song. Berlin finally relented to Ezra's urging and composed another song for him. Entitled "The Army's Made a Man Out of Me," Ezra was to be backed by Sergeant Phil Truex, Private Julie Oshins, and a vocal chorus of 110 men.

However, a problem arose concerning the ending of Ezra's new number. Berlin allowed the song to trail off inconclusively. He knew the song needed a coda, vocal and orchestral, to end so the singers would elicit applause on their exit, but he was too busy to finish it. In desperation, Ezra approached Rosenstock, Robin, and Lynn Murray, a top radio choral arranger and composer, to help him find a suitable ending for his song. But just as they completed their work, Berlin walked onstage and heard Ezra singing words he had not written. He rushed over to the piano and ripped apart the pages recently completed by Robin and Murray. "It has always been and always will be, 'Words and Music by Irving Berlin!' And nobody else!"

The next day, Berlin presented Ezra with his own version of the ending, a coda very much like Robin and Murray's creation. The completed song worked well, but the relationship between the two men had been further damaged.

The next struggle between Ezra and Berlin concerned the staging of the finale. Berlin intended to end the show with "God Bless America." Following this, he wanted the men to file down the steps of the stage and through the audience and out the front of the house singing "We're on Our Way to France," a song popularized in *Yaphank*. He planned for the men to wear combat gear, helmets, rifles, and light packs, which he hoped would bring the audience to tears. Women in the audience would cry, he predicted, believing that during every performance a different crew would do the show and immediately leave on a troopship for Europe or the South

Pacific. Ezra, however, did not like this idea, because he thought it merely imitated the former show. More importantly, he believed the audiences of the forties were too sophisticated for such cheap theatrics and that no one would believe these men were leaving for combat directly from the theater.

A private battle of wills ensued, and every few days Berlin asked his director when he intended to stage the number. Ezra avoided the issue by explaining that Bill Horne, the operatic tenor chosen to be the soloist, and the men all knew "God Bless America." He would stage "We're on Our Way to France" after they had learned the new material. During the final week of rehearsal, when Ezra still had not staged the number, Berlin again approached him. This time Ezra explained his objections, maintaining that "We're on Our Way to France" did not at that moment seem relevant to World War II. Reluctantly, Berlin wrote a new finale.

"This Time" was the largest number in the entire stage production, and Ezra had only a few days to coordinate the words and movements of the entire cast. To expedite rehearsals, he devised a military gimmick: as a higher ranking soldier, he could bring the entire company to attention. He then called individual platoons to stand at parade rest, which meant they could stand at ease but without speaking. He and the choreographer then worked with one or two platoons at a time, finally developing a march in time to the music.

The final effect greatly pleased Ezra, who later explained his technique as follows:

> I had Platoon One march in a circle on the stage level and then up onto the first level in time to the music with their bayonets fixed on their Enfield Rifles at shoulder arms . . . the platoon below them also with fixed bayonets walked the opposite direction. Other platoons were doing the same thing on a higher level. So it gave the illusion of a continuous line of cross-bayonets, one on a level higher than the other. . . . Out front, it looked like an endless chain of soldiers going up a mountainside.

To complete the effect, Ezra instructed his lighting designer, Lieutenant John Koenig, to light the number in a way that hid the soldiers' faces in darkness. Ezra did not want the audience to see actors, singers, and dancers but only infantrymen in full gear on their way to battle.

As Ezra had feared, Berlin did not like his staging, and he imported John Murray Anderson, Flo Ziegfeld's top lighting designer and director, to doctor the finale. But just as Tours had vindicated Rosenstock, Anderson informed Berlin that the number was already extremely effective. His one suggestion was that they change the gel color in the lights, a recommendation that Ezra readily accepted since it intensified his desired effect to highlight the steel bayonets and metal helmets.

Similarly, Berlin also brought in Moss Hart to doctor the most outstanding performance segment of the show, the Hollywood canteen number, in which Burl Ives sat reading a newspaper throughout the entire twelve-minute scene. After rehearsal, a few of the men, including Burdick, Hart, and Ezra went into the greenroom to chat. "I don't really quite understand why Irving brought me in," Hart said. That's in very good shape." He felt that he might have contributed a couple of laughs but nothing substantial. Later at lunch, Hart continued with "Ezra, I just don't feel that it was necessary for me to have come in and improve upon what you've already done."

The conflict between Ezra and Berlin was now open and obvious to the entire company. Having brought in Tours, Anderson, and Hart indicated Berlin's lack of confidence in Ezra's work. Berlin also solicited a response from Broadway director Josh Logan. Ezra was humiliated. He was more than hurt. Berlin had wounded him, and the wound did not heal.

In an interview Dick Burdick said, "My feeling was that it was like an injured animal, and if you approach it, it fights back." Throughout his life, if Ezra sensed any injustice, he had a tendency to expose it. In this case, he turned almost violent in his reaction. "So I felt that he harbored this justifiable resentment," continued Burdick. "It festered, and he built upon it."

Despite mounting tensions, rehearsals continued as scheduled. The day before their first preview, Ezra took time to stage the curtain call. Following the finale, Ezra and the actor playing the company commander walked to center stage and called the company to attention and to shoulder arms.

Upon command, the whole unit presented a short manual of arms, which was visually and audibly very effective— especially with 110 gun bolts simultaneously being opened and closed for the inspection of arms. While the company faced the audience and held the present arms mode, Ezra and the company commander saluted the audience. Ezra then called them back to parade rest. After doing this sequence a second time, the soldiers turned left to present arms to Berlin, who appeared downstage left in his World War I uniform and campaign hat. Ezra then saluted Berlin before commanding the company to address the audience for the last time.

As Ezra finished staging the call and was about to release the company, Berlin asked what had happened to "God Bless America." Ezra perceived the song to be anticlimactic, but out of a sense of duty to Berlin he inserted it at the beginning of the curtain call. Although beautifully sung, the song could not match the power of "This Time" and failed miserably in previews. Berlin grudgingly relented and cut it from the show, but he later reinserted it into the film with Kate Smith singing and Ezra's old friend from *The Aldrich Family*, Jack Miller, conducting.

The feud between Stone and Berlin was put on hold while *TITA* opened on July 4, 1942, at the Broadway Theatre. The packed house paid up to $27.50 for the privilege of attending. The production raised more than forty-five thousand dollars on opening night for the Army Emergency Relief, a nonmilitary organization, now headed by General Phillipson and established to give prompt financial help and other short-term assistance to all soldiers and their dependents. Relief took the form of money or aid in kind, such as fuel, hospitalization, medical and dental care, other emergency services such as assistance with reemployment, allotments, and insurance. Several sources reported that Kate Smith had paid ten thousand dollars for two tickets to the opening night performance. No one at the time knew, but Ezra paid out of his own pocket five thousand dollars for Governor and Mrs. Lehman's tickets. Of opening night Ezra wrote,

> The audience was expectant but skeptical. They had paid high prices for their seats. . . . It had better be good. Before long we knew they thought it was. Joe Lipman's magnificent arrangement for the overture, played by the entire orchestra under Rosenstock's direction, received a tremendous ovation. There was another spontaneous salvo of applause when the curtains parted to reveal a living backdrop of two hundred men on the minstrel stands. Then in turn, "Stumpy" Cross and the Harlem number, Eddie Barclift's dancing, Jimmy MacColl's impersonations, Alan Manson as Jane Cowl, and the Allon Trio, all brought down the house. We finished the second act and took our curtain calls in a golden glow. We had a hit.

Critics unanimously gave Irving Berlin, Ezra Stone, and *This Is the Army* high marks. Richard Watts, Jr., of the *New York Herald Tribune* wrote,

> *This Is the Army* is not merely a magnificent soldier show. It is one of the greatest musical shows of any description ever produced in this country. To Irving Berlin, who wrote it; to Ezra Stone, who directed it; to all of the soldiers who are in any way participating in it and to the United States Army which was intelligent enough to realize the value of such a production to the wartime spirit of all of us, there must go more credit than it is possible to set down here.

"Under the uniforms, beneath the military decorum, there is an abundance of life in this show," wrote Brooks Atkinson of the *Times*. "It leaves the audience in a glow of enjoyment and loyalty. . . . He has contributed another memorable show to the genius of America." "Perhaps Sergeant Stone deserves even more praise than the indefatigable Mr. Berlin, for the most winning thing about *This Is the Army* is a swift and sustained tempo, which succeeds admirably in keeping the audience in an Oliver Twist mood until the final curtain," wrote Harry Lorin Binsse of the *Commonweal*. "As wise an ingredient as any in the Stone recipe is what seems to be a rule against encores, for which strong-mindedness audiences should be, if they are not, properly grateful." Perhaps the highest praise came from Kyle Crichton of *Collier's Magazine* when he claimed that, "the American theater has never known a greater success."

As described in Burdick's autobiography, following most performances, film, stage, and sports luminaries, political figures, and War Department brass visited the men back stage. There was much ogling of the men dressed as chorus girls "with their provocative, gossamer costumes, their soft, flowing coiffeurs, and deceptive ersatz bosoms. Some of the guys were absolutely stunning."

> Ty Perry, uncannily impersonated the great stage star and beauty, Lynn Fontanne. He was greatly abetted by realistic makeup, an ivory-colored pillbox hat with a matching shroud that draped in back to his shoulders, and a long, clinging jersey gown. One night during intermission, a celebrated four-star general came backstage to chat with Irving Berlin. He detoured to the men's room, and as he opened the door, Ty, in full costume, was in process of hoisting his skirt at the urinal. "Oh, my God, excuse me!" the general gasped, and quickly made a smart retreat.

After three highly successful months on Broadway, *TITA* moved to Baltimore to break in the touring production. While there, Staff Sergeant Stone, protesting his unit being detached without proper ratings and having to live on a WWI per diem rate for lodging, food, laundry, and transportation, formally requested transfer to a combat unit. When General Phillipson learned of his request, he came up to Baltimore, took over a dressing room, and summoned Ezra to report to him.

At the doorway, Ezra saluted and stood at attention. The general always laughed at Ezra's salutes and never bothered returning the gesture. "What are you doing to me, Ezra," he sighed. The staff sergeant then told his superior officer that if what his men were doing was important and needed, then they should be set up with ratings and a proper per diem. Phillipson told Ezra to trust him, and he went to work. A couple of weeks later, during the first week of October, army officials organized the company of *TITA* into two separate military police units, which meant that they received ratings for two first sergeants, four or five master sergeants, six or seven tech sergeants, and so on down the line. The administration justified its actions by pointing to the army's intention of eventually sending the show overseas. The logical plan was to break the company into two tab units rather than send one large and cumbersome unit, which would be more costly both in manpower and gear. Berlin was to head one of the units, while Ezra was to be in charge of the other.

From Baltimore, the troupe traveled to the National Theatre in Washington, D.C., the second stop on its nationwide thirteen-city tour, which included stops in Pittsburgh, Philadelphia, Boston, Cleveland, Cincinnati, St. Louis, Detroit, Chicago, and eventually also in San Francisco and Los Angeles. Even before the show left Manhattan, theater patrons in the nation's capital had purchased every available seat. A *New York Times'* reporter wrote, "A portable box office was set up opposite the theater, and as early as 7 o'clock this morning lines started forming. Most of the day a double line stretched the length of the block."

Reportedly, the opening in Washington on Tuesday, September 29, was attended by more top military brass than any previous theatrical event. The following day, General George C. Marshall, chief of staff, penned a letter to Berlin, which was later published in several newspapers, praising *This Is the Army*:

> Last night you and the cast of your show faced perhaps as critical an audience as you will find on your tour. In the ovation which you received I hope you found some measure of reward for the great talent and tireless effort which all of you have devoted to *This Is the Army*. . . . In addition to expressing my appreciation to you for contributing to Army Emergency Relief and for providing an effective stimulus for civilian morale, I thank you for an electrifying evening in the theatre.

During the show's Broadway run, Eleanor Roosevelt took a particular interest in *TITA*. On several occasions, while her sons visited her on a furlough, she took them to see a performance. "I used to get a kick out of standing in the wings and peeking out and watching her reaction to the show that she'd seen three or four times by then," Ezra later told a group of Rotary members. "She'd be watching the acting on stage, and then when she knew that there was a particularly funny thing going to happen, out of the corner of her eye, she'd watch whichever son was accompanying her to enjoy his reaction."

Sometime during the first week of their engagement in Washington, Mike Reilly of the Secret Service in the White House pulled Ezra to the corner of the stage and said, "There's some rumblings going on about the old man coming to see this show." President Roosevelt was notably fond of attending the theater but for security reasons had forgone this pleasure since the United States had entered the war. It was also a well-known fact that presidents had particularly poor luck attending theaters in that city. Reilly said, "I'd like to ask you a few questions about it to see if we can iron out the details." His inquiry mostly concerned logistics, especially those involving the 110 Enfield rifles used in the finale of the show. Having the guns twenty feet away from the commander in chief of the United States understandably caused him some anxiety. Ezra explained that if he looked closely he would find some of the original Cosmoline on most of the rifles, and the actors naturally did not use live ammunition. Still, Reilly said that his men would have to inspect every gun prior to the performance.

The KP sketch that occurred in the beginning of the show also concerned Reilly. In it Ezra directed Hank Henry, a wonderful burlesque comic, to enter from stage right holding a meat cleaver and cross to another GI who was peeling potatoes on stage left. Reilly asked Ezra, "How well do you know this guy, Hank Henry?" "Oh, he's a wonderful guy," Ezra responded. Reilly then said, "Have you ever heard him say anything derogatory about the president?" Ezra quickly rebutted with, "No! What's your problem?" "Well, he's gonna be standing there about five feet from where the president is going to be seated," Reilly explained. "He's doing a lot of waving around with that meat cleaver." Understanding his apprehension, Ezra said, "Forget it—it's out. We'll give him a turkey leg." Incidentally, the turkey leg actually worked better than the meat cleaver; it got a much bigger laugh and stayed in the show for the rest of the run.

Following this routine interrogation, it was decided that the company would put on a command performance for the president, a special matinee, the audience of which would be made up entirely of military service personnel from the Washington area. Reilly and his men took over security in the theater as soon as the curtain dropped on Wednesday, October 7, the eve of the command performance. They inspected every rifle, and Reilly had men posted in the projection booth, the orchestra pit, backstage, and in the front of the house.

A member of the audience later said that they [the audience] were scared to death that day because most of them were "desk jockeys" from the Coast Guard, the navy, the marines, and the army. Without explanation, they received orders to report to a convoy of busses. They thought they were going overseas. After a short ride on a bright, sunny day, the sixteen hundred hand-picked soldiers found themselves sitting in a theater. This, they assumed, must be part of a briefing concerning some superior, secret troop movement in which they were to be involved. Even when the orchestra moved into place, the men still could not shake this belief. When the pit orchestra went into the flourishes and rumbles and the house left exit door opened over the stage box revealing the commander in chief, however, they realized that this special event was intended for their benefit. A surge of applause swept through the house as the president waved to the troops. Later during the intermission, the soldier orchestra played "Home on the Range," which had been publicized as one of the president's favorite songs.

Throughout the show, President Roosevelt obviously had a good time, as the actors could hear his laughter above that of the large audience. He made a point of continuing his ovation after each number—even as the majority of the audience's applause began to dwindle. "He just kept clap-ping," Ezra recalled. "Everybody looked up, so we got two rounds of ap-plause because of his showmanship."

Although they were certainly aware of his presence, the performers made no direct reference to their distinguished guest until after the final curtain, when the entire company, with fixed bayonets, presented arms and the orchestra gave a ruffle and flare of drums. When the performance concluded, Ezra heard the president say in reference to the honor units of uniformed men present, "This is the greatest audience that has ever been assembled . . . and the greatest show."

During an earlier intermission break, Reilly had come into Ezra's dressing room and asked, "How'd you like to meet the old man?" Ezra thought that he certainly was not going to receive that invitation every day of his life, so he responded with, "I sure would. When?"

After the finale, Reilly took Ezra by the hand through the pass door on stage right where one of his men identified and cleared both Ezra and him. By the time they ascended the stairs, the door to the alley had already been opened. Only a short distance from Ezra sat President Franklin D. Roosevelt—hat on and his cigarette in the cigarette holder at the well-known angle. Beside him stood a lady and a couple of military aides, while John Roosevelt pushed his father's wheelchair. With little hesitation, Reilly pulled Ezra toward the commander in chief and said, "Mr. President, I'd like you to meet Ezra Stone." As he had been taught in basic training, the intimidated soldier-actor inexpertly snapped to a salute. Like General Phillipson, the president did not return the gesture. Ezra did not know whether to drop his hand, scratch his head, or simply hold it in position. After an awkward moment, Roosevelt half-heartedly signaled for him to relax.

Though Ezra was only 5'3", he had to look down upon the president. He was extremely jovial, but Ezra noticed that the powerful man looked strangely at him and seemed to study his face. Roosevelt said some com-plimentary things about the show and that Eleanor was right to make him come to see it and get away from all the problems in the White House. He then turned to Admiral William Leahy, his top military aide, and said, "Oh, you know we're having the whole company over this evening for supper." By that time, Ezra knew that White House staff had scheduled the dinner for Friday night, not Thursday. He therefore faced a protocol problem— should he correct the president of the United States or should he simply show up both nights? He opted to say nothing and simply show up at the scheduled time. Small talk followed, and then Ezra watched John Roose-velt wheel his father toward the limousine.

Following Friday's performance, the column of 310 men formed and marched eight or nine blocks to the White House. The men entered through the eastern entrance, and marched up the marble stairs to the Great Hall. As Master Sergeant Stone finally turned the corner into the large room, he captured his first glimpse of the reception line, which consisted of the president, wearing a dinner jacket and seated in a carved high chair, Eleanor Roosevelt, who wore an evening gown, and two military aides. Every man, from the lowest private to the highest ranking officer in the column was introduced by name to the president.

As Ezra approached he said, "I'm sure you're glad to see me, Mr. President—I'm the last man in the formation." Roosevelt laughed and then turned to his wife and said, "Eleanor, this was the strangest looking soldier I've ever seen in my life." Ezra then understood the strange look that he had received from the president in the alley following the matinee performance. He had been in battle dress for the finale of the show, complete with side arms, but he had also been in full stage makeup, which in the sunlight turned a vivid orange. He had also donned red lipstick and shadow over his eyes. "You could well imagine that the president had never seen any of his soldiers looking like that," Ezra laughed.

The first full week of October 1942 represented the biggest week in Ezra's young life. Not only did he receive a promotion to master sergeant, open a show in the nation's capital, play before F.D.R. in a command performance, and attend a special White House dinner, but he and Sara were married. Sol Feinstone still did not approve of Ezra's relationship with Sara; therefore, the young couple had made plans for a secret wedding.

At the time, Sara was appearing on Broadway at the Plymouth Theatre in *Vickie*, starring Jose Ferrer and Uta Hagen, with Red Buttons and John Forsythe in smaller roles. The company played two performances on Sundays and remained dark on Mondays. Meanwhile at the National Theatre in Washington, Ezra and the cast of *TITA* were dark on Sundays. Once again to save money, Ezra bunked with his old friend Charles Moos, now a young lawyer in the Department of Labor.

On Monday, October 5, Ezra picked up Sara at Union Station around 3:00 P.M. and took a cab to the home of Judge Mattingly, a justice of the peace brought out of retirement to handle the wartime wedding traffic. Ezra later joked that he was literally hooked, for Mattingly had no right hand—just a hook. All necessary paperwork and arrangements had been taken care of beforehand by Charles on a pro bono basis. The couple pulled up in front of Mattingly's home in Chevy Chase, where Ezra told the cab driver to wait. They were only going to be married, and they would be right back.

A few minutes later, Mattingly rattled off the official words, while looking at the marriage license for their names: "Do you, E. C. Feinstone take Sara Frances Seegar. . . ." Suddenly, Ezra realized that his everpresent Marsh Wheeling stogie was still in his mouth. When he took a step away to place it on the judge's mantle with the ash end safely hanging over the edge, the judge's hook shot out to Ezra's wrist and drew him back to the marrying marks in time for the "I do's." Mattingly signed the papers, collected his fee and one for his wife, who served as witness. Ezra grabbed his still lit cigar, and he and Sara promptly returned to the waiting cab.

The newlyweds had a quick dinner at the Shoreham before Sara dropped him off at the stage door of the National just in time for the half-hour call. She then checked into the Willard Hotel, just down the street from the theater. She was supposed to leave a message with their room number with the stage doorman, but Ezra never received the note. The couple almost spent their wedding night separately, for Sara had registered as Mr. and Mrs. Feinstone. Upon arrival, Ezra Stone had a difficult time persuading the hotel night manager that he was E. C. Feinstone. Ezra finally coaxed him into calling his wife to verify his identity. Tuesday morning, Sara boarded the train to Manhattan so that she could perform in *Vickie* that evening, while Ezra had to report to the Ellipse by the Washington Monument for drill and calisthenics.

Meanwhile, the feud between Ezra and Berlin, after having been in temporary remission, had erupted again during the final curtain call of the command performance. For this matinee, Ezra had first presented arms to the military personnel in the audience. Then on cue, he ordered the company to turn right to address President Roosevelt. Finally, they turned left to present arms to Berlin. This special curtain call had not been rehearsed; Ezra merely directed the men from the stage. But he apparently did not ask Berlin to delay his entrance, which usually came directly after the company addressed the audience. Just as the composer walked on stage for his bow, the entire company, following Master Sergeant Stone's orders, was turning away from him toward the president.

"Berlin thought that I had screwed him on purpose in the presence of the president," Ezra recalled. "I tried to explain to him that it was a last minute sudden realization on my part, that I hadn't acknowledged the presence of the president. In retrospect, what the hell was he so mad about? Shouldn't he have been proud to have come out of the wings and salute the president too?" But Berlin never thought that way; with him it was always Berlin first and foremost.

The next minor incident between Ezra and Berlin occurred in Philadelphia, the third stop of their national tour. Before one of his performances, Virginia Davis, an ex-girlfriend from Oak Lane Country Day School, invited Ezra to dine with her family in Center City, just a few blocks from their host theater. After the meal, Hilda Davis, Virginia's mother, proudly displayed her recent birthday gift, a signed manuscript of George Gershwin's "Bess, You Is My Woman Now" from his folk opera *Porgy and Bess*. Upon his return to Mastbaum Theatre, Ezra excitedly told a group of his friends what he had just seen. He did not realize, however, that Berlin stood behind the door of his dressing room and overheard the story. From the other room Ezra and the others heard, "What's so wonderful about that? To put it down on paper just takes a musical secretary. That doesn't take any talent; it's like typing a letter." Apparently, Berlin thought that Ezra was belittling him for being musically illiterate. Many people, including Ezra, ascribed Berlin's deep-rooted inferiority complex to this. While Berlin continued this particular tirade, Ezra and his friends simply stood in befuddled amazement.

St. Louis at the time was one of the best road stops in the country. Coming from Cincinnati, the company of *TITA* arrived in St. Louis, their eighth city in two and one-half months, on December 13. Tensions had remained high between Ezra and Berlin since Philadelphia, but it was while they were in the Gateway City that their feud culminated in an open war of threats.

Even before they had arrived, Ezra was angry with Berlin about publicity and bookings in St. Louis. In a letter to his parents, Ezra wrote, "Well Berlin and his incompetent advance men insulted these St. Louisians by not even asking their advice or giving them enough time to arrange for ticket sales." As a result, opening night on December 14 in the Municipal Auditorium was ghastly—twelve hundred empty seats, a cold audience, and condescending newspaper reviews. "All of this makes me laugh," Ezra wrote in another letter to his parents. "I warned him of it in New York, and he wasn't very interested."

Within a few days, the conflict came to a head. Laurence Bergreen quotes Alan Manson, a performer who reveled in his opportunity to participate in the cast, "I was very, very upset by the feud between Ezra and Mr. Berlin, . . . I didn't know who was right, but after all, if it weren't for Irving Berlin, we'd all be in the shithouse." In an interview Richard Burdick said, "The company naturally sided with Ezra because we all loved him so much. We respected his professionalism, and we felt he was badly treated. . . . It was my feeling, and everyone else's, that it was Berlin who initiated it."

By this time, the two men were no longer on speaking terms, so Berlin informed First Sergeant Alan Anderson that he intended to reaudition all the nonprincipal and nondancing roles. This frightened the men, for if they left the show, a combat unit was perhaps awaiting them. The performers came to Ezra and pleaded with him to forestall this action. Finally, Ezra urged Anderson and Rosenstock to arrange a conference with Berlin after one of the performances.

At the meeting, Ezra immediately questioned the composer's intentions. Berlin's initial response was, "You put all your friends in the show." Ezra most certainly had a few friends involved with the production but not three hundred. Besides, the director felt that each was a qualified professional who performed his job well. "Are you accusing me of packing the show with my friends?" Ezra asked. "Should we go down the roster and check off those guys who got into this unit in exchange for plugs for the Irving Berlin Music Company?" Berlin flushed when Ezra said he could produce names.

Next, Berlin, a first generation Russian Jew, informed the group that the unit had "too many Jews." He predicted that the American public would criticize them for this. To this accusation Rosie quietly suggested, "Actually, Mr. Berlin, there are more Italians in the orchestra than Jews." All of Berlin's accusations against the company apparently stemmed from his quarrel with Ezra.

Following this incident, Ezra became withdrawn. He sulked about the situation and seemed to divorce himself from the show. "I've been sleeping in the theater as I've wanted to be alone for a while and get some thinking done," he wrote to his parents. "Strangely enough the theater has been the best place. Since everyone dashes madly to get away each night, it is quiet here early and I always had a yen to live in a theater anyway."

From St. Louis, the show moved to the Shrine Auditorium in Detroit on December 20 and played through the holiday week. While there, Ezra, in his customary fashion, sent unusual Christmas cards to the entire company. "Berlin is heard to have said that my sending X-mas cards to all the men was another plan on my part to show him up," Ezra noted in a letter from Detroit. "He just sent one to the company in general which was posted on the board. It was a dull card saying 'May all your days be merry and bright and may all your X-mas' be white'—copyright, Irving Berlin, Inc." This last item became the joke of the company. "I think all the boys appreciated my card, as they came up to thank me, almost to the man, and commented on how clever they thought it was."

Despite the threats and accusations, the company remained intact. *This Is the Army* closed in Chicago on January 16, and the company boarded a slow-moving Union-Pacific train headed for Los Angeles. "We've been traveling since 4:00 A.M. Saturday and have only gone about a thousand miles," Ezra wrote late Monday evening. "Everything passes us, including milk trucks."

Concerned about maintaining the men's morale, Ezra called an informal meeting with Anderson, Rosenstock, and Sara, who traveled with the company aboard the civilian car. They discussed at length Ezra's reconciliation with Berlin. It was decided that Anderson would pave the way. He was to tell Berlin that he felt the so-called feud had now reached such proportions that it was hurting the cast. He would then suggest that Berlin and Ezra should talk matters over.

Later that evening, Ezra penned another letter to his parents.

I will then explain that I felt I was wrong to allow the situation to have continued as it has for so long. That my concern now is for the welfare of the men and the show as I'm sure his is too. That I feel there are certain people who are thriving on the friction between us and perhaps have kept it stimulated, resulting in bad publicity for all concerned.

Ezra, believing Berlin would be rational at this point, planned to explain his fears of being misused professionally in the upcoming motion picture. He also planned to outline his desire to leave the company after the film and secure a commission in Special Services for overseas duty.

The planned meeting between Berlin and Ezra apparently never occurred, and the company arrived in Los Angeles on Wednesday or Thursday of that week. Following some California engagements, *TITA* reached the end of its national tour on February 13, 1943. By this time, the show had exceeded all financial expectations, having earned over two million dollars for Army Emergency Relief.

Soon afterward, the company took root in a Hollywood lot dubbed "Camp TITA." "It is made up of about eight tents and a flagpole and is guarded twenty-four hours a day by soldiers whose guns are too rusty to fire," wrote Sara in a letter to the Feinstones. "I think Gilbert and Sullivan could have made it pay, but it seems a little unnecessary in the middle of the Warner Brothers lot."

Despite the artistic and financial success of the New York production and national tour, Ezra still harbored ill feelings. He loved the men and the show, but Berlin and his faction had wounded him. As shooting began on the film, Berlin significantly reduced Ezra's artistic involvement. Ezra was told that Warner Brothers did not intend to use his name in the billing, which was to include Ronald Reagan, George Murphy, George Tobias, Joan Leslie, Joe Louis, and members of the army. Ezra was also told that Berlin had made some rather nasty unofficial remarks about his ability to some military brass. Berlin reportedly said that Ezra's popularity had slipped and that he was not as funny or important a comedian and actor as he might think.

Finally, when the magazine section of the Sunday *Los Angeles Times* did a spread of pictures from the movie, it credited Irving Berlin with writing and directing the stage version of *This Is the Army*. "I think that in the event of a London and Africa showing he will have my credit completely dropped," Ezra wrote in a prophetic letter to his parents. Although Ezra did not have proof at the time, Irving Berlin did eventually delete his name from all subsequent programs and posters. It was only in 1991 that Ezra could prove this fact. A friend mailed him a Southwest Pacific Area *TITA* program which read: "Entire production staged under the personal direction of Mr. Berlin."

Ezra was so upset by these events in Hollywood as well as the previous confrontations that he decided he wanted his song, "The Army's Made a Man Out of Me," omitted from the movie. Believing the film was too long, Jack Warner quickly agreed to Ezra's proposition.

A short time after this, Ezra had his final encounter with Irving Berlin. "How well I remember how shocked I was when Berlin came up with the new number, 'Dressed Up to Kill,' for the close of the film," Ezra recently wrote. "I found I was not alone in my revulsion." His strongest ally was Private Vance Campbell, who graduated from Princeton Seminary after the war and started his ministry. The two men prompted an opposition campaign against the lyrics to Berlin's song, which suggested that killing was the only path to victory.

Campbell and Ezra planned and executed a strategy that alerted the mass church organizations. Following this, various religious groups sent a great number of telegrams and letters to Warner and Berlin, protesting against the song's lyrics because they could stir up hatred of Jews, blacks, and Japanese in America. People also claimed that the lyrics ran counter to the national philosophy built on the concept of the inalienable rights of all human beings.

Berlin and his supporters argued that the notion of "killing 'til the world is free" fit rather well with the doctrine of unconditional surrender. War, they argued, is not about singing and dancing; it is about killing, death, and the ultimate price of freedom. Although Ezra took a purely moral stance against Berlin's lyrics, some of the *TITA* cast perceived Ezra's attack as his attempt to undermine Berlin and get the final word in this prolonged confrontation.

Due to this pressure, Warner implored Berlin to change the lyrics to "dressed up to win" because "when mass church organizations start after you, you haven't a leg to stand on." In the end, the altered lyrics contradicted the visual display of soldiers poised with bayonets ready to enter into battle, but the effect still opposed what Ezra and the religious groups had attempted to rectify.

It was also during the filming of *This Is the Army* that Ezra—out of moral opposition to another movie—faced possible court-martial. Warner Brothers' newly released *Mission to Moscow* revolved around Ambassador Joseph Davis' kudos to Joseph Stalin. Ezra had long been an anti–Stalinist and signed a petition against the film. Warner's press vice president, Charles Einfield, summoned Ezra to a meeting with him and Ezra's commanding officer, Major Ambrose. In that meeting Ezra was asked to release a statement saying that his name had been used without his permission. He refused. When he was threatened with a court-martial, he said, "Fine! Please do! That'll be fine publicity for our cause of protest."

This Is the Army, the greatest soldier show ever produced, continued to run until the end of the war, but its director left the company after the film. Despite the unbearable feud with Berlin, however, Ezra later recognized *This Is the Army* as a tremendous step in his directing career. "It was my first major organizational challenge as a director," he reminisced. "I virtually produced it also. I didn't raise the money for it, but I was functioning during that period as Berlin's right-hand assistant. . . . It was very important for me."

In March 1944, the War Department hoped to get the majority and minority leaders of the House of Representatives to pass a bill to give congressional recognition to Irving Berlin for his patriotic contributions to the war effort. During an investigation, however, the War Department unearthed information that certain members of the company and relatives of the men in *This Is the Army* resented the drive by Berlin's agents for his glorification under false pretenses. They believed the billing of the show as *Irving Berlin's This Is the Army* was a misrepresentation. They felt he deserved credit for his music but that the rest was entirely a U.S. Army contribution — sponsorship, sketch writing, equipment, orchestra, programs, and administration. They believed it should have been known as *Uncle Sam's This Is the Army*, with songs by Irving Berlin.

From the beginning, however, Berlin had believed that his appearance in the show was necessary to assure its success. "His presence on the center of the stage at each final curtain merely served to deprive the boys in uniform of the applause which was theirs," stated a 1944 memo circulated in the War Department. "On the road he monopolized the publicity and thus deprived the soldiers and the army of credit which rightfully belonged to them. Mr. Berlin went to England in order to get an introduction to royalty which he craved."

Berlin contended that his participation in this project had forced him to sacrifice fantastic sums of money. The memo reported that the soldiers and their relatives considered this to be sheer myth. "Considering his normal vast income and the high tax brackets in which the additional income from the *TITA* songs would have fallen, his actual loss was negligible, surely less than that of many of the soldiers in the company." Moreover, they believed the publicity his press agents gained from his other interests by exploiting his connection with the war effort was worth more to him than any money he might otherwise have earned.

According to the official archives at the Irving Berlin Music Company, in 1945 President Harry S Truman presented Irving Berlin with the U.S. Army's Medal of Merit, its highest award for civilians.

8. The Postwar Transition

Sometime during the filming of the Warner Brother's movie, *This Is the Army*, Berlin heard of and completely rejected the army's plan to split the company into two tab units—one to be headed by him and the other by Ezra. "There's only one *TITA* unit, and that's the one that I will join when I can," he demanded. This meant that the chosen men had to play in every scheduled European and Pacific theater of operation, and the so-called surplus would get transferred to other units. When Ezra realized that Berlin repudiated the army's concept, he immediately went to work to protect his own future. To stay ahead of military red tape, he sent word to his old friend Lieutenant Louis Simon saying that he would be available as soon as the filming was finished. Simon "rescued" Ezra by having him transferred to the Fourth Air Corps and to March Field, located near Riverside, California, about one hundred miles from Los Angeles.

This Is the Army, incidentally, played more than one thousand performances before two and one-half million spectators, and during its worldwide tour the company logged over seventy thousand miles and earned over twelve million dollars for the Army Emergency Relief. It made its final appearance in Honolulu Stadium on October 22, 1945; Berlin, naturally, made special arrangements to appear in the cast.

Meanwhile, Ezra and Sara lived a comfortable life in noncom quarters on the base. Ezra produced and directed several important military productions including *At Your Service, Bonds Away!* and *You Bet Your Life*. Based on McClellan Field, *At Your Service*, like *This Is the Army*, was a revue show of songs and sketches. Written by Richard Burdick, Edward Heyman, and Louis LaFrance, the show was to tour the West Coast and raise money for the Army Athletic and Entertainment Fund. Lieutenant Larry Cotton, formerly the top tenor soloist with Horace Heidt but now working as the public information officer in charge of putting this show together, transferred a dozen or more actors, singers, and dancers from *TITA*, including Ty Perry and Jimmy MacColl, to McClellan Field.

To give the production a strong directorial hand, Cotton arranged for Ezra to be placed on detached service from March Field. "We put together a rousing show. It lacked the sheer size impact of *This Is the Army*, as well as the Berlin songs," wrote Richard Burdick in his autobiography. "But with

Sara Seeger and Ezra Stone at home in March Field, 1945.

a cast of seventy-five seasoned professionals, and Ezra's zestful staging, it had an intimacy and an exuberance that captivated audiences in every city on the West Coast tour."

One weekend while stationed at McClellan Field, Ezra received a three day pass, so he made arrangements to visit Sara, who was pregnant with their first child. A B-25, which had recently received an overhaul,

Ezra and Little Joe "The General," March Field, December 1944.

prepared to take off from McClellan to March Field, so Ezra quickly paraded to the flight line and got himself assigned to that plane. Picking up his parachute, he headed out to the aircraft.

Closely behind Ezra in line stood a sailor trying to hitch a ride down to San Diego. The sailor thought that if he could get as far as March Field, he could hitchhike the rest of his trip. He was granted permission to board the plane, but Ezra had received the last parachute. The sailor decided to take the risk.

Only a skeleton crew boarded the plane—a captain, who was piloting; a first lieutenant, who was copiloting; and a tech sergeant, who served as the crew chief on a flight with no crew. As this was his first flight in a military bomber, Ezra excitedly climbed aboard and looked about. When the plane reached cruising altitude, the crew chief granted Ezra permission to explore the cabin at the back of the plane. To get to the tail, he had to walk along a narrow beam through the bomb bay. There were large signs on the doors located beneath him on either side of the beam warning "DO NOT STEP." Ezra knew the repercussions if he were to slip off the plank, but the roundness of his body and the narrowness of the passage forced him to take off his parachute.

When he had reached the back cabin, Ezra decided to play waist-gunner as he had seen Harry Carey do in the movies. He figured out how to unlatch the port of the waist-gun and how to hinge, fold, and fasten it into the hanging lock in the cabin roof. He was, however, not tall enough to make it catch in the lock, so he concocted a makeshift stepladder out of an empty Coca-Cola crate. While he was standing on the edge of the crate trying to latch the waist-gunner's port, the pilot for some reason decided to turn the plane. Had the box tipped, Ezra probably would have fallen out of the plane.

Suddenly, the sight of the empty bottles that he had taken out of the crate inspired Ezra to some mischievous activity. Realizing that there was a small hole in the plane's belly at the tail-gunner's position ordinarily used for photo reconnaissance, Ezra, in juvenile fashion, began to play bomber by dropping bottles through the opening. At that moment—unbeknownst to Ezra—the crew chief appeared at the bomb bay. "Captain wants you up forward right away," he yelled. Sensing danger, Ezra peered out the window and saw that the outboard motor on the left propeller was absolutely rigid. A line of smoke trailed behind. The plane had four engines, and Ezra sighed with relief when he noticed that the left inboard engine continued to spin without hesitation. He then looked to the right wing and saw the identical situation; the inboard engine spun with regularity while fire consumed the outboard.

Ezra had to make a choice to either put on the parachute and remain in the tail of the plane or run like hell through the bomb bay carrying his parachute. He chose the latter. Once at the front of the plane, Ezra quickly put on his parachute. He looked around and suddenly realized that he was the oldest person on board. The captain and lieutenant were in their early twenties, and the crew chief and the sailor were mere teenagers.

With one engine gone and another burning, the pilot turned the plane around for the final approach. The crew chief ordered the men to prepare themselves to eject. Upon receiving the order to eject, the men would have to exit through the bomb bay. After securing his straps, Ezra noticed that the sailor with no parachute looked at him with a rather desperate gaze. If they received the word to jump, Ezra figured that the sailor would either try to steal the back pack from him or that he would climb aboard and float "piggyback" down to earth.

A thunderous noise suddenly erupted from the plane. In his mind, Ezra knew the aircraft was splitting apart. Navigation maps and other paraphernalia flew about. The crew chief, who busied himself in the cockpit, yelled for Ezra to grab and secure the turret hatch. The lock and the turret gun had flicked open sucking the air downward. As instructed, Ezra grabbed the appropriate lever, while the sailor clutched Ezra to prevent him from falling through the opening. They held this position as the plane approached the runway. Out of the corner of his eye, Ezra caught a glimpse of the landing strip, where a couple of ambulances and fire trucks stood ready to handle the emergency.

Fortunately, they landed without incident. The crew dropped the hatch under the navigator's position allowing three steps to roll to the ground. So low was the small passageway that no adult could get through without kneeling. The captain looked around and began to tick off the order of debarkation. "You better go first Stone, and the medics are right there." Ezra didn't know why he had been chosen to go first, but he did as he was told and crawled under the plane's belly. Immediately, one of the medics, who was a friend of Ezra's from the base hospital, yelled, "Ezra, what the hell happened to you?" "What do you mean?" Ezra responded. "You're all blood. You better lie down."

The medics placed Ezra on a stretcher, carried him to a waiting ambulance, and escorted him to the emergency room — all the while searching for his wound. A goodly amount of blood soaked Ezra's shirt, so the medics assumed the injury was severe. Following a thorough inspection, they deduced that Ezra had sustained no injuries. During the incident, the sailor had gotten cut, and it was his blood that covered Ezra's clothing.

A couple of months after the tour of *At Your Service*, Ezra engaged Burdick — and others — to write another show. *Bonds Away!* was a touring show for the Fourth Air Corps in cooperation with the United States Treasury Department to sell bonds for the 4-War Loan Bond Drive. Opening at the War Memorial Opera House in San Francisco, this production boasted a mock B-25 airplane with three machine guns — which shot blanks — in the waist, turret, and tail positions. *You Bet Your Life*, also written by Burdick, toured staging areas up and down the West Coast. Originally conceived and designed by Ezra's close friend, Harry Horner, a Viennese artist who had designed scenery for *Reunion in New York*, the show helped Army Air Corps engineers perfect the techniques of camouflage.

In addition to directing these major productions, Ezra organized smaller weekly revues for the enlisted men and club shows for the officers and noncommissioned officers. He also booked U.S.O. troupes, including Bob Hope's first G.I. show, announced fight nights, and worked as the promotional director for the Fourth Air Corps Flyers champion football team.

Just before the end of the war, however, Ezra, together with Horner, received orders to report for duty to MacArthur's headquarters in the theater of operations. They had been assigned to provide morale on a troopship headed for Okinawa. A few days before the ship's departure, however, the Americans dropped atomic bombs on Hiroshima and Naga-saki, and the long war came to an end. Still, Ezra found himself with orders to head out to sea. On the basis of having served for over four years in the military, he knew he could apply for immediate discharge if he could secure the paperwork before becoming entrapped in military red tape. Without delay, he went to the Los Angeles Red Cross and applied for an emergency thirty-day furlough, which gave him sufficient time to move his family back to the East Coast. He then returned to March Field to process the necessary documents.

Meanwhile, Ezra contacted Paul Mosher and the William Morris Agency and alerted them of his impending discharge. By this time it was the middle of August, and *The Aldrich Family* was in summer repeats, with Raymond Ives now playing the irresponsible teenager. The 1945–46 sea-son was scheduled to begin in October. Because of a clause in his original contract, General Foods was obligated to rehire the original Henry at no less than the salary and benefits he had received before his departure. Mosher began the publicity campaign, and Ezra had only to secure his final discharge papers.

Upon his return to March Field, Ezra realized that he had to obtain the base commander's signature to make his release official. At that point he saw his entire plan falling apart, for the colonel was regular army and extremely disdainful of drafted personnel. With the help of his neigh-bor in the noncommissioned officer's quarters, Sergeant Major Raymond Ponce, he arranged a meeting with his commanding officer. Ezra later recalled,

> I remember him looking up at me and saying, "What happens if I don't sign this for you, and we find other work for you to do here for another couple of months?" I said, "Well, I've certainly enjoyed my tour of duty here at March, Colonel. And personally I'd be very happy to stay here in my quarters with my family. . . . But I haven't earned enough to take care of my family in the four and a half years I've been in the service. And there isn't that much more life in my radio series. It isn't just me going to be out of a job, but there's a whole company." I was giving him the full pitch. . . . He kind of chuckled and said, "Don't worry. You go back to your radio show. Good luck to you."

By sunset, Ezra had departed from the army and boarded an airplane headed for the East Coast. Before leaving Riverside, however, he purchased a yellow sport shirt, tan slacks, and loafers, which he carried in a box onto the airplane. After takeoff, he dashed into the rest room, stripped off his military garb and changed into his new "civies." When he returned to his

Postwar Aldrich Family portrait.

seat, the stewardess could not figure out what happened to the fat little Master Sergeant who had boarded on military orders. He flew into Washington's National Airport, where he was to meet Sara and their son, Little Joe, "The General." She searched the debarking passengers for her soldier husband, but like the stewardess, failed to recognize him. Little Joe did.

According to a brief announcement in the *New York Times*, Ezra Stone returned to *The Aldrich Family* as Henry Aldrich on October 19, 1945, the same week Ives' contract expired. General Foods Grapenuts Cereal now sponsored the program, which had moved to Friday at 8:00 P.M. on the CBS Radio Network. Ezra's transition back into radio was painless. In fact, after a few weeks he felt as if he had never left. Henry remained sixteen years old, and the series still explored his relationship with his family, friends, and community. And, of course, House Jameson, Kay Raht, and Jackie Kelk had remained in the cast. Mary Rolfe, another of his school-mates from the American Academy of Dramatic Arts who had previously — thanks to Ezra — performed in a *Brother Rat* road company, now replaced Charita Bauer, the future "Queen of the Soaps," as Henry's sister Mary. Nevertheless, *The Aldrich Family* was, in a sense, a casualty of the war, for it never regained its number one ranking. It did, however, continue to enjoy respectable success, maintaining a rating between eleven and sixteen percent throughout the next six seasons.

Several months after his release from the army, Ezra, now a market-able stage director, was befriended by producer Michael Todd, who signed him up for an unusual three-play contract. This unfortunate arrangement obligated him for two years. Before rehearsals began for Ezra's first assign-ment for Todd — a production of William Roos' comedy, *January Thaw* — producer Max Gordon asked Ezra about directing a musical revue on the subject of GIs returning to civilian life entitled, *Call Me Mister*. Because of his obligation to Todd, Ezra had to tell Gordon that he was unavailable. Subsequently, he set to work on the Todd project.

Ezra rehearsed *January Thaw* — a story that pits the Rockwoods against the Gages in the age-old battle of country versus city — in the top floor of a building Todd had recently purchased on 56th Street in Manhattan. In fact, Todd housed his entire organization in that building. The producer dropped in on rehearsals on the top floor every so often, but for the most part left Ezra in charge. Of the script and cast, the director later said,

> It was really a one-joke plot . . . a very slim concept for a three-act play. It had some very funny scenes in it. The casting was adequate, serviceable I'd say, not distinguished. The two male leads, one was a superb farcier, Robert Keith, father of Brian Keith. Charles Middleton did the farmer. He was a screen actor and very frozen-faced, which we all thought was right for the character. But he was essentially dull, with no sense of comedy. Lulu Mae Hubbard played the wife. A serviceable performance, but with Lulu I fell victim of placing friendship above talent. She was the widow of a marvelous actor and person, Paul McGrath, a friend from the *Room Service* flop in Philadelphia and a fellow Equity rebel. . . . So it didn't have the magic of an Abbott cast.

Ezra realized these problems before the show opened but still believed he could save the show. "You try to make it as funny as you can based on reality and characters and the situation," he explained. "You try to keep it moving." But these problems proved insurmountable, and the production opened in Boston's Colonial Theatre on January 15, 1946, to cool reviews.

After two weeks in Boston and a thorough reworking of the script, *Thaw* moved to Newark, New Jersey, where it met with a slightly warmer reception. Unable to secure another out-of- town theater, Todd opened his comedy on Broadway on Monday, February 4, where it met with mixed but predominantly negative evaluation in the newspapers. Seymour Peck of *PM Exclusive* called it "an empty-headed, hyperthyroid little farce . . . obviously hoping that if it moved fast enough, no one would notice it was pretty much ado about nothing." "It is based on a threadbare, wholly improbable plot and has to resort to distortions for its laughs," wrote a critic from *Variety*. "The comedy in *Thaw* results neither from slick lines, sufficient absurdities in the characters, nor from hilarious situations, but rather from playing to the hilt upon contrived differences."

For Ezra, *January Thaw* presented an uphill directorial assignment, and the reviewers mercifully treated him kindly. In fact, most of them seemed to sympathize with his dilemma. Herrick Brown of the *Sun* wrote, "His direction obviously sought to keep the play rolling merrily, but even he can't help stretches from meandering nor hold the script together." Peck of *PM Exclusive* wrote "They deserve a better play. And so does Ezra Stone, whose staging of *January Thaw* shows that he has learned well from the master director of farce, George Abbott." Despite the predominantly pessimistic notices, most critics agreed that Todd could expect some financial return from *Thaw*. The 1945–46 Broadway season found a large number of box office patrons who seemed extraordinarily tolerant of mediocrity, and Todd had an innate sense of knowing what would appeal to public taste. The show closed at the Golden Theatre on March 16, after forty-eight performances, and although he did not make any money on the production, Todd managed to break even financially.

After *January Thaw* closed in New York, Ezra purchased the rugs and other knickknacks from the set. With Little Joe as his helper, Ezra drove their farm truck to pick up the dressing at the stage loading dock. His friends, the union teamsters, graciously looked the other way. "The real prize," Ezra wrote, "was a gift of the two piglets that I had written into the play. They made very good hams." Years later, when Mike Todd on a visit to his son at the Lawrenceville Academy in New Jersey stopped by to see Sara and Ezra, he spotted the *Thaw* items and wanted to buy them back. "Sorry Mike," Ezra said, "they're now part of our home. Sara and I love them! Even you don't have enough money to buy them back."

Although he received little if any bad press from *January Thaw*, Ezra never got another directorial assignment from Todd. Since he had signed a three-play contract, Ezra could not direct another major production for the next two years. Naturally he did not remain idle during that time. He directed a variety show called *Film Fun* and a three-act farce entitled *The Milky Way* for the U.S.O., then headed by his friend Louis Simon, and he staged a production of *My Heart's in the Highlands* for the University of Virginia's Summer Theatre. And he continued as Henry on radio's *The Aldrich Family*.

Just after the 1948 New Years' holiday, a group of first-time producers including Oliver Smith, Paul Feigay, Herbert Kenwith, and David Cummings, asked Ezra to direct Gertrude Berg's *Me and Molly*. "I didn't have too much hope for that production mainly because the producers were so inexperienced and were constantly arguing among themselves," Ezra later recalled. He thought he was headed for disaster, but he knew that Gertrude Berg was a well-recognized property, which helped justify his decision to take the job. Berg's radio soap opera, *Rise of the Goldbergs*, had begun in 1932 and chronicled the life of the Jewish family from the Bronx for sixteen seasons. It had millions of faithful listeners and featured Mama (Molly), Papa (Jake), Samalee, and Rosalee Goldberg.

Born Gertrude Edelstein, Berg was a rather large and fascinating woman. She had black hair, dark eyes, and an attractive face, and she certainly knew the characters she had created. They were, in fact, her milieu. A firm and hard woman, many of her colleagues viewed her as a contrary but gifted person whose talent enabled her to write, direct, and star in her own radio series. *Me and Molly* represented Berg's debut on the legitimate stage, and because of her intimidating reputation several directors had refused the assignment before the producers approached Ezra. "When the play was finally offered to me, my first challenge, along with trying to fix the script, was to try and establish a working relationship with Gertrude Berg," he later explained. "I spent lots of time with her, and she was generous with her time. We visited sections of New York where these characters might have lived and worked." Ezra felt comfortable with the people and language, for the Goldbergs mirrored his own family and childhood experiences. His time and research with Berg thus allowed him to acquaint himself with the author and star and to obtain creative ideas for the production.

By Ezra's own admission, *Me and Molly* was nothing more than an elongated radio script with a weak plot, but it accurately and warmly displayed the lives of this Jewish family, and it afforded him an opportunity to work with his former teacher and close friend Philip Loeb, who portrayed Jake. Surprisingly, Loeb, an opinionated man under the best of circumstances, treated his former pupil with the utmost respect. He remained within the established boundaries of an actor, thus allowing Ezra to direct in a manner reminiscent of Abbott. The early working rehearsals proceeded smoothly.

By the time Ezra received the offer to direct *Me and Molly*, he had become a seasoned Broadway director. Over the years, he had come to incorporate parts of the methodology of Abbott, Loeb, and other veteran directors with whom he had worked; however, his approach to both script and production was somewhat different. Ezra was almost fanatical about his preproduction preparation. He often spent long and uncomfortable meetings trying to convince playwrights, such as Berg, to rewrite or eliminate a scene or add an extension to humorous points. He blocked the script on paper and then decided on such points as what he wanted the audience to see when the curtain rose, the placement of key scenes, the movement of actors, the essential properties, and the overall mood of the production.

Because of the trend toward spontaneity, improvisation, and subtext, Ezra over the years became unhappy with his working methods. He later said, "That whole syndrome has imposed a sense of guilt on me because I don't do any of that. I've tried on several projects. I'd say, 'Well, I'm really going to do this now the way some of my other friends who are so successful are doing it. I'm going to take side notes of the beats of every scene, break it down and give the actors full reign to express what they have evolved.'" However, in this process Ezra became so frustrated and irritable with himself, he soon returned to his old system — the Abbott way.

During the time of *Me and Molly*, he gave little thought to subtext or to dividing scenes into motivational units. Where dialogue seemed false and contrived, he noted it and tried to find logical substitutions. If the author supplied awkward exposition — i.e., characters telling each other information they already knew for the benefit of informing the audience — or if the script demanded illogical or impossible situations, Ezra tried to think like a playwright. With *Me and Molly*, Berg sometimes used her radio script technique of letting the audience imagine the action. In one key scene, she used only four lines of dialogue.

> TRUCKER: (*At door*) Goldberg? Apartment 2B?
> UNCLE: That's right!
> TRUCKER: We've got a piano for you.
> (*A piano is moved into the living room.*)
> UNCLE: Play, Rosie.

Here, with the help of Harry Horner's design, Ezra had to create a whole scene with the truckers hoisting the piano through the bedroom window, unhooking it, and rolling it into the living room while neighbors and kids converged upon them to witness the event and kept getting in the way. At first the actors improvised the scene and later set the action and dialogue. Ezra's new scene took about five minutes to perform.

One trick Ezra learned in dealing with playwrights was never to mark notes visibly in the script. "Usually you're working at a table," he explained. "They see the buzz words, and already they're building a defense." Therefore, he coded his remarks on every page with letters. Then on a separate sheet, he wrote corresponding notes. When a playwright said, "No, I don't go for that," Ezra, if he deemed his point important, responded with, "Hey, when we get into rehearsal, give me first crack at it. Let me show it to you my way. If you're still unhappy, I'll restage it your way, or we'll have the line read this way." And sometimes Ezra opted for, "Give me opening night of the tryout performance for my version; you [the playwright] take the second performance."

Following several weeks of rehearsals in Manhattan, *Me and Molly* opened in Philadelphia. A rash of bad reviews caused the production to fare poorly at the box office. These troubles led to one of the most traumatic experiences of Ezra's professional career as a director. After one performance, a producer took the director aside and informed him that they had invited Harold Clurman, the celebrated theoretician and director of the Group Theatre, to doctor his production. Under the circumstances, Ezra felt this meant that they intended to release him. "I cracked," he recalled. "When I got hold of Philip in his hotel room he said he knew about it but that I shouldn't worry." Loeb informed his friend that the program would still list him as director and that Clurman had no intention of re-directing the show; he simply wished to speak privately with the actors. Thus, the leader of the Group Theatre visited the cast for two days while Ezra nervously awaited an invitation to return. "I was beside myself," he said. The incident was not only embarrassing to his professional integrity, but it also involved Leob, one of his mentors and closest friends, although he had nothing to do with the decision. Upon returning to rehearsals, Ezra saw no noticeable differences; Clurman had made no substantive changes. "If any great magic occurred," he said, "I couldn't tell."

As frightening and embarrassing as the incident seemed at the time, it quickly passed and the show opened on Broadway on February 26, 1948, at the Belasco Theatre. Both the production and the director received warm notices. For Ezra, *Me and Molly* represented a departure from the rapidly paced, Abbott-type farces, because this production possessed a leisurely, intimate aura. Brooks Atkinson called it "a cheerful portrait of interesting people, and the humor is kind-hearted. It is something for the playwright to preserve that much personal integrity amid the gag traps of Broadway." The production entertained audiences through 156 performances, and John Chapman included it among his ten best plays of the 1947–48 season, a period that saw over fifty new shows open on Broadway.

Soon after *Me and Molly* had premiered, Ezra got his first taste of Off Broadway. At 159 Bleeker Street, Norman Rose and David Heilweil assembled New Stages, a company of young professionals who sought to produce original artistic scripts. Eva Wolas, who had recently completed a respected and popular translation of Jean-Paul Sartre's *The Respectful Prostitute*, wrote an imaginative play entitled *To Tell You the Truth*, which reported on the battle of the sexes in the Garden of Eden. Ezra was engaged to direct the small cast, which included young Tony Randall.

After the first week of rehearsals, Randall informed Ezra that he was not pleased with his role and intended to leave the cast. Ezra decided Randall was embarrassed about his physique, much of which would be revealed by the skimpy costume he would wear as Adam. More importantly, Randall did not believe he could successfully perform comedy. He had trained as a dramatic actor and feared this role would compromise his artistic integrity. Ezra, who had struggled with the same dilemma as a young actor, coaxed him to return to work. When *To Tell You the Truth* opened on April 18, the critics praised Ezra for giving the production professional polish and the actors for creating imaginative portrayals. Tony Randall realized that he could play comedy, and Ezra gained more dear friends and colleagues—Eva, David, and Jean Gillespie, and their "super stage manager," Lamar Casselli, who went on to become director of TV's *College Bowl* and then chairman of the television department at Loyola-Marymount University in Los Angeles. The show, however, never found a substantial audience and closed after fifteen performances.

Less than two weeks after his first play opened Off Broadway, Ezra received an offer from his old friend José Ferrer to replace an actor in a New York City Center production. After a late night repeat of *The Aldrich Family*, Ezra and Sara arrived in the early morning at their home in Bucks County, Pennsylvania. They had just fallen asleep when the telephone rang. Half dazed from exhaustion, he heard Ferrer's voice saying, "Ezra, I've got a problem. You've got to help me. I'm in rehearsal with Ben Jonson's *The Alchemist*, and I had to fire the actor playing Sir Epicure Mammon, and I know you'd be perfect for the role. Do you know the play?" Ezra said he would read it, but Ferrer needed an immediate response. Sleepily, he said, "Well, if you think I can do it, Joe. When do you open?" It was to debut in a little over one week, and Ezra had never been a quick study. He said, "Well, you know I need all day Thursday for my radio show." "That's no problem," Ferrer replied. "The matinee's on Wednesday; we'll hold the curtain for you on Thursday. And it's a limited engagement." Ezra agreed to give it a try, saying he would report for work the next day.

Ezra knew next to nothing about Jonson or *The Alchemist*, but at the time he thought he was saving his friend from artistic ruin. The next morning, he turned up a copy of the script to peruse over breakfast. When he came to Mammon's entrance, he began to feel slightly queasy, for the character's first speech occupied the majority of three pages of text. But he had made a commitment and would not back out. "I eventually got three rounds of applause during and concluding that speech," Ezra later said.

Ezra worked extremely hard at rehearsals. In fact, he quickly grew fond of the character and knew if he could conquer the text, he would

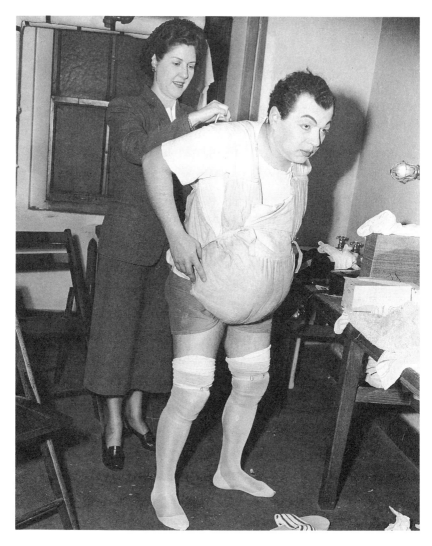

Sara Seeger helps Ezra with his belly pad before the New York City Center production of *The Alchemist* (1948).

immensely enjoy performing it. Mammon's opening scene is a comic aria
in which the character controls the action while the others more or less
supply straight lines to his jokes. As the plot progresses, however, Mammon drifts away from the primary action. Ezra wished to do something to
give the character distinction. In a scene in the fourth act, Mammon is
aroused from an upper chamber that he has temporarily occupied with a
courtesan. Herbert Brodkin's set design provided a balcony overhanging

Ezra (Sir Epicure Mammon) demonstrates his head-first slide during the New York City Center production of Jonson's *The Alchemist* (1948).

a shop with a flight of stairs at right angles leading to the footlights. Ezra decided to devise a fall down those steps that would grab the audience and provide his character with a memorable piece of business. Without telling anyone, he choreographed the maneuver after rehearsal. Using a belly pad, he faked a trip and slid down the steps face first, practicing the maneuver a number of times until he felt he had it under control. At the final dress rehearsal, without informing anyone, he performed his fall. Upon landing,

Ferrer, who was also onstage, yelled for the stage manager to call a doctor. By this time all the actors had circled around Ezra, who sheepishly looked up and said, "Can I keep it in, Joe?"

When *The Alchemist* opened its limited engagement on May 6, many audience members found the bawdy lines and subject matter to their liking. Several critics, however, did not appreciate the script, noting that "good intentions . . . cannot bring the old play back to life." As for Ezra, the reviewer from the *New York Times* reported that he had added style to his interpretation of the voluptuous and licentious Mammon.

As much as he enjoyed his participation in Jonson's classic play, Ezra did have a minor confrontation with a talented but pretentious British actor named George Coulouris, who played the alchemist Subtle. "It may have been a jealousy kind of thing," Ezra said. "Maybe I was being a snotty egotist in rehearsal. I was really so caught up in getting that text down and getting the show up." During act four, scene five, the two men shared a moment on stage alone. As this was a night scene, the lighting designer—again Brodkin—sparsely illuminated the actors with thin shafts of light. Coulouris as Subtle entered the stage, grabbed Ezra (Mammon) by the lapel, and shook him for some unchaste activity. After the first few performances, however, Ezra realized that when Coulouris grabbed him, he was pushing him out of the light. Ezra had been playing his portion of the scene in darkness. Rather than complain to the stage manager, Ezra decided to take matters into his own hands.

During the next performance, when Coulouris grabbed for him, Ezra backed away. The British actor moved forward and again reached for him, finally realizing that he too stood in darkness. He therefore moved back into the spot and played the scene as if his counterpart stood in close proximity. Ezra, in the meantime, walked offstage and over to the stage manager, Walter Wagner—a friend from the *Brother Rat* days—and asked him where they were in the script. "His double take was a classic." He had made his point, and Coulouris, who had to improvise the rest of the scene that evening, shared the stage light with him for the remainder of the run.

Soon after this engagement, Ezra became involved with television for the first time in his directorial career. The rising television industry seriously threatened live drama as well as radio. Actors and directors trained on the legitimate stage, however, handled the transition to TV with relative ease compared to their counterparts who had only worked behind a microphone. Ezra believed his somewhat unique background served him well. He later explained, "Directing on television . . . the basics are the same. Whether it's film, stage, or television. It's also the same with actors. The proscenium opening is different; you have a close-up lens. But that's your proscenium arch. No point acting in the wings or under frame. You have to act in the picture."

Even as a young man Ezra had been fascinated by the idea of working in television. In 1939, he had confessed to a student reporter that he favored movies over the stage as an instrument for bringing drama to the public, but he felt "television will in time take the place of movies." His first direct exposure to the new medium had come during the 1939 World's Fair in New York City. Philco exhibited a camera and allowed visitors to stand under hot lights and see the new technology transmit their images to a monitor positioned a short distance away.

In 1940, Ezra had worked for the first time as an actor in front of a television camera, when NBC produced an experimental presentation of *The Aldrich Family* for the Federal Communications Commission. "The enormous lamps were so close and hot that the stage became a stifling sauna," he said. Because of the low resolution black and white transmission, the makeup artists used extremely odd colors on his face to give it definition between scales of gray. Ordinary lip rouge would not have defined his lips, so they painted them a deep maroon, almost black. His base makeup was an ostentatious lavender, and they shadowed his eyes red in order to transmit identifiable variations. "It just looked absurd," he recalled. "It was like a clown makeup. You're playing a scene with another actor, and all you can really react to is this garish makeup."

Then during the war, Ezra and his comrades from the Opry House had successfully petitioned NBC to produce for television excerpts from their soldier show, *We're Ready*. Like the FCC demonstration of *The Aldrich Family*, *We're Ready* was a one-performance engagement and only seen on the East Coast.

After Ezra's discharge from the army, the William Morris Agency had grand hopes for him as both a stage and TV director. In 1948, the agency arranged for him to make his television directorial debut on ABC with a pilot series, *L'il Abner*, adapted from Al Capp's popular comic strip. During the engagement, he met and worked with Capp, Eva Marie Saint, Joe Marks, and Jon Sypher. No sponsor purchased the series, and Ezra's prime-time TV debut ended after the pilot show.

He did not return to this medium for almost two years, and *L'il Abner* seemed to him at the time rather uneventful. In retrospect, he acknowledged that it marked an important transition in his career. He had been purposely turning away from acting, and with this assignment he had established a foundation from which to market himself as a director in both entertainment media. Naturally, he had no way of knowing then that television would consume his life for more than two decades. Following the failure of his TV directorial debut, he turned his attention back to the legitimate stage.

In January 1949, Jerome E. Rosenfeld, a young student attending Yale University, came to Ezra's radio dressing room with a play entitled *At War with the Army*, a farce-comedy by James B. Allardice, who went on to become the creator and sole writer for the acclaimed, witty Hitchcock spots on TV's *Alfred Hitchcock Presents*. A group of actors had produced the script at Yale the previous season and thought it had Broadway potential. Considering his training in farce with Abbott and his recent experience in the United States Army, Rosenfeld and his associates, Henry May and Charles Ray McCallum, believed Ezra to be the best director for their venture. After reading the script, Ezra thought it had much potential, but he also believed it had many weaknesses. As typical throughout his married life, he had also passed the typescript over to his wife for her professional assessment and approval.

Sara had read *At War with the Army*—which chiefly concerns the chaos resulting from army discipline, red tape, and regulations during the boredom of preparing for war in a Kentucky army camp in late 1944—and thought it had little chance of surviving the rigors of Broadway. Although she admitted it contained humorous dialogue and characters, she told her husband he would be wasting his time with this vehicle. Nevertheless, Ezra needed a creative outlet. As was his habit throughout his career, when a job assignment came his way, he generally accepted the position if he had no better offers. Once he had committed to the project, he reveled in the challenge to beat the odds. He knew that the probability of success was always slim; certainly more Broadway shows failed than were hits. This challenge and the need to keep busy actually inspired his creativity—sometimes even beyond what he believed himself capable of—for he never thought he was a genius or even a master director. In most instances, he approached directing as a technical, practical task peppered with flashes of inspiration. But with *At War with the Army*, he reached deep into his bag of tricks to try to make it successful.

When Ezra cast the production, he agreed to give the original company from Yale a fair chance to recreate their roles on Broadway. He hired several of the initial members, but the cast was made up primarily of his former associates from the American Academy of Dramatic Arts, previous Broadway productions, and *This Is the Army*. The final cast that went into Boston previews included William Mendrek, Mike Kellin, Jerry Jarrett, Ty Perry, Maxine Stuart, William Lanteau, Bernard Kates, Norma Lehn, Sally Gracie, Ernest Sarracino, John Shellie, Sara Seegar, Tad Mosel (who later won a Pulitzer Prize for his *All the Way Home*, a dramatization of James Agee's novel *A Death in the Family*), and Steve Elliot as First Sergeant Johnson.

Although an extremely handsome radio actor, Elliot had an unpleasant stage disposition that did not become apparent until after the play had opened in Boston. Ezra decided to replace him. Following some investigation, he located his old friend Gary Merrill from *See My Lawyer* and *TITA*.

Merrill had just finished the film *Slattery's Hurricane* in Hollywood and was on his way back to New York when bad weather forced him to lay over in St. Louis. There, he took the opportunity to visit Jack Goldman, whom he had met while playing in St. Louis during the third touring production of *Brother Rat*. "He [Stone] called to ask if I would replace an actor in a show currently playing in Boston, *At War with the Army*," Merrill recalled in his autobiography *Bette, Rita, and the Rest of My Life*. "I told him about my option with the Fox Studio, but he said, 'That's O.K., I'll take my chances. Just help me get the show to New York.' I agreed."

For the next few weeks Merrill split his time between his New York soap operas and *At War with the Army* in Boston. From there the show went on to Philadelphia, but the director still did not believe it was ready to open on Broadway, and the show went back to Boston for another two-week engagement. The day before its Broadway debut, however, Fox Studio optioned Merrill's contract; therefore, on opening day he gave the production manager his two-week notice. "In my experience," he wrote, "a terrific way to open in New York."

While in previews, Ezra, who was continuously searching for ways to overcome the script's deficiencies, choreographed a running gag involving the company's soft drink machine. In Donald Oenslager's original set design, a cabinet (noncoin) Coca-Cola tub was indicated in the dayroom of the company headquarter's set. Ezra, however, wanted a coin-operated machine like the one the cast of *This Is the Army* had in the alley of the Broadway Theatre. During the run of *TITA*, Ezra had assigned Private Alan Lowell to stock the machine. He in turn began to store his personal supply of juice, milk, and turkey—all of which were sometimes ejected instead of Cokes. Ezra believed this would make a wonderful piece of comic business for *At War with the Army*. In the show, officers and the lesser ranking personnel periodically placed money in the machine. When nothing materialized, they angrily went about their business. This transaction continued for most of three acts until the silent Lost Private [Tad Mosel] made his final appearance.

> . . . *Private notices Coke machine and his face lights up. Rises, places bags on bench, struggles and tickles himself as he searches for a coin in his money belt. Puts coin in machine. It buzzes and flashes five times, but no Coke. Private looks around to see if he is being watched, then hits the machine. Still no Coke. He is about to give up and as he turns a Coke comes out; overjoyed, he starts to open it. Another Coke comes, followed by five more. He is overwhelmed and places his hand over the opening to stop the flow, then plugs the opening with the sleeve of his coat. He opens his barracks bag, empties it of a complete uniform, unplugs the opening and rhythmically begins placing Cokes in his bag as they come from the machine. About the tenth one is a milk bottle, which startles but does not disconcert him. He bends over and looks into the opening, a Coke hits him in the eye. He gathers*

his baggage and is about to leave when several coins come out of the coin return. He plunges his garrison cap under the slot and a torrent of coins fill it. Finally they stop. With difficulty he picks up his cap and rapidly starts off Left leaving a Coke on the Captain's desk as he passes above it and exits Left.

Ezra even added a turkey leg to the business. The Coca-Cola machine was eventually replaced when Pepsi offered a better marketing package.

Ezra's creation became so popular in the New York theater district that the machine was a subject of a full-page color photograph when *Life Magazine* did a feature story on the production. At the end of each performance, Ezra gave a solo star curtain call to the machine. Although several critics concluded that the machine overshadowed the performances, most of them agreed it was an outstanding piece of comic business comparable to the pinball machine setup in William Saroyan's *The Time of Your Life*. Ezra contended that many patrons came back to see the Pepsi machine's performance.

At War with the Army opened on Broadway on March 8, 1949, at the Booth Theatre. "Mr. Stone likes his actors to run fast and constantly, emitting their lines in full stride and at the top of their voices," wrote John Lardner of the *New Yorker*. "With a one-way track at his disposal, he brings out their full athletic talents. Even the master under whom he studied, George Abbott, never staged a piece more loudly and rapidly. In the result, *At War with the Army* shows the mark of the Stone-Abbott school." No doubt, the speedy execution sometimes made a line or a bit of business seem funnier than it actually was. But without a strong central theme to unify the production and hold it on a rising line, most critics agreed the speed eventually became rather wearisome. Ezra's effort and creativity turned what many deemed a certain failure into a modest success, and it entertained audiences through 151 performances. *At War with the Army* later became a movie starring Jerry Lewis and Dean Martin, their first film collaboration.

Following *At War with the Army*, Ezra maintained his characteristic hectic schedule in theater and radio throughout the next year. During this period, he also became a teacher at the American Theatre Wing, which had established a professional acting training program primarily for veterans whose lives and careers had been interrupted by the war. Working alongside such theatrical legends as Alfred Lunt and Guthrie McClintic, Ezra, who predominantly taught scene study courses, instructed and retrained young professionals like Peter Falk, James Earl Jones, Mimi Benzell, Lincoln Kirkpatrick, Paul Dooley, Sidney Lumet, and Hal Holbrook.

Later that same year, Maurice Evans invited him to participate in an all-star production of Oliver Goldsmith's *She Stoops to Conquer* at the City

Center, where he had recently found success in Jonson's *The Alchemist*. The cast included Burl Ives, Celeste Holm, Brian Aherne, Carmen Mathews, and Evelyn Varden. On opening night, Varden and Ezra received thunderous applause after their first acrobatic chase scene. They came offstage and collapsed in the down left wing with joy and relief. Holm and Aherne, in the meantime, were standing in the wings waiting to enter. When Holm restrained Aherne from stepping in on their ovation, he grudgingly muttered, "Well, that's the *first* round of the piece." Nonetheless, Brooks Atkinson in his *New York Times'* review called Ezra's portrayal of Tony Lumpkin both "exuberant and inventive."

During the New Year's Eve performance of *She Stoops to Conquer*, Ezra, with his fanny facing the audience, took an upstage leap onto a settee, splitting the rear seam of his trousers from his waist to his crotch revealing his jock strap and shorts. A deafening and sustained roar came from the audience. During the intermission, the wardrobe mistress hastily mended the seam. But when Ezra repeated the settee business as staged in the second act, the new stitches ripped apart. Ezra had mooned the viewers twice in one night. The audience, who obviously thought this was part of the intended business, responded with another round of applause. "Carmen, with whom I had played the scene, thought I was being my naughty self by rigging the seams. She complained to George Schaefer, who was in charge of the series for Maurice Evans," Ezra said.

Incidentally, every Thursday evening during these two City Center projects, Ezra had to go to his radio show in full period costume and makeup. "Our Aldrich audiences really had to stretch their imaginations," he remembered. "They had to watch me as Henry dressed up as Mammon or Lumpkin."

Ezra's transition to television seemed to flow naturally from his stage and radio careers. With Broadway steadily losing the nucleus of its devoted audience and with his and other radio series falling by the wayside, he had long predicted that the entire industry would gravitate toward the new medium.

As a television director, Ezra certainly utilized his past artistic training, but the rapidly changing technology of the medium presented him with new and exciting challenges. Since programs at that time were typically broadcast live in front of both studio and television audiences, TV in its early days shared an ephemeral quality with legitimate theater and most radio shows. Because few authentic TV studios had been constructed, most programs were broadcast from converted legitimate stages. For example, *The Olsen and Johnson Buick Hour*, Ezra's first directorial assignment of the 1950–51 season, appeared live from the Colonial Theatre on Columbus Circle in Manhattan. The control booth, built in one of the larger dressing rooms on the second floor, brimmed with tube-burning equipment, which

emitted a tremendous amount of heat. With monitors and electronic de-
vices racked and wedged against the walls, Ezra the director, his assistant,
and the technical director sat on a small bench on a riser. The three men's
shoulders touched, leaving little room to maneuver around the switch-
board located only a short distance away. This forced the engineers, who
shaded and controlled the visual and audio output and maintained camera
balance, to sit on the dressing room floor in front of the riser. Watching his
technical director do all the fades, dissolves, and camera cuts, Ezra once
said, "You really have to have six fingers to be a TV TD." But after casually
glancing at his cohort's left hand, he sat mortified—it had six fingers.

For *The Olsen and Johnson Buick Hour*, a variety program starring Ole
Olsen and Chick Johnson, Ezra used an extraordinary number of cameras—
one on the street, one in the lobby, one backstage, and three onstage—in
order to capture the zany antics of Olsen, Johnson, and their cast of so-
called stooges. Since he could not see well from the control booth, Ezra
blocked each show from the stage. He then repositioned himself in the
booth for run-throughs. Ezra quickly learned, however, that the technical
expertise and limitations of engineers profoundly affected the artistic output of television. "You can't put three cameras on the air simultaneously;
the engineering can't take it," the technical director informed the director.
When Ezra naively inquired as to why they could not perform maneuvers
such as this, they answered in terms of wattage and megahertz. The somewhat frustrated director then said, "Just show it to me. Put it up on the
screen. Get me a super of three images from three cameras." With this, he
could see the loss of visual clarity. Thus, writers frequently had to revise
sketches, and the director had to alter his artistic vision because the
engineers refused to compromise clarity. "Sometimes it was a mess. So as
a director blocking it and laying it out, I had to be aware of the technical
limitations, the equipment, how close a boom mike could get without being in the shot or in the track of the camera," Ezra later recalled. In his
early years as a television director he never completely mastered the technical aspects of the craft, but he nevertheless did not stop trying to learn.
He simply hoped he would comprehend enough to get through each episode with the help of his technical experts.

The 1950–51 season provided Ezra with a quick initiation into the new
medium. As part of NBC's *Four-Star Revue*, which later changed its name
to *The All-Star Revue*, he directed many top-name entertainers in several
variety programs. Within a seven-month period, he directed *The Danny
Thomas Show*, *The Martha Raye Show*, *The Ed Wynn Show*, *The Fred Allen
Show*, and *The Ezio Pinza Show*, programs that were styled to the talents
of the host and guests. In this same season, Ezra also directed for television
The Colgate Comedy Hour with Herb Shriner, a variety program formatted
like those of *The Four-Star Revue*.

Many radio programs such as *The Jack Benny Show* successfully made the leap to TV, and it came as no surprise when on June 3, 1949, General Foods and Young and Rubicam announced tentative plans to convert *The Aldrich Family* to a prime-time series. "Its future next fall apparently depends on its potentialities as a television attraction," a *New York Times'* reporter wrote. "A video run-through of the program was made last week on kinescope film. If the film meets with a cordial reception from the sponsor, the program probably will be renewed. If not, it may be dropped. The sponsor's theory, of course, is that he wants to have a package which will be suitable to either medium." Nevertheless, the advertising agency announced its intention to replace Ezra as Henry Aldrich. "The passing of the years has made him a little too mature for the part, a consideration which has not been too vital on radio but is important in a visual art," wrote the reporter. *The Aldrich Family* television series, however, did not take shape at that time, and General Foods quickly announced its return to NBC radio with Ezra as the eternal teenager in the fall of 1949.

After twelve seasons on radio, *The Aldrich Family* finally began its short and yet auspicious television tenure in the summer of 1950. Following a series of auditions, Young and Rubicam chose film star Jean Muir for the role of Mrs. Aldrich. The press release three days before the scheduled premiere on Sunday, August 27, stated, "Miss Muir's wide experience as a mature actress and the real-life mother of three young children has ideally equipped her for the role of Mrs. Aldrich, who guides her family with a loving and understanding hand."

On the morning of Saturday, August 26, shortly after hearing of Muir's appointment, Theodore C. Kirkpatrick, a former FBI man turned secretary-treasurer of the most feared organization in radio and television known as the American Business Consultants, met in Manhattan with his partners. For three years they had been issuing a weekly newsletter called *Counterattack*, which had the exclusive aim to expose the communist menace. Three months earlier the group had released a paperbound booklet entitled *Red Channels: The Report of Communist Influence in Radio and Television*, which listed 151 names of persons associated with the industry, along with the so-called communist or communist front organizations each reportedly had been affiliated with at one time. Muir's name appeared in *Red Channels* followed by nine alleged communist affiliations including the Congress of American Women, Southern Conference for Human Welfare, *The Negro Quarterly*, and Progressive Citizens of America. She was also chastised for sending a congratulatory cable to the Moscow Arts Theatre in honor of that troupe's fiftieth anniversary.

Kirkpatrick and his associates, utilizing supporters of their publication, immediately inaugurated a telephone campaign against Muir. Within hours, executives of Young and Rubicam and General Foods began receiving calls at home. Many callers claimed to speak for large groups. As a result, the television debut of *The Aldrich Family* was delayed one week, and Muir's contract was terminated with a cash settlement. The decision, which made headlines in the entire country, came from the highest echelons of General Foods. The company did not investigate, asked for no explanation, claimed no disloyalty on her part. She, in the meantime, denounced six of the allegations and claimed the other three were innocent of communist conspiracy. General Foods, however, wished to avoid controversial people on programs it sponsored. Following the incident, Muir found her career virtually destroyed by the blacklist.

The blacklist did not directly affect Ezra's career, but it destroyed the lives and careers of many of his closest friends and associates. José Ferrer, Garson Kanin, Norman Corwin, Burl Ives, Sam Jaffe, Zero Mostel, and Harold Rome represented only a few of his friends affected by *Red Channels*. Shortly after the Muir incident, General Foods fired Ezra's mentor, Philip Loeb, from Gertrude Berg's popular television series, *The Goldbergs*. The American Business Consultants had branded him as a controversial figure, and the sponsors responded by refusing to hire him. Following this, Loeb seemed to die a spiritual death. His sparkling personality, which had once roused fellow equity members to action, changed dramatically. He lost the drive, energy, and verve that had made him so popular among his peers. He became reclusive.

On September 1, 1955, at 8:45 P.M., a maid discovered the body of a man in the cheapest room of the Taft Hotel in New York City, Room 507. He was registered as "Fred Lang." When the police arrived, they uncovered a bottle containing fourteen pills on a dresser table but found no explanatory note. Fred Lang was Philip Loeb, actor, director, trade union leader, teacher, and Ezra's cherished friend, his second father. Dr. Aaron Plachta, assistant medical examiner, later examined the body and reported that he had died of visceral congestion from an overdose of sleeping pills.

On Tuesday, May 24, 1988, *Equity News* published its special 75th anniversary edition; in it Ezra penned a touching account of Philip Loeb, the man who had opened doors for him that led to a productive career path and his happy life. The following story, "Who Was Fred Lang?" was written by Ezra Stone and is here partially reprinted from *Equity News* with permission of Actors' Equity Association.

> If you want a generous sample of Philip's rare, off-the-wall humor, listen to Carl Harms' audio recording of the dedication program of the Loeb Conference room on July 7, 1981. . . . I was there, too, and I recounted Phil's reply to me during sweltering rehearsals of the Theatre Guild's *Parade* (1935), which he was directing, when I reminded him that his fly was open. "Ventilation!" he snapped, "I am protesting the management's

lack of air cooling." For the rest of that day he refused to button (prezip-pers) up.

Then there was the time we went to a matinee together with a pair of first-row, free tickets given out at equity. Shortly after the curtain rose, a very prominent and prodigiously amply upholstered character lady of the day, who was also an equity councillor and a fierce, very vocal foe of Philip's entered to an embarrassingly small hand from the sprinkling of actors in the audience. She had been directed (or perhaps misdirected) to cross downstage center and with her rear facing front, to open a small foot locker, reach into it and extract a hidden liquor flask. When she bent over, her posterior seemed to practically fill the entire proscenium arch. Whereupon, Phil leaned over to me and in his best projected stage whisper so as to be sure that the freebie audience and the actress heard him, he proclaimed, "And that's not the biggest ass on council!" But that was certainly the biggest laugh that flop show got in its three-day run.

The work of Philip Loeb, the actor and director, spans some 40 years. His greatest mass audience impact (and his last) was as Jake in the popular television series, *The Goldbergs* (1949). He first created his version of the warm, weary, and witty Jake Goldberg in Gertrude Berg's play *Me and Molly* at the Belasco Theatre in 1948. Gertrude and Philip meshed beauti-fully both onstage and off. The last thing they needed was a director, especially me. The same magic was created when Philip supported Ezio Pinza in a summer stock package of *The Play's the Thing*. Once again, I was the unneeded director. My show business ineptness was never felt more than on those occasions when I was charged with directing Philip, or my mentor, boss and benefactor, George Abbott.

The classic, masterful eating scene in the Abbott production of *Room Service* (1937) was almost entirely the result of Phil's comedic genius. RKO brought him out to Hollywood just to be the comedy consultant for the Marx Brothers' screen version. . . .

Philip loved to teach; he loved young people and always maintained that a good teacher is always in the state of learning. He was a stern, unrelenting, demanding teacher. [Ezra then goes on to recount several of his stories concerning Loeb while a student at the academy, as an actor under Loeb's direction in *Parade* and recognizes his role in helping Ezra land a position in the Harris production of *Room Service* and in recom-mending him for his position with George Abbott.] Along came the showy role of "Mistol" Bottome, the hazed VMI cadet in *Brother Rat*. . . . In that show, I got my first favorable mention from Brooks Atkinson in the *New York Times*. When the early edition hit the street at 1:30 A.M., I woke Phil up in his room at the Lincoln Hotel (now the Milford Plaza) to read it to him. "Don't resign your seat in the Abbott office," he snapped and hung up on me.

When lightning struck and Abbott cast me as Henry Aldrich, . . . Phil sent me an opening night telegram: "No matter what Atkinson says, don't wake me up. Stop. And don't resign your seat at Sardi's." When Henry and *The Aldrich Family* became a top radio network sitcom, Phil made no bones about reminding me that I could certainly afford to buy him a good meal now and then. Invariably, he would pick The Lobster on 43rd Street and order the most expensive dinner ($4.75). Ever the teacher, it was here that he made me eat my first oyster and my first clam.

"Eat it," he ordered. "You're in a rut. You gotta take chances, risk, dare, venture, try! Are you going to spend the rest of your life cracking your voice as Henry Aldrich for easy laughs?"

Although he never said it in so many words, I knew Phil was proud of me when Mr. Abbott announced that my Broadway directorial debut would be his production of *See My Lawyer*, . . . I knew because at another one of our seafood dinners to mark my good fortune, he asked how old I was. "Are you old enough to vote yet? When's your birthday?" I replied, "If you must know, I'll cast my first vote in the next presidential election and I was born on December 2, 1917." "Well, aren't you going to ask me when my birthday is?" "Why should I?" "Because," he said, "it's next Friday, March 18, and I think in celebration of your directorial debut you should buy me a nice present—something I need, like a gold wrist watch."

Three days later I went up to his room and I put three gold watches on his hotel room bureau. When he finally came out of his shower, I said, "Phil, here's your gold watch, pick the one you like." "Where did you get them?" he asked. "Are they hot?" I explained that my cousin was in the jewelry business and he was letting me have any one of the three at the wholesale price. "How much?" Phil asked. I wouldn't tell him. "It's a present, Phil. You don't leave the price tag on a present." He insisted. I refused. He finally made the hard decision and chose one after trying on all three, standing naked in front of the mirror. "Happy Birthday, Phil!" I put the other two in my pocket and headed for the elevator. He wrapped himself in a towel and followed me down the public hall, still trying to get me to confess. As the elevator door closed, I said, "Happy Birthday, Phil! You picked the cheapest one!" "Fink!" he screamed, beating on the closing door. "You're nothing but a Fink! My rotten pupil is a Fink!" . . .

The last time I saw Phil alive was early in August of 1955 on the Northeast corner of Barrow and Hudson in Greenwich Village. He had insisted on walking me back to my parked car. The day before, I had been summoned with a phone call from Phil's childhood friend Mrs. Linda Meyers. Phil was recuperating in Linda's apartment from his second cataract operation. "He wants to talk to you," she explained, "it's very important! Can you come in from Bucks County tomorrow for brunch?"

Phil was not his usual irrepressible, ebullient self. No wisecracks. No fiery tirades. He was grim, taut—vocally almost monotone. His left eye was still bandaged. He muttered that he was probably going to end up a blind, old man with a cane. I said that with a stick as a weapon he would be an even more formidable adversary against his blacklisting foes: *Red Channels*, the House Internal Security Committee, General Foods and even the less than courageous board of trustees of his beloved American Academy of Dramatic Arts. They had summarily relieved him of his contract as codirector of the executive committee of the school although his mentor, Charles Jehlinger, was on record with the statement that Loeb was the best teacher equipped to run the Academy.

Finally, I said, "I've been watching you eat Linda's brunch, Phil. You're a long way from being a blind man. Even with just one eye, your knife never once missed the butter dish, or the jelly jar, or your slice of toast." He remained silent—not even a trace of a smile.

Finally we left the table and adjourned to the living room, where he got down to the important business. He asked me if I remembered my promise to act as executor of his estate. "Of course I do," I assured him, "but I'm in no hurry!" He ignored my joke and asked if I still had my copy of his handwritten, unwitnessed last will and testament, bestowing all of his assets to me to hold until I was certain that his schizophrenic son was cured. Then he gave me another scrap of paper with several handwritten paragraphs, witnessed by Linda. It said that if his son never recovered, he wanted his estate divided between his sister Sabina, Sam Jaffe, Linda and Barbara Ames, his one-time academy pupil, and then devoted companion for many years.

As it finally turned out, his estate was even less than modest. In today's market, it wouldn't buy a new Chevy; a sad accounting for a person who had entertained millions, had taught hundreds of young students, and who had successfully fought for better working conditions for all performers. Where did it all go? Phil was not a gambler. He never owned a home; his entire wardrobe would fit in a rooming house closet. Oh, yes, his books and files filled two ancient humpbacked steamer trunks. But that was it.

Phil's life earnings and savings had all gone to support his divorced wife, former actress Jeanne "Johnny" La Gue who died in 1942 and their only child, (John) Daniel Loeb. I now have a faded snapshot of me and young Daniel (much later he added "John" to his name), taken by his mother. I found it in Phil's files before I turned over all of his papers to George Freedley, then curator of the Theatre Collection of the New York Public Library. (They are now catalogued and available for scholars and researchers in the Lincoln Center Library of the Performing Arts.) I did not yet know that I would someday be John's legal guardian until his still mysterious death at the Montrose New York Veteran's Mental Hospital in 1962.

Phil was heavily in debt. He had "borrowed" from Sam Jaffe, Linda and my folks—none of whom expected or wanted repayment. Keeping John in a private sanitarium in Washington, D.C., hoping for a cure, became financially impossible. Phil had to give up and have his son's mental illness declared service-connected and have him committed to the V.A. Hospital in Brockton, Massachusetts, where I visited him regularly.

The brunch was over. Phil insisted on walking me across the street to my car. I got in, rolled down the window and said, "Goodbye!" He reached in, touched me on the shoulder and mumbled, "Thanks. Thanks for coming in." In the rearview mirror I watched him wait for the green light and when he was safely across Hudson Street, I pulled away from the curb. One last look in the mirror and he disappeared around the corner. That was the last time I saw him.

That night instead of driving back to our farm, I stayed over in the family apartment in Brooklyn Heights where Phil had visited frequently and had enjoyed many of my mother's home-cooked meals. He loved her borscht and gefilte fish. I told my father how concerned I was about Phil's state of mind and what seemed to me to be his plans for imminent death. My father explained that such depression after what was then major surgery was normal and that in Phil's case, with all his other problems, it could be expected.

About a week later I called Linda from the farm to check on Phil. He had left the day before and had gone up to stay with Zero and Katie Mostel

on West 86th Street. This was good news. Next to Sam Jaffe, Zero was
Phil's closest friend. I knew that Zero's craziness was just what Phil
needed.

It was the last day of August, about 9:30 in the evening. I was back
on the farm. Zero called me to ask if I had heard from Phil. He had left
their house after lunch and said he'd return at dinner time. For the rest
of the evening we were on the phone trying to track down Phil's other
friends. I finally reached Sam. I had also gotten hold of Jack Gould, a good
friend of Phil's ever since Gould was on the drama desk of the *New York
Times*. I asked Jack how to go about releasing the report that Phil was
missing. Through the police? To the city desks of the afternoon papers?
We were too late for the last editions of the morning papers. My hope was
that since the popularity of *The Goldbergs* television series, Phil's face was
known to millions of people in the greater New York area, maybe someone might have seen him and could provide a lead to his whereabouts.
We finally decided to wait until morning.

The next night Sam called with the terrible news. Philip Loeb was
Fred Lang. He had earlier told friends that he wished his name were Fred
Lang, which in German translates into "long peace." Phil's final irony
as a union activist was to pick Labor Day to die. A check of the hotel
telephone log showed that the night before, two uncompleted, long-
distance calls were placed from Room 507. The line had been busy. It was
mine!

The coffin was closed for the service held in an upstairs funeral
chapel on lower Amsterdam Avenue. It was standing room only. Bill Ross
spoke eloquently of Phil as friend, actor, director. Sam Jaffe shared his
memories of Phil as friend and Equity colleague.

Then it was my turn. I told of Phil as my friend and teacher. I said
he taught me many things: how to be a better actor, director, teacher;
how to be an effective trade unionist; how to appreciate the master
painters, sculptors, architects; how to enjoy good food, including clams
and oysters.

But the most important thing he taught me was how not to die!

Although Ezra supported many of the same causes as Loeb and his
other friends, he believed he avoided persecution by *Red Channels* and
other communist witch-hunt organizations by following some simple advice from his father, a strong anti–Stalinist and an early democratic socialist. In 1938, while playing Henry on stage and radio, Ezra attended a
political meeting to raise money for the loyalists of the Spanish Civil War.
The rousing and so-called subversive rally took place in the Roof Garden
Theatre atop the 44th Street Theatre at midnight following that evening's
performances. The next morning, Ezra, who had contributed a nominal
amount of money to the cause, informed his father of his actions. Feinstone
inquired about the sponsors, to which Ezra replied, "All my friends were
there." His father then said, "You find out who's in back of them before you
become a part of good causes. If you see any name of known communists
or suspected fellow travelers, forget it." He suggested his son find another

organization, such as *The Christian Science Monitor*, which backed the same cause, and pledge his allegiance through them.

Ezra's transition from professional actor to professional director was complete when he was hired as the second director of *The Aldrich Family* television series during the first half of the 1951–52 season. He gained this job as a result of several factors. First, the industry had only a few qualified directors during its infancy. Second, although Ezra certainly could not physically portray Henry, he knew the characters and situations more intimately than anyone else—except Clifford Goldsmith—and he knew well the rhythms and technique of such members of the acting company as Kelk and Jameson. General Foods and Young and Rubicam obviously counted on Ezra to add imagination and insight to the programs, all of which were now under Goldsmith's strong and close supervision. If an actor became too harsh or unrealistic or became overinventive, Goldsmith instructed the director to inform the actor to make appropriate changes. Additionally, the sponsors probably hoped Ezra's ear for the leading role could somehow transfer to Bob Casey, the young man with rather limited acting abilities whom they had chosen to play Henry. Ezra found Casey to be a pleasant and attractive person with an all–American look but with no real sense of comic timing or imagination. He memorized the lines and moved as Ezra directed, but he had little flair for interpretation. "If he tried to imitate me," Ezra later said, "it was a very weak, noneffective impersonation that just didn't work."

The Aldrich Family never found a consistent television audience. Ezra claims that Kelk, Jameson, and Ed Begley, who remained as Homer's father, saved several episodes from dismal failure, but those in the television audience, who had grown up with Henry Aldrich on radio simply could not equate this visual image with what they had previously heard. Gene Leitner wrote, "On TV, everyone sees the same picture. On radio, each listener maintained their own mental picture; everyone envisioned the characters and situations differently. And that made a difference." Ezra, on the other hand, argued that the show fell victim to the natural evolution of situation comedies. Other programs, borrowing many of Goldsmith's original concepts, had a fresher audience appeal. But many people could not accept the series without the power and magic of Ezra's vocal interpretation. Loyal fans simply could not hear anyone but Ezra Stone as Henry. This chapter of Ezra's life finally came to a close when after thirteen episodes he quietly stepped down as the director of the TV program that on stage and radio had brought him fame.

9. Epilogue

In the early 1950s, Ezra, Sara, Joe, and now Francine settled on their 170-acre farm in Newtown, Pennsylvania, just north of Philadelphia. Between jaunts to New York City, Ezra and Sara maintained a herd of ninety-five purebred Ayrshire dairy cattle, most of which were named after Shakespearean characters. In this decade, Ezra sustained his customary hectic schedule, directing *Wake Up, Darling* by Alex Gottlieb and *Curtain's Up!*, a one-woman show starring Ethel Barrymore Colt, on Broadway as well as programs for a number of early classic television series including *I Married Joan, Love That Guy, The Danny Thomas Show, The Martha Raye Show, The Ezio Pinza Show, Life with Father and Mother, Caesar's Hour, Joe and Mabel* and appeared in several episodes of *The Eternal Light*. He also directed the *Auto Light Easter Parade* in 1953, and in 1957 he produced a Texaco special "Command Performance" starring Ed Wynn and another starring Ethel Barrymore Colt for the American Theatre Wing.

As a stage director, he turned his attention to regional productions at various nearby theaters. For instance, at the Bucks County Playhouse, then a favorite theater of his located near his home, he performed in *Middle of the Night, Once More with Feeling,* and *The Man Who Came to Dinner* and directed such productions as *Count Your Blessing, Half in Earnest, Blue Danube, The Mistress of the Inn,* and Will Glickman and Joseph Stein's *Mrs. Gibbon's Boys.* He directed summer stock touring packages of *Loco,* starring Dagmar and Arthur Treacher, *The Play's the Thing,* starring Ezio Pinza and Philip Loeb, *God Bless Our Bank,* with Ann Sothern, and staged a nightclub revue at the famous Blackhawk Restaurant in Chicago. In 1953, he was brought in to doctor and redirect the Broadway tryout of *The Pink Elephant* in Philadelphia, which starred Steve Allen, and the Theatre Guild hired him to direct the pre–Broadway production of *Comin' Thru the Rye* at the Westport Country Theatre. On June 30, 1958, Ezra directed his wife and two children in a Bucks County Playhouse stock production of *Season in the Sun,* which also starred Paul Lynde and himself.

In a few short years, however, television production moved from live programs to film and video tape, and the industry moved from the east to the west coast. For both personal and professional reasons, Sara decided that Ezra should follow the "biz." Leaving their land in the hands of their

Ezra, Francine and Josef (circa 1950).

Bucks County working farmer *cum* manager, William Campbell, Ezra and family packed their belongings and headed for Hollywood. Ezra struggled for several years but eventually directed hundreds of episodes of popular television programs. "I made a damn good living in episodic TV, and I was very productive," he later wrote. "But I did have to hustle to get as many bookings as possible."

In one sense, the number of programs he produced and directed seemed

The Stones (circa 1950), Sara, Ezra, Josef, Francine.

to demonstrate his continuing success, but on the other hand it also manifested some of the frustration he found in the West Coast television community. His cohorts were not as receptive and compassionate as the relatively close-knit New York stage and radio performers had been. He had a wife and family to support, and jobs became increasingly difficult to secure. Ezra never discussed the issue, but while in California he suffered a nervous breakdown.

In March 1963, at a low ebb in his career, he stumbled into a position that gave him new strength. On a whim, he interviewed for an opening at IBM to stage the annual Data Processing Division's Western Region "Hundred Percent Club" award and recognition convention in San Francisco. At the time, IBM boasted over three hundred thousand employees worldwide. In gratitude, the company, several times each year, paid tribute to individuals through these Hundred Percent Club conventions, or as Ezra called them—"Those One-Shot, High-Risk, Blue-Ribbon Babies." These were enormous events, as IBM brought in over one thousand employees to partake of twenty-four hours of staged presentations over a three-day period. Ezra, who essentially served as executive producer and director, was a vital part of every decision concerning these presentations. From the creation of costumes to developing scripts, Ezra's concentration was total.

Stone family portrait (circa 1950), Francine, Sara, Josef and Ezra.

"We had elegant stage sets," said Art Kane, a fellow producer at IBM. "We had live bands. We had audiovisual productions. Ezra taught us how to work it. . . . In fifteen years with Ezra at the helm we never had a flop. We always had a hit, and that was big time."

Ezra actually spent twenty-four years with IBM as general director of 105 conventions and as the producer and director and consultant for over 250 films and audiovisual projects including ". . . a better way," *Area for*

Julia in Las Vegas at the Sands Hotel, July 1970. Ezra Stone (director) with Diahann Carroll.

Action, Take Five, and *The Know-How People,* and *The Reel World,* which won the Grand Prize at the Barcelona Festival in 1972 plus dozens of Cine Gold Eagles and other awards.

In 1969, he and Sara were instrumental in helping to found the American College Theatre Festival (ACTF) — the national gala held each year at the John F. Kennedy Center for the Performing Arts in the nation's capital. In 1972, actress Irene Ryan established a foundation to award scholarships to outstanding student performers in each of the nation's regions. At that time, the national festival emphasized only full-scale college productions,

Sara Seeger and Ezra Stone.

but Sara, assisted by Ezra, devised a way to give the Irene Ryan awards a special quality. Her concept was entitled "An Evening of Scenes," a program featuring the work of the best student actors in five-minute episodes. Each student actor, who had finished first in his or her regional competition, received the best professional coaching. For the first few years, Sara produced the program and served as the mistress of ceremonies while Ezra chaired a panel of professional judges consisting of agents and casting directors.

Ezra with daughter, Francine Bakewell-Stone (Photographer: Kristen Peterson).

Ezra and Sara remained in their modest redwood ranch home on a shelf in the outpost of Hollywood Hills, with a sensational view of the Los Angeles basin and, on a clear day, of the Catalina Islands and the other channel islands, until 1980 when circumstances brought them back to Bucks County. In a local interview in 1982, Ezra explained, "It was mostly because of the grandchildren." At the time they moved back to Bucks County, Ezra and Sara had two grandchildren, Kimberly Joyce Stone and Petra Meade Bakewell-Stone. Jennifer Stone and Lorenzo Isaiah Bakewell-Stone were born soon after. This, however, did not represent the only reason for their return, for Ezra had made a promise to his father, who at the age of ninety-two had been suffering from ill health.

Always the dutiful son, Ezra had throughout his life placed his father on a pedestal. Sol Feinstone was both stern and demanding with his children—a strict disciplinarian. "He was not easy to live with, with his academic demands upon Ezra," said Charles Moos speaking of Ezra's childhood. "Despite Rose's unremittingly gentle efforts to mollify, the stress could be devastating. His sister, Miriam, vividly recalls the anticipation of school report cards as a period of such high anxiety that he ran away." Strangely enough, even after Feinstone's death, it seemed that Ezra still sought his father's intellectual approval.

As a mentor, Feinstone placed a great deal of pressure on his son. Ezra stood in awe of his father's scholarly and pragmatic insights into business and negotiations. Feinstone had controlled much of his life, and Ezra had never made a career or personal move without first consulting him. This often worked out well for Ezra, but it seemed to strip him of self-confidence. In January 1993, Don Dee sent a brief letter to Ezra soliciting his response to the question "What has been your worst failure during your life and how has that failure helped advance your career?" Ezra began his answer with "My life has been blessed much beyond what my limited intellect and talent deserves."

Although Feinstone was by nature an unaffectionate husband and father, Ezra loved him unconditionally. Feinstone was undoubtedly the most influential person in his son's life, but Ezra's respect for his father seemed to get in the way of emotion. Dick Burdick, a longtime friend, recently told the curious story of Ezra's reaction to one of his frequent visits to Buckstone Farm, where Sol and Rose Feinstone resided. Sometime after the Second World War, Burdick and his family had moved to Bucks County. Subsequently, Burdick adopted Feinstone as a surrogate father of sorts. "It was a strange thing," Burdick said. "We would be together, and I would be leaving, or when I'd arrive, I would put my arms around Sol and Rose and kiss them." On this occasion, as Ezra walked his friend to the car, he said, "Richard, I envy you; I could never kiss my father."

Several stories written by Harry Harris in his revealing article "Sol the Eccentric," recently published in the *Philadelphia Gazette*, further illustrate Ezra's austere, colorful, and puzzling father. In his last days, Feinstone chattered incessantly to his round-the-clock nurses. The old man kept recalling with pride that when he accompanied his son, then a minor, to Hollywood for his role in *Those Were the Days*, Paramount Pictures financed their airfare, hotel, and living expenses. He lamented that he had embarrassed a young Soviet guide by correcting her translation of a Russian phrase. What he most regretted, however, was that he had rejected a $300-a-month teaching post at Syracuse for a $500-a-month job at the Philadelphia Navy Yard. "It was my biggest mistake," he sighed. "My whole life would have been different."

A paradoxical philanthropist who contributed millions of dollars to laudable projects, Feinstone—as a matter of principle—left no inheritance to his children and grandchildren. "He worked hard at giving his money away and he did a good job because there is nothing left," Ezra explained to another reporter. Harris went on to explain that Feinstone was an agnostic who shunned membership in any synagogue; however, he treasured his Jewish heritage. He spoke Yiddish (and wrote the world's first chemistry textbook in that Diaspora-unifying language), gave his children biblical names, and hobnobbed with rabbis.

Despite his wealth, the old man lived a prudent lifestyle. He ate little and owned only two suits—including a hand-me-down from Ezra. He furnished the family's successive homes in Philadelphia, New York, and Washington Crossing, Pennsylvania, with "bargains" acquired at auctions, rented out floors of his residences, and deplored pretentious displays. Among his taboos were such indulgences as costly cars, boats, and jewelry. When his wife purchased a fur coat from a friend, he became so irate that to pacify him she converted the fur into the lining of a cloth coat. Once he complained to the manager of a Horn and Hardart automat because a saucer contained five prunes, instead of the usual six.

Despite his unaffectionate disposition, operatic and classical music and visual beauty moved Feinstone to tears. An Oxfordian, he was convinced that the sonnets and plays normally attributed to Shakespeare, were actually written by Edward de Vere (1550–1604), the seventeenth Earl of Oxford—an opinion also held by Ezra. Feinstone shrank from family hugs but was not opposed to kisses from attractive women—unless they wore too much lipstick.

An eccentric man, Feinstone at times possessed a rather feisty nature. On one occasion, he received information from Sam Levene that a restaurant in Cape May, New Jersey, had refused to give him a menu because it "didn't serve niggers or Jews." Feinstone went to Cape May, purchased the entire block of stores, and instructed a local agent to renew every other lease at a reduced rent but to cancel the restaurant's lease. When the indignant restaurant owner rushed to Philadelphia to confront his new landlord, the unyielding Feinstone said, "Before, you didn't serve niggers and Jews; now you don't serve anybody."

Nevertheless, Feinstone also had a softer side. He rarely posed for photographs and in the few portraits displayed in his home he looked rather foreboding and stern; however, he loved to laugh. He enjoyed a good joke, especially one with a Yiddish punchline. Before undergoing surgery at Mercer Hospital in Trenton, where he died on October 17, 1980, Feinstone's last words to his wife were, "Tell everybody to have a good time."

Feinstone's early auction sorties involved furniture, stuffed birds, incomplete sets of plates and wine glasses, miniature Hebrew books, and assorted *objets d'art*. He then began to collect memorabilia about his "personal heroes in every field," including English poets. But Feinstone had loved America since his childhood in Lithuania, and the American Revolution became one of his obsessions over the last thirty years of his life. When he bought his three-hundred-acre farm near the site of Washington's historic crossing of the Delaware River, he focused his collecting on America's early history. As a younger man, he had let a Thomas Jefferson get away because he could not afford a four-hundred-dollar bid. In the early 1970s, however, a wealth of historical documents offered for sale by the Long Island Historical Society, piqued his attention. The treasure consisted of

127 letters written by President Washington to the managers of the man-sion and farmlands at Mount Vernon. Feinstone offered $100,000 for the lot but advised the sellers that they could undoubtedly get more if they sold the letters individually. At the subsequent Parke-Bernet auction, however, he decided that the collection should remain intact; therefore, to prevent fragmentation of the entire Mount Vernon estate, he bought all the letters for $250,000. He then offered the documents as a gift to the Ladies Asso-ciation of the Union at Mount Vernon—if President Gerald Ford would formally accept the gift in their behalf.

Feinstone often attached qualifications to contributions. For example, upon donating a building to the Opportunities Industrialization Center, he demanded as payment "one full cup of coffee and a slice of black bread." He insisted they fill the "cuppa" to the brim, because he drank his coffee sugarless and black. To show his appreciation for the support of a Quaker neighbor when the proposed naming of the Sol Feinstone Elementary School evoked anti–Semitic slurs, Feinstone, who had already insisted on a separate children's library (with a plaque in untranslated Hebrew letters referring to the biblical injunction "Let there be light"), added another stipulation: To commemorate the neighbor's son, killed in action during World War II, the institute was to display the tallest elementary school flagpole in the state of Pennsylvania.

Over the years, Feinstone amassed an impressive collection of impor-tant manuscripts of the American Revolution, which he initially housed at Washington Crossing Historic Park. But in 1973 he gave his entire farm and manuscript collection and created a generous endowment to fund the David Library Foundation, which he had incorporated in 1972 as a bi-centennial gift to the nation. "He wanted the library, with its lecture hall to serve as a research institution for scholars and members of the public who are interested in America's Revolutionary War era," Ezra later said. He named the library after David Golub, the developmentally disabled son of his daughter, Miriam, and her husband Nate Golub, of Washington Crossing. To this day, the library is supported by Feinstone's foundation.

Today, the David Library of the American Revolution has developed into a unique treasure trove dedicated to the last half of the eighteenth cen-tury. Feinstone, in decades of collecting, had amassed over twenty-five hundred documents, including letters written by Alexander Hamilton, Thomas Jefferson, Sam and John Adams, Lafayette, and many others, plus more than three hundred manuscripts and letters of George Washington. About one hundred items are kept in a vault at the David Library, while the rest, for reasons of space and security, are kept at the American Philo-sophical Society Library in Philadelphia. Microfiches of Feinstone's entire collection can be found at the library; approximately seven million pages of documents are preserved there on some ten thousand reels. Unique

Ezra Stone, president and director of the David Library of the American Revolution.

items in the collection that draw scholars of the Revolution to the David
Library include President Washington's correspondence with his secre-
taries of state from 1789 to 1796 as well as Indian treaties from 1722 to 1801
and papers of Revolutionary War financier Robert Morris, naval officer
John Paul Jones, political leader Aaron Burr, and Declaration of Indepen-
dence signer John Hancock. Each year, more than a thousand visitors take
advantage of the library's many resources.

Shortly before he died, Feinstone appointed his son president and
director of the David Library of the American Revolution. In 1979, Sara
planned and executed the renovations on their house on Stone Meadows
Farm in Newtown Township, but they commuted from the West Coast until 1981, when she and Ezra again settled in this historic area. "She made
the decision to move back to Bucks County," he later wrote. "She knew
before I did that our show biz careers were over." After this time, the
library consumed the majority of his hectic schedule, but in an interview
he admitted his passion for the collection never matched that of his late
father.

Feinstone often referred to the library as his "third child," and it now
became Ezra's mission to administer the library programs and ensure that
his father's goals of telling the Revolutionary War story were met. Ezra's
days as an actor and director had for the most part come to an end, although he and his wife remained active participants in the theatrical scene
through another Feinstone legacy associated with ACTF.

In 1973, Michael Kanin had asked Feinstone to sponsor multiple annual awards, which were given to winning student playwrights across the
country—the criteria being freedom and Americana. They presented the
first coveted award, for Jeff Pate's *Booth*, produced by St. Cloud University,
at the national ACTF convention at the Kennedy Center. Two other David
Library award recipients also went to the national festival, *Sideshow* from
Angelo State University and Sean Clark's *Eleven Zulu* from theUniversity of Missouri–Columbia. Each year, Ezra and Sara traveled to colleges
throughout the country judging entries and teaching workshops. Of all the
facets of show business, Ezra told an Indianapolis reporter, he enjoyed
legitimate theater the most. "But then I love to teach too," he exclaimed.
Working with young people invigorated him and his wife. "We don't handle them with kid gloves," he said. "We're tough on them, but what you
always have to remember is if you break one of these young actors apart,
you must put them very carefully back together."

This concept was evidenced as Sara worked with a female student
from Indiana University–Purdue University at Indianapolis. Under Sara's
stern and demanding eyes, the young actress collapsed in tears. "That's all
right dear. I've shed more than a few myself. You wouldn't have much
future in this business if you didn't have enough emotion to cry." The

session ended as the girl smiled through her tears. In conjunction with this program, the couple conducted workshops and seminars at the universities of Missouri, Minnesota, Montana, Washington, Portland, San Diego, Salt Lake City, Florida State, South Dakota, Flagstaff, New York, Las Vegas, California at Los Angeles, Temple, Columbia, Yale, George Washington, James Madison, Brigham Young, Michigan State, Arizona State, and dozens of others.

After twenty-four years with ACTF, during seventeen of which the David Library-ACTF Playwriting Awards were distributed and over $250,000 contributed by Feinstone—not counting over one thousand hours donated by Ezra and Sara—their workshops and the original script competition were abandoned at the end of the 1980s because of a difference of opinion on how the awards should be apportioned.

Even in his mid-seventies, Ezra worked tirelessly at his father's old position. He held memberships in no less than ten entertainment unions and guilds, including the American National Theatre and Academy West of which he served as chairman of the board and created, produced, and directed the memorable "Golden Wedding Anniversary Tribute" for the famous acting team, the Lunts. As recently as August 1989, he received an honorary doctorate of fine arts from theUniversity of Missouri–Columbia for his contribution to both the professional entertainment world and to educational theater programs across the country.

On August 12, 1990, Sara Seegar passed away. "So many years, so many memories, so many fine friends, and so many blessings," Ezra wrote. "Now it's *my* turn to learn how to handle the downside of life." He never fully recovered from the loss of his loving wife. Many of his close friends had recently passed away, and now, with the loss of Sara, he felt alone. He therefore poured himself into his work—his way of enduring the pain.

Randy Kelly, a 1982 AADA student who had been tutored by Ezra after receiving the Philip Loeb Scholarship, recently shared a special remembrance of Ezra. "I never forgot his advice on making things happen myself and in 1987 I founded the Village Theatre Company, a not for profit Off-Off-Broadway company," said Kelly.

> In 1989, having never forgotten my friend in spirit Phil Loeb, and being outraged at the attempts by the then conservative administration and fundamentalist coalition to pressure the NEA into censoring the work of its recipient artists, I decided to produce a revival of Eric Bentley's play *Are You Now or Have You Ever Been.*
>
> When I tried to secure the rights, however, Mr. Bentley refused to grant them, citing his reason as knowing nothing about me or The Village Theatre Company. When I told Ezra this he immediately wrote and called Mr. Bentley and in two days I had the play.
>
> During rehearsal for the play I invited Ezra to speak with the cast

about Phil and others he had known who had suffered during the fifties. At one point as he spoke to the enraptured cast he began a story by saying "One time Sara and I went to a cocktail party . . . ." He began to cry. After a moment or two he looked up at the cast and said, "I'm sorry, Sara was my wife of many years. She recently died and I miss her." That was it, that was all he said, simply, humbly, and went on with his talk.

When he got into that old stationwagon in front of the theater to go home I said to him, "Ezra, I had no idea about your wife. Had I known I would certainly not have bothered you about my problems with the play or asked you to come to the city and talk."

He just looked at me with those twinkling eyes and said, "Randy, I miss her and I'm lonely, but nothing would have stopped me from helping you. It is important that you do this play. What happened to Phil and the others can never ever happen again."

Following Sara's death, Ezra still had many plans, many dreams to be fulfilled. He took great pride in his work with the Director's Guild and the completion of the Feinstone Conference Center on the grounds of The David Library. His greatest joy, however, came through his family. His four grandchildren—Kim, Petra, Jennifer, and Lorenzo—were his crowning achievement. He loved them endlessly.

Snow and ice pelted the northeast on Tuesday, March 1, 1994. By Thursday, however, all major roads leading to New York City had been cleared. As usual, Ezra drove his brown Chevy Caprice station wagon to work and conducted his morning business. He spoke with David Fowler, research director of the library, then called Marilyn Huret, library administrator, who had stayed home because of the weather. He gave her some final instructions before driving into the city for the day to attend a Director's Guild meeting and to see the Frank Lloyd Wright exhibit at the Museum of Metropolitan Art on 5th Avenue. Although the roads were not bad, Huret, as usual, concluded the phone call with, "Drive carefully." Ezra laughed and said, "Oh, don't worry. I will."

Associated Press reported that Ezra drove his station wagon into a New Jersey Turnpike guardrail near Interchange 11 in Woodbridge. Emergency personnel said his car flew eighty-two feet and crashed into a bridge abutment. Trapped inside the wreckage, Ezra grabbed the hand of a young highway patrolman who had quickly arrived on the scene. ". . . grandchildren . . . love my grandchildren . . . I love my grandchildren . . . ." With these words he died.

Radio and newspaper reporters who made cursory announcements that a Pennsylvania man named Ezra Stone had died in a car crash did not realize the significance of the event. Their older listeners and readers, however, knew immediately. "To a generation a half century ago he was the star of the top-rated *Aldrich Family* series heard on national radio for fifteen years," wrote Art Thompson of the *Advance of Bucks County*. "To his neighbors in Bucks County where he lived, . . . Stone was a familiar, friendly figure, encountered at the post office, the hardware store or super-market, recognizable by his trimmed white beard, fisherman's cap and everpresent pipe."

As for Henry Aldrich and the character's effect on Ezra's life and career, his mentor, George Abbott, wrote in his autobiography, "Ezra Stone typed himself forever with 'Coming Mother.' He made a great deal of money out of it but it undoubtedly hurt his career." Certainly, Ezra had carried Henry's shadow with him for the remainder of his years in and out of the profession, but Abbott's assessment falls well short of the truth. Ezra admitted to a reporter that Henry "shaped my life, my wife's life and my children's lives." Truthfully, Henry opened doors for Ezra that otherwise might have remained closed. The role gave him an edge, a marketable leverage. In early 1990, he said, "I know after all these years, virtually every assignment I've had since the creation of Henry Aldrich in some way was a result of that one shot." He spent twenty-three years with IBM, all of which began because those executives remembered Henry. Of course, Ezra delivered; otherwise there would never have been more than two decades of employment. As recently as May 1991, Louis Peccarelli, an IBM disciple of Ezra's, employed him to coproduce, direct, and cowrite with Robert Orben — the nationally known humor writer and former head speech writer for President Gerald Ford — a high-risk, complex project for the IBM Golden Circle involving five separate video crews and five Direc-tor's Guild Association directors — all friends and DGA colleagues of Ezra.

At the height of his popularity, Ezra was a national star. For an actor whose career seemed secure, one might speculate why he had vanished into relative obscurity after 1953; that is, his name no longer appeared regularly in gossip columns or the theater or entertainment sections of newspapers and magazines. Although he began as a child actor, Ezra always seemed to be preparing himself for work behind the scenes. He felt his acting career was a fluke, and he found continuous satisfaction creating his art from the wings. At any rate, his ego did not demand visibility in the eyes of the audience or in the gossip columns of the newspapers.

Of his life's work, he said,

> I think that if I had incipient genius, theatrical genius, it certainly would have become evident before now. That essentially my so-called success and limited recognition, and still probably more than I deserved, was for the quantity and variety of my work that I achieved. But that's only as a result of that kind of puritan ethic of always having to be working. Un-doubtedly, had I been more selective in the assignments that I undertook, I might have come up with a product that was on the level or approached the level of the work of some of my colleagues functioning in the same period of time.

Although he unquestionably mastered more forms of media than most entertainers, his work, to him, never merited the stamp of enduring worth. Individual portions of his career exemplified top-notch comedic inspiration, general vitality, and energy, but he attributed these accomplishments to his organizational skills and his do-or-die attitude toward work. On stage and off, Ezra tried to utilize every minute, every second to discover better and quicker ways of accomplishing his goals. "Jiggy [Robin] used to kid me about how during the army days I would button my five-button Eisenhower jacket with two hands, two buttons at a time," Ezra recalled. "And so it wouldn't be a total loss, I would button the fifth one with one hand and use the free hand to find an itch to scratch."

His friends, however, disagree with Ezra's assessment of his own career and his contribution to the industry. His childhood companion, Charles Moos, wrote, "In the sixty years we've known each other I have consistently found Ezra to be a deeply compassionate and sensitive human being who unfortunately depreciates his achievements to such an extent that he is deprived of much if not most of the gratification one would normally expect. He is compulsively modest. . . ." Joseph Tomes, who worked with Ezra on *At Your Service* while they were both stationed in California during World War II, wrote, "My admiration and respect for Ezra are unbounded." Hal Prince recently wrote, "I was a kid hooked on 'Henry! Henry Aldrich!'"

> Some years later, I ended up literally sitting in Ezra's chair in the Abbott office tending to odd jobs. In those days you filled the cooler with *heavy* bottles of water and you opened the windows in the summer to cool things off. Then you graduated to script reading and casting calls. I was one of a long line of Abbott interns, which included not only Ezra, but Garson Kanin. Over the years, I got to see Ezra sporadically—never enough—and though the list of his accomplishments grew, to me, he and Garson and I will always be the Abbott boys.

In a 1990 interview, Eddie Bracken said, "When the word Ezra Stone comes up, I tell everybody what a wonderful, talented human being that man is. I love him."

Bibliography

Abbott, George. *Mister Abbott.* New York: Random House, 1963.
————. "Not the Original Cast." *New York Times,* June 28, 1936, section 9, p. 1.
"Abbott System Turns Up a Stone." *New York Times,* September 24, 1939, section 9, p. 2.
"Aldrich Family Loses Ezra Stone." *New York Times,* August 13, 1942, p. 21.
Allardice, James B. *At War with the Army.* New York: Samuel French, 1948.
Allen, Fred. *Treadmill to Oblivion.* Boston: Little, Brown, 1954.
American Academy of Dramatic Arts: New York Catalogue, 1990–91. New York: American Academy of Dramatic Arts, 1990.
Arthur, Thomas H. "Ezra Stone/Sara Seegar." *Dramatics.* January 1982, pp. 28–43.
"Artist Group to Study Dropping of Actor from Television Version of *Goldbergs.*" *New York Times,* January 9, 1952, p. 10.
Bannerman, R. LeRoy. *Norman Corwin and Radio: The Golden Years.* Tuscaloosa: The University of Alabama Press, 1986.
Bannister, Harry. *The Education of a Broadcaster.* New York: Simon and Schuster, 1965.
Barnouw, Erik. *The Golden Web: A History of Broadcasting in the United States.* Vol. 2. New York: Oxford University Press, 1968.
Benny, Jack and Joan Benny. *Sunday Nights at Seven: The Jack Benny Story.* New York: Warner Books, 1990.
Bergreen, Laurence. *As Thousands Cheer: The Life of Irving Berlin.* New York: Viking Penguin, 1990.
Berle, Milton and Haskel Frankel. *Milton Berle: An Autobiography.* New York: Delacorte Press, 1974.
Broadcast Advertising. Vol. 2. New York: National Broadcasting Company, 1930.
Brockett, Oscar G. *History of the Theatre.* 5th ed. Boston: Allyn and Bacon, 1987.
Brown, Les. *The New York Times Encyclopedia of Television.* New York: The New York Times Book Company, 1977.
Burdick, Richard S. *Next Time I Want to Come Back as a Yellow Bird: A Shirtsleeve Memoir.* Tampa: Axelrod, 1992.
Buxton, Frank and Bill Owen. *Radio's Golden Age.* New York: Easton Valley Press, 1966.
Chapman, John. "The Happiest Man on Broadway." *Saturday Evening Post,* January 9, 1943, pp. 15, 81.
Chester, Giraud, Garnet R. Garrison, and Edgar E. Willis. *Television and Radio.* 4th ed. New York: Appleton Century-Crofts, 1971.
Coghlan, Frank "Junior." *They Still Call Me Junior: Autobiography of a Child Star; With a Filmography.* Jefferson, North Carolina: McFarland, 1993.

Cogley, John. *Report on Blacklisting*. Vol. 2, *Radio and Television*. New York: The Fund for the Republic, 1956.

Collins, Dan. "Actor Juggles Eight Jobs at Once, Yet Thrives; Finds Only Five Hours Sleep a Night Is Enough." *New York World-Telegram*, n.d.

Copeland, Norman. *Psychology and the Soldier*. Harrisburg, Penn.: Military Service Publication Company, n.d.

Cott, Ted. *How to Audition for Radio*. New York: Greenberg Publisher, 1946.

Creative Education at Oak Lane Country Day School of Temple University. Philadelphia: Oak Lane Country Day School of Temple University, 1932.

Crichton, Kyle. "Little Giant." *Collier's Magazine*. April 27, 1940, p. 11, 60.

_____. "This Is the Army." *Collier's Magazine*, October 17, 1942, pp. 14–15, 28.

Csida, Joseph and June Bundy Csida. *American Entertainment: A Unique History of Popular Show Business*. New York: Watson-Guptill, 1978.

"Culling Room Service." *New York Times*, July 25, 1937, section 10, p. 2.

Dorfman, Nat N. "It Still Is the Army." *New York Times*, January 31, 1943, section 2, pp. 1–2.

Douglas, Kirk. *The Ragman's Son*. New York: Simon and Schuster, 1988.

Dryer, Sherman H. *Radio in Wartime*. New York: Greenberg, 1942.

Duerr, Edwin. *Radio and Television Acting: Criticism, Theory, and Practice*. New York: Rinehart, 1950.

Dunning, John. *Tune in Yesterday: The Ultimate Encyclopedia of Old-Time Radio, 1925–1976*. Englewood Cliffs, N.J.: Prentice-Hall, 1976.

Edwards, Anne. *Early Reagan*. New York: Morrow, 1987.

"Equity Would Have *Goldbergs* TV Show on 'Unfair' List as Long as Loeb Is Barred." *New York Times*, January 12, 1952, p. 10.

Eustis Morton. "The Director Takes Command." *Theatre Arts Monthly* 29 (February 1936): 120–23.

Ewen, David. *The Story of Irving Berlin*. New York: Holt, 1950.

"Ezra Stone and Sara Seegar Have Come Home." *Advance of Bucks County*, October 28, 1982, p. 3.

Fass, Paula S. *The Damned and the Beautiful: American Youth in the 1920's*. New York: Oxford University Press, 1977.

Feinstone, Sol. *Fellow Passengers: A Letter to My Grandchildren and to All Grandchildren*. New York: Vantage Press, 1972.

Flanner, Janet. "The Real Parents of Henry Aldrich." *Ladies Home Journal* 59 (September 1942): 132–33.

Folkart, Burt A. "Ezra Stone; Played Henry Aldrich on Radio Show." *Los Angeles Times*, March 6, 1994, p. A26.

Fonda, Henry and Howard Teichmann. *Fonda: My Life*. New York: New American Library, 1981.

Fowler, David. Introduction to "A Guide to the Sol Feinstone Manuscript Collection of the David Library of the American Revolution." Washington Crossing, Penn.: The David Library of the American Revolution, forthcoming.

Frances, Eugene. Interview. "The Oral History of Philip Loeb." Philip Loeb Award Audio Tape Collection. New York: American Academy of Dramatic Arts, n.d.

Francis, Robert. "Broadway Dynamo." *Brooklyn Eagle*, n.d.

Freedland, Michael. *Irving Berlin*. New York: Stein and Day, 1974.

Fussell, Paul. *The Great War and Modern Memory*. New York: Oxford University Press, 1975.

Gagnier, Mary. "Documenting Birth of a Nation." *Philadelphia Inquirer*, November 2, 1989, section BC, p. 4.

"George Abbott." *Current Biography: 1940*. New York: Wilson, 1940.

Gianakos, Larry James. *Television Drama Programming: A Comprehensive Chronicle, 1947–1959*. Metuchen, N.J.: Scarecrow Press, 1980.

Goldsmith, Clifford. "Life with the Aldrich Family." *New York Times*, July 1, 1945, section 2, p. 5.

_____. *What a Life*. New York: Dramatists Play Service, 1939.

Goldsmith, Oliver. *The Vicar of Wakefield and She Stoops to Conquer*. New York: Harper and Row, 1965.

Gould, Eleanor Cody. *Charles Jehlinger in Rehearsal*. New York: By the author, 1958.

_____. "The Genius of Jehlinger." *Americada*, Summer 1984, pp. 6–7.

Gould, Jack. "Actor Is Dropped from Video Cast." *New York Times*, January 8, 1952, p. 29.

_____. "Portrait of the Sad Visionary." *New York Times*, March 17, 1940, section 10, p. 3.

Green, Abel and Joe Laurie, Jr. *Showbiz from Vaude to Video*. New York: Holt, 1951.

Gregory, Thomas West. *Adolescence in Literature*. New York: Longman, 1978.

Grimes, William. "Ezra Stone, 76, Henry Aldrich on the Radio." *New York Times*, March 5, 1994, p. 38.

Harmon, Jim. *The Great Radio Comedians*. Garden City, N.Y.: Doubleday, 1970.

Harris, Harry. "Sol the Eccentric." *Pennsylvania Gazette*. November 1993, pp. 35–39.

"Henry the Third." *Newsweek*, September 6, 1943, p. 88.

The History of the Theatre Guild: The First Fifteen Years. New York: The Theatre Guild, 1934.

Holm, John Cecil and George Abbott. *Three Men on a Horse*. New York: Samuel French, 1935.

Hutchens, John K. "Hen-ry! A Bow to Mr. Goldsmith's 'Aldriches' with or Without an Anniversary." *New York Times*, April 11, 1943, section 2, p. 7.

_____. "On the Abbott of Times Square." *New York Times*, December 6, 1936, section 12, pp. 5–6.

"I Gather No Moss." *Hilltopper*, Jamaica, N.Y., March 8, 1939, p. 3.

Jenks, Edward. "Have a Cigar, Henry." *New York Times*, May 24, 1942, section 8, p. 8.

Jonson, Ben. *The Alchemist*. Edited by Peter Bement. London: Methuen, 1987.

Koppes, Clayton R. and Gregory D. Black. "Blacks, Loyalty, and Motion-Picture Propaganda in World War II." *Journal of American History* 73 (September 1986): 383–406.

Lamparski, Richard. *Whatever Became of. . .?*. New York: Crown Publishers, 1985.

"Lecturer Into Playwright." *New York Times*, July 10, 1938, section 9, p. 2.

Lerner, Alan Jay. *The Musical Theatre: A Celebration*. New York: McGraw-Hill, 1986.

"Life as It Now Runs on a Cooperative Basis." *New York Times*, February 26, 1939, section 9, p. 3.

"Loeb and Red Channels." *New Republic*, January 21, 1952, p. 8.

"Loeb Autopsy Held." *New York Times*, September 3, 1955, p. 32.

McArthur, Benjamin. *Actors and American Culture, 1880–1920*. Philadelphia: Temple University Press, 1984.

McCaleb, Kenneth. "Collegiate Nostalgia: Vintage '04 *Those Were the Days* at Paramount's Old Siwash." *New York Mirror*, March 31, 1940, Sunday Mirror Magazine Section, p. 15.

Maibaum, Richard and Harry Clork. *See My Lawyer*. New York: Dramatists Play Service, 1939.

Manumit School: A Demonstration Labor School, Where Education Is Life, Not Lessons. Pawling, N.Y.: Manumit School, 1929.

Martin, John. "The Dance: Army Style." *New York Times*, September 13, 1942, section 8, p. 8.

Merchant, Abby. "Your Loving Son." Typescript, 1940.

Merrill, Gary. *Bette, Rita, and the Rest of My Life*. Augusta, Maine: Lance Tapley, 1988.

Miller, Merle. *The Judges and the Judged*. Garden City, N.Y.: Doubleday, 1952.

Monks, John, Jr., and Fred R. Finklehoffe. *Brother Rat*. New York: Dramatists Play Service, 1937.

Mott, Kay. "Shakespeare Named These Cattle." *Philadelphia Inquirer Magazine*, April 23, 1950, p. 12.

Murray, John and Allen Boretz. *Room Service*. New York: Dramatists Play Service, 1937.

Nathan, George Jean. "Blitzfarce." *Newsweek*, October 9, 1939, p. 35.

Navasky, Victor S. *Naming Names*. New York: Penguin Books, 1981.

O'Neill, Eugene. *Ah, Wilderness!*. New York: Random House, 1933.

"Origin of Brother Rat." *New York Times*, December 13, 1936, section 11, p. 5.

"Ousted Video Player Gets *Goldberg* Fee." *New York Times*, January 25, 1952, p. 13.

Patterson, James T. *America in the Twentieth Century: A History*. 2d ed. San Diego: Harcourt, Brace, Jovanovich, 1983.

Paul, Eugene. *The Hungry Eye*. New York: Ballantine Books, 1962.

"Philip Loeb Dead; Prominent Actor." *New York Times*, September 2, 1955, p. 38.

Pinza, Ezio and Robert Magidoff. *Ezio Pinza: An Autobiography*. New York: Rinehart, 1958.

Pitts, Michael R. *Radio Soundtracks: A Reference Guide*. London: Scarecrow Press, 1986.

Poteet, G. Howard. *Radio!*. Dayton: Pflaum, 1975.

"President Roosevelt Roars with Laughter at 'Command Performance' of *This Is the Army*." *New York Times*, October 9, 1942, p. 23.

Program. *Brother Rat*, by John Monks, Jr., and Fred R. Finklehoffe. New York: George Abbott, December 16, 1936.

Program. *Parade*, by George Sklar and Paul Peters. New York: Theatre Guild, 1935.

Program. *Reunion in New York*, by Lothar Metzl and Werner Michel. New York: The American Viennese Group, 1940.

Program. *This Is the Army*, by Irving Berlin. New York: United States Army. *The Playbill*, July 1942.

"Radio Artists Win Approval of Equity." *New York Times*, July 31, 1937, p. 6.

Red Channels: The Report of Communist Influence in Radio and Television. New York: American Business Consultants, 1950.

Redifer, Rex. "Ezra Stone's Come a Long Way Since 'Coming, Mother!' Days." *Indianapolis Star*, February 27, 1984, pp. 17–18.

Russell, Norton. "Henry Aldrich Is in Love." *Radio and Television Mirror* 13 (January 1940): 16–18.

Settel, Irving. *A Pictorial History of Radio*. New York: Bonanza Books, 1960.

Shepard, Richard F. "Ezra Stone (Henry Aldrich) Still Deep in Americana." *New York Times*, August 10, 1980, p. 52.

Shipp, Cameron. "Army Troupers Invade Hollywood." *New York Times*, March 28, 1943, section 2, p. 3.

Siepmann, Charles A. *Radio, Television, and Society.* New York: Oxford University Press, 1950.

Sorgen, Carol. "From Howdy Doody to Henry Aldrich." *Baltimore Jewish Times*, October 8, 1982, pp. 61, 115.

Spewack, Samuel and Bella Spewack. *Boy Meets Girl and Spring Song.* New York: Dramatists Play Service, 1936.

Spitzer, Marion. "Being a Few Notes Comparing *This Is the Army* with Its Predecessor *Yip! Yip! Yaphank.*" *New York Times*, July 12, 1942, section 8, p. 1.

"Sponsor Disclaims Dropping of Loeb." *New York Times*, January 15, 1952, p. 34.

Stanton, James E. "Ezra Stone Is Devoted to Keeping Dad's Dream Alive." *Courier Times*, December 16, 1992, p. 1B.

Sterling, Christopher H. and John M. Kittross. *Stay Tuned: A Concise History of American Broadcasting.* Belmont, Calif.: Wadsworth, 1978.

Stewart, R. W. "A Typical Boy at the Mike." *New York Times*, July 28, 1940, section 9, p. 10.

Stone, Ezra. "A Man of Iron Named Jehli." Typescript, November 21, 1952.

Stone, Ezra. "Who Was Fred Lang?" *Equity News* 74 (May 24, 1988): 43–49.

_____ and Weldon Melick. *Coming Major!* New York: Lippincott, 1944.

Strauss, Theodore. "Salute to *This Is the Army.*" *New York Times*, August 1, 1943, section 2, p. 3.

_____. "So *This Is the Army.*" *New York Times*, June 14, 1942, section 8, pp. 1–2.

Summers, Harrison B., ed. *A Thirty-Year History of Programs Carried on National Radio Networks in the United States: 1926–1956.* New York: Arno Press and The New York Times, 1971.

Terrace, Vincent. *Radio's Golden Years: The Encyclopedia of Radio Programs, 1930–1960.* New York: Barnes, 1981.

_____. *The Complete Encyclopedia of Television Programs, 1947–1976.* Vol. 1 and 2. New York: Barnes, 1976.

"That Old Music Master, G. Abbott." *New York Times*, February 21, 1937, section 10, p. 2.

Thomas, Bob. *Golden Boy: The Untold Story of William Holden.* New York: St. Martin's Press, 1983.

Thompson, Art. "Can It Be? That Lovable Henry Aldrich Turns 75." *Advance of Bucks County*, December 3, 1992, p. 33.

_____. "Ezra Stone: His Life a Stage for His Many Talents." *Advance of Bucks County*, March 10, 1994, pp. 1, 16.

"Those Abbott Tourists." *New York Times*, July 31, 1938, section 10, p. 2.

"Those Brother Rats Look South." *New York Times*, July 25, 1937, section 10, p. 2.

"Typical Boy at the Mike." *New York Times*, July 28, 1940, section 9, p. 10.

"What a Family." *Time*, April 12, 1943, p. 49.

"What a Life, Fun in a High School." *Life*, June 6, 1938, pp. 48–51.

"What Is the Junior Theatre?" *New York Times*, December 27, 1931, p. 4.

Wilson, Garff B. *Three Hundred Years of American Drama and Theatre.* Englewood Cliffs, N.J.: Prentice-Hall, 1982.

Woolf, S. J. "Sergeant Berlin Re-enlists." *New York Times Magazine*, May 17, 1942, pp. 17, 27.

————. "This Is the Army Irving Berlin Saw." *New York Times Magazine*, August 20, 1944, p. 17.

Index

Abbott, Bud 87

Abbott, George 2–5, 45–54, 56–59, 61–69, 71, 72, 75, 77, 78, 82, 90, 91, 93, 95–99, 122, 125, 129, 130–137, 140, 141, 147, 148, 154, 180–184, 190, 192, 197, 198, 217, 218; directorial trademarks of 63, 129–131; post show parties of 66, 67; working methods of 58, 59, 68, 69; worklight readings of 68, 69, 132, 134

Academy of Music (Philadelphia) 9

Actors' Equity Association 35, 43, 71, 88, 89, 149, 196, 197, 200

Actors' Forum 88, 89, 180

Actors' Fund 98

Adams, John 212

Adams, Sam 212

Advance of Bucks County 216

Affairs of Anatol (television) 5

Agee, James 190

Ah, Wilderness! (Eugene O'Neill) 41–43

Aherne, Brian 193

Air Corps (U. S. Army) 150

Akins, Zoe 33, 43, 44

Albert, Eddie 44, 58, 59–62, 97

Albertson, Frank 58, 60, 62, 63

Albright, Hardie 40

The Alchemist 185–188, 193

The Aldrich Family (radio) 3, 4, 41, 82–87, 89, 101, 103–125, 142–146, 160, 178, 179, 180, 182, 185, 195, 197, 216; bidding war for 85; cast of 113–117; debut of 82–84; format of 107, 110, 111; Hollywood performances of 124–125; *The Jack Benny Show* summer replacement for 101, 103–105; *The Kate Smith Hour*, as part of 85–87; live performances of 120–121; opening signature of 105,

106; postwar performances of 178–180; rehearsals for 119, 120; situation comedies, predecessor of 106, 107; sponsored by 106; success of 107–111; World War II performances of 142–146

The Aldrich Family (television) 189, 195, 196, 200, 201; communist witchhunt on set of 195, 196, 200, 201

"Alexander's Ragtime Band" 149

Alfred Hitchcock Presents (television) 190

The All-Star Revue (television) 194

All That Glitters 75

All the Way Home 190

Allais, Charles 15

Allardice, James B. 190

Allen, Fred 5

Allen, Steve 5

Allon Trio, The 160

Alvin Theatre (New York City) 17

Ambassador Theatre (New York City) 67

American Academy of Dramatic Arts, The 3, 11, 21–33, 38, 41, 44, 47, 53, 54, 71, 76, 81, 99, 101, 102, 180, 190, 197, 198, 215

American Broadcast Company (ABC) 189

American Business Consultants 195, 196

American College Theatre Festival (ACTF) 207, 208, 214, 215

American National Theatre and Academy 5, 215

American Philosophical Society Library (Philadelphia) 212

American Theatre Wing 192, 203

America Viennese Group 136–140

Ames, Barbara 199

225

Index 239